797,885 Books

are available to read at

www.ForgottenBooks.com

Forgotten Books' App
Available for mobile, tablet & eReader

ISBN 978-1-330-00978-9
PIBN 10003034

This book is a reproduction of an important historical work. Forgotten Books uses
state-of-the-art technology to digitally reconstruct the work, preserving the original format
whilst repairing imperfections present in the aged copy. In rare cases, an imperfection in
the original, such as a blemish or missing page, may be replicated in our edition. We do,
however, repair the vast majority of imperfections successfully; any imperfections that
remain are intentionally left to preserve the state of such historical works.

Forgotten Books is a registered trademark of FB &c Ltd.
Copyright © 2015 FB &c Ltd.
FB &c Ltd, Dalton House, 60 Windsor Avenue, London, SW19 2RR.
Company number 08720141. Registered in England and Wales.

For support please visit www.forgottenbooks.com

1 MONTH OF
FREE
READING

at
www.ForgottenBooks.com

By purchasing this book you are
eligible for one month membership to
ForgottenBooks.com, giving you
unlimited access to our entire
collection of over 700,000 titles via
our web site and mobile apps.

To claim your free month visit:
www.forgottenbooks.com/free3034

* Offer is valid for 45 days from date of purchase. Terms and conditions apply.

English
Français
Deutsche
Italiano
Español
Português

www.forgottenbooks.com

Mythology Photography **Fiction**
Fishing Christianity **Art** Cooking
Essays Buddhism Freemasonry
Medicine **Biology** Music **Ancient
Egypt** Evolution Carpentry Physics
Dance Geology **Mathematics** Fitness
Shakespeare **Folklore** Yoga Marketing
Confidence Immortality Biographies
Poetry **Psychology** Witchcraft
Electronics Chemistry History **Law**
Accounting **Philosophy** Anthropology
Alchemy Drama Quantum Mechanics
Atheism Sexual Health **Ancient History**
Entrepreneurship Languages Sport
Paleontology Needlework Islam
Metaphysics Investment Archaeology
Parenting Statistics Criminology
Motivational

PREFACE.

THE Translation of the *Politics* of Aristotle,
which is now given to the world, is, I hope,
only an instalment of a larger work. It has
always seemed to me that anyone who would
do full justice to the *Politics* has indeed a
threefold task, viz. to translate it, to write a
commentary upon it, and finally to publish a
series of essays on subjects connected with it.
It is only the first, and perhaps the easiest
part of the task that I have now undertaken.
For the second I have already made much preparation; but I am not unaware that other
scholars, more distinguished than I can hope
to be, are labourers in the same field, and it
is possible that the materials which I have
already collected in order to an edition will

not at present or for a long time see the
light.

The text of the present Translation is that
of Bekker's octavo edition published in 1878.
No other text of the *Politics* is at once so
accurate and so accessible to ordinary readers.
The variations from it which I have adopted
are generally such as are justified by the
best MSS. authority, but sometimes conjectural emendations of previous editors or trans-
lators, and in two or three instances my own.
Following Bekker's text, I follow also his order
of the Books. There is much to be said for
it, and it is advisable not to burden a mere
Translation with the discussion of a problem
which belongs properly to critical scholarship.

I have had many helps in preparing this
Translation. I trust I have made some use
of all the recent, and most of the more
ancient works which throw any light upon
the interpretation of the text. A modern
translator of the *Politics* need hardly express
his primary obligation to the labours of Suse-

mihl. But apart from the general sources of information, I enjoyed the privilege, as an undergraduate, of attending the Lectures of Professor Jebb and Mr Henry Jackson upon this book; no doubt they will pardon me, if I have sometimes made their thoughts and even their words my own. Many friends in Cambridge and elsewhere have supplied me with critical opinions on particular passages, and I am grateful to them all. But there are two especial acknowledgments which I must make; the first to Mr Henry Jackson, Fellow and Praelector in Ancient Philosophy in Trinity College, Cambridge, who not only introduced me to the *Politics*, as I have already said, by his Lectures several years ago, but has done me the signal kindness of reading my whole Translation, as it was passing through the press, and aiding me with suggestions which I have often accepted, and never neglected without remembering Hermann's remark about Lachmann; and the second to my relation, the Rev. M. B. Cowell, Vicar of Ashbocking in Suffolk, whose pleasant home has been to me a haven of rest during many weeks that I have devoted to the study of Aristotle.

It only remains to add that corrections or criticisms of the Translation will be gratefully and gladly received.

King's College, Cambridge.
  March 31, 1883.

N.B. The marginal references are to the pages of the Translation, the references in the foot-notes to the pages and lines of Bekker's text.

The words italicized, except in a few self-evident instances, are inserted in order to make the original fully intelligible.

Domestic Economy includes,

    (1)   the relations of a slavemaster to his slaves (δεσποτική),

    (2)   the relations of husband and wife (γαμική),

    (3)   the relations of a parent to his children (τεκνοποιητική or, as it is afterwards called, πατρική),

and (4)   the Art of Finance (χρηματιστική), the nature and scope of which are disputed.

We consider first the relations of master and slave.

CHAPTER IV.

Property (ἡ κτῆσις) is a part or element of the household, and the Art of Acquisition (ἡ κτητική) a part of Domestic Economy. For a householder, like any artist, must have his proper instruments, and every property (κτῆμα) is an instrument conducing to life (ὄργανον πρὸς ζωήν).

Instruments are either animate or inanimate; they are also either instruments of production (ποιητικά) or of action (πρακτικά).

A property is an instrument of action, and a slave is an animate property.

A slave then is an animate instrument or an assistant in the sphere of action (ὑπηρέτης τῶν πρὸς τὴν πρᾶξιν).

As a property is not only the property of its owner but wholly belongs to or depends upon him, so a slave is not only the slave of his master but wholly belongs to him. And thus a natural slave is a human being who is naturally not his own master but belongs to someone else.

CHAPTER V.

Are there then natural slaves, persons for whom a condition of slavery is expedient and just?

The principle of rule and subjection pervades all Nature. We may instance the natural subordination of body to soul (ψυχή) and within the soul itself of appetite (ὄρεξις) to intellect (νοῦς), of the lower animals to man and of females to males. We infer that the same principle is true of human beings generally. Where we find persons as far inferior to others as the body to the soul or as beasts to man, these are natural slaves.

(The slave differs from his master in not possessing reason and from the lower animals in being able to understand it. There is little or no difference between the uses of domestic animals and slaves.)

But this natural absolute distinction between slaves and free persons—a distinction which should be equally conspicuous in their bodies and souls—is not always apparent; hence a dispute as to the justice of slavery.

CHAPTER VI.

There are two kinds of slavery, natural ($\phi\acute{v}\sigma\epsilon\iota$) and conventional ($\nu\acute{o}\mu\varphi$) which are properly distinct but are popularly confused. The reasons of this confusion are (1) that none are so well able to employ force as the virtuous, if they possess adequate external means, and thus virtue appears to imply force, (2) that the stronger are always superior in respect of some Good which is wrongly identified with virtue, and thus force appears to imply virtue. Not perceiving that the existing state of things is partly right and partly wrong, people either identify justice with benevolence and thereby reprobate all slavery, or define justice as the rule of the stronger and thereby justify all slavery. A third theory—a sort of compromise—according to which all such slavery as is the result of war is just, is clearly illogical, as a war may be unjust in its origin.

We conclude that slavery is in itself an institution natural and right, its justification consisting in the intrinsic moral superiority of the master, although the doctrine is not capable of universal application. Where the true relations exist, the institution of slavery is equally beneficial to master and slave.

CHAPTER VII.

It is now clear that the functions of a slavemaster and a constitutional statesman are not the same, as Plato supposed; for in the one case the subjects are slaves and in the other free persons.

It is not a particular science (ἐπιστήμη) but the possession of particular qualities (τῷ τοιόσδ' εἶναι) that constitutes the slave-master. At the same time we may speak of a science proper to the slavemaster, meaning by it the science of using slaves, i.e. of giving them orders about their regular duties.

CHAPTER VIII.

Coming to Finance (χρηματιστική) we have first to consider the true relation of Finance to Domestic Economy.

They are not identical; for it is the business of the former to provide and of the latter to use what is so provided.

Is Finance then a part of Domestic Economy?

As Finance is concerned with the means of acquiring property and property is of various kinds, it is possible that some branches of Finance are parts of Domestic Economy, while others are not. Let us take one main branch of Finance, viz. agriculture or the acquisition of food generally, and examine its relation to Domestic Economy.

(The different kinds of food produce varieties in the lives of animals and human beings. Men live either by grazing, as nomads, or by the chase, whether as brigands, fishers or sportsmen, or by agriculture and the cultivation of fruits, or by a combination of two or more of these pursuits.)

It is the intention of Nature to supply Man with the means of subsistence, or in other words with property, so far as it is necessary to his life. Therefore the Finance by which man appropriates Nature's gifts, i.e. such articles as are necessary to life or useful to persons associated in a State or household, is naturally a part of Domestic Economy. And it is these which constitute genuine wealth.

CHAPTER IX.

There is however a second or unnatural kind of Finance which arises in the following way.

Every commodity admits of two uses (1) its proper use, (2) its use as an article of exchange. The Art of Exchange (ἡ μεταβλητικη) was originally limited to the barter of one commodity against another for the mutual supply of wants, and so far it is not unnatural nor is it a species of Finance in the bad sense. But at a later date it was developed by the invention of a currency (νόμισμα) and took the form of Retail Trading (ἡ καπηλική).

(The idea that Finance is mainly concerned with the acquisition of money arises from the common confusion of money with wealth.)

In a word, the first kind of Finance is natural and necessary, it is a branch of Domestic Economy, and money is only its means; the second is unnatural and unnecessary, and the unlimited acquisition of money is its end.

The two kinds of Finance are apt to be more or less confused, as they both make use of the same material, viz. money, although not in the same way. But the desire of constantly accumulating money arises from an anxiety about the means of living rather than of living well or from an inadequate conception of living well.

CHAPTER X.

We are now in a position to determine more exactly the relation of the good or natural Finance to Domestic Economy. In one sense it is and in another it is not a part of Domestic Economy. The householder or statesman is in a certain sense concerned with the financial means, as he is also with the health, of his household or State; but in either case there is a subordinate art—the Art of Finance or the Art of Medicine—which deals directly and specially with the subject. In strictness however financial means are pre-requisites which it is the business of Nature to provide and of the householder or statesman to use.

Of all the forms of unnatural Finance none is so objectionable as petty usury (ἡ ὀβολοστατική); for in it money is put to a wholly unnatural use, being employed not as a medium of exchange but as a direct means of gain. Hence the name τόκος (lit. offspring); for children are like their parents, and interest is money born of money.

CHAPTER XI.

Finance regarded from the practical side.

(A) The subdivisions of Finance in the natural or proper sense are

(1) Stockfarming.

(2) Husbandry, including both agriculture and the cultivation of trees.

(3) Beekeeping.

(4) The management of fish and fowls.

(B) Unnatural Finance, i.e. Finance which consists in exchange, comprises

(1) Commerce, including marine trade (ναυκληρία) inland trade (φορτηγία) and shopkeeping (παράστασις).

(2) Usury (τοκισμός).

(3) Hired labour (μισθαρνία).

(C) Between these lies a third kind of Finance, to which belong all such arts as depend upon the earth or those products of the earth which are useful, although they do not yield fruit, e.g. wood-cutting (ὑλοτομία) and mining (μεταλλευτική) generally.

The various subdivisions of practical Finance have been treated by particular writers. Among financial schemes the advantage of a monopoly is illustrated by anecdotes of Thales and a Sicilian speculator.

CHAPTER XII.

Of the divisions of Domestic Economy two, viz. the relations of a master to his slaves and Finance, have now been considered. There remain the relations of a father to his children and of a husband to his wife. The rule of a husband over his wife is like the rule of a statesman over the citizens of a constitutional State (πολιτική) except that it is permanent. That of a father over his children is like the rule of a king over his subjects (βασιλική).

CHAPTER XIII.

A question arises as to the capacity of slaves and of women and children for virtue. Is the virtue of master and slave, husband and wife, father and child and generally of natural ruler and natural subject the same or different? The answer is that they are all capable of virtue, but there are different kinds or degrees of virtue, and each must possess it in such a manner as is suitable to the performance of his proper functions.

We have still to consider whether a certain virtue is necessary to the mechanical artisan (βάναυσος τεχνίτης).

The position of the artisan differs from that of the slave. He lives in a state of limited slavery, not sharing his master's life nor having a natural existence, as the slave. Hence his virtue is but a fraction of the slave's virtue.

The virtue of which a slave is capable must be produced in him by his master, not by the mere teacher who instructs him in his duties. And as slaves are capable of a certain virtue and are able to understand reason, it is right to advise them rather than always to order them, as Socrates suggests.

Conclusion :

We have considered Slavery and Finance. The right relations of husband and wife, father and children can only be determined with reference to the polity under which they live. It is necessary therefore to describe the best polity. And a review of celebrated polities whether projected or actually existing will form a natural preface to this description.

BOOK II.

EXAMINATION of polities projected by individual thinkers or existing in States.

CHAPTER I.

The citizens of a State must have
either (1) nothing in common,
or (2) everything in common,
or (3) some things in common and not others.

But the first case is clearly an impossibility, as a polity implies community or association (κοινωνία), and the citizens must at least live in a common locality.

The second is proposed in the *Republic* of Plato, where Socrates argues for a community of wives, children and property.

CHAPTERS II—V.

Criticism of the *Republic* of Plato.

CHAPTER II.

The objections may be ranged under three general heads, viz.

(I) The unification of the State, which Socrates regards as his end, is not proved to be desirable.

(II) Unification, if it were desirable, would not be produced by community of wives, children and property.

(III) The proper limits of this community are not stated.

W. A.   *b*

hh

We take these heads in order.

(I) The unification of the State is not the true end.

For

(1) a State implies a number of people, and as a State approaches unity, it ceases to be a State and becomes first a household and then an individual; so that the unification of a State means its destruction.

(2) The members of a State are not only numerous but different in kind. For it is just this diversity of the component elements which distinguishes an organic whole such as a State from a military confederation.

(N.B. Hence the true preservative principle of States is reciprocal equality (τὸ ἴσον τὸ ἀντιπεπονθός) which among unequals leads to perpetuity of rule or subjection and among equals to alternation of office.)

(3) A condition of more independence is preferable to one of less, and a household is a more independent body (αὐταρκέστερον) than an individual, a State than a household.

CHAPTER III.

(II) Even if it be granted that the unification of the State is the true end, it will not be attained by the means proposed.

According to Socrates the test of unity is that "all simultaneously term the same object *mine* or *not mine*" (ἐὰν πάντες ἅμα λέγωσι τὸ ἐμὸν καὶ τὸ μὴ ἐμόν).

But the word "all" is ambiguous.

"All" may mean either "each individually" or "all collectively."

If in this case it has the first meaning, the formula, however specious, is incapable of realization ; if the latter, it is far from conducive to harmony.

After this verbal criticism Aristotle proceeds to objections of fact.

(A) Community of wives and children.

(1) The sense of individual possession will be absent. People love what is their own ; what belongs to everybody belongs in fact to nobody. But every citizen in the *Republic* is supposed to have 1000 sons, who are as much the sons of any other citizen as his own ; hence no parent will feel more than a remote fractional interest in any child. Besides, no citizen will be able to feel sure that even one of the 1000 sons is really his ; for it will always be possible that no child was born to him or that his child did not survive.

(2) Despite the community of wives and children, it will be impossible to prevent suspicions of relationship arising from the personal likeness of certain children to certain parents.

CHAPTER IV.

(3) If the relationships *are* unknown, it will be difficult to prevent murders of kinsfolk and other impieties ; nor will the proper atonements be made after such deeds.

(4) The community of wives and children will tend to weaken mutual affection in the class among which it prevails. It is therefore a system better suited to the Husbandmen (γεωργοί) or subject class of the *Republic* than to the Guardians (φύλακες) or rulers for whom it is instituted by Socrates.

(5) There will be a difficulty in providing for the transference of children, as Socrates ordains, from one class in the State to another e.g. from the Husbandmen to the Guardians; and in the case of children so transferred there will be especial danger of the impieties above described.

CHAPTER V.

(B) Community of property.

(The question may be considered without reference to the community of wives and children.)

(1) It will occasion constant disputes as to the relation between the labour done and the amount of produce to be enjoyed. The existing system of private tenure would be far preferable, as it gives every man an interest in his own possessions, if a generous disposition were fostered in the citizens. We shall thus gain the benefits of both principles.

(2) It will destroy the pleasure arising from the sense of private property.

(3) Without private property the virtue of liberality is impossible; as also is continence, where there is community of wives.

In a word, the community proposed by Socrates would make life impossible.

His mistake lies in not perceiving that it is a *moral* unity of the State which is alone desirable, and that this unity must be effected by moral, not by mechanical means, i.e. by education rather than by community of property.

Further, the evidence of History is an argument against the Socratic community of wives, children and property; for had it been a beneficial institution, it would have been already devised.

And lastly, the attempt to create a polity of the Socratic type, were it once made, would demonstrate the impossibility of complete unification.

(III) The incompleteness of the polity proposed in the *Republic*.

(1) It is not stated whether the community of wives, children and property is to extend to the Husbandmen as well as to the Guardians. If it is, how will they differ from the Guardians? If it is not, there will be two opposing principles within the State, in fact two States in one, and mutual recrimination, law suits &c. will be as frequent in this State as elsewhere.

(2) The theory of Socrates that his citizens will be so educated as to need few legal regulations is unjustifiable, as he assigns the education to the Guardians alone.

(3) Nothing is said about the political constitution, laws and education of the Husbandmen, although their character is

important to the maintenance of the community among the Guardians.

(4) The Husbandmen, as having an absolute ownership of their estates on condition only of paying rent to the Guardians, will be arrogant and intractable.

(5) If there is to be community of wives, and at the same time private possession of property, among the Husbandmen, who will attend to the domestic affairs, while the men work in the fields?

(IV) Minor objections.

(1) The illustration which Socrates draws from the lower animals, to show that the pursuits of men and women should be the same, is inapposite, as the lower animals are incapable of Domestic Economy.

(2) The proposed perpetuity of rulers, which is a necessary feature of the Socratic polity, will be a cause of political disturbance.

(3) Socrates denies happiness to the Guardians, and yet teaches that the State as a whole ought to be happy. But this is impossible; for if the Guardians are unhappy, à fortiori happiness will be impossible to the other classes, and the happiness of the whole State is incompatible with the unhappiness of all its parts.

CHAPTER VI.

Criticism of the *Laws* of Plato.

The polity of the *Laws* is in numerous respects open to the same strictures as that of the *Republic*. For although it professes to have more affinity to existing States, it is gradually assimilated to the polity of the *Republic*, except in regard to the community of wives, children and property.

The objections are as follows:

(1) Socrates assumes the number of citizens who possess heavy arms to be five thousand, a number preposterously large.

(2) He argues that the legislator ought in his laws "to have regard to the country and the people." It would have been proper to add "to neighbouring lands also."

(3) The amount of property to be held by any citizen is defined as "enough for living temperately" (τοσαύτην ὥστε ζῆν σωφρόνως). But the word "temperately" is ambiguous, it does not exclude penurious living. A better definition would be "temperately and liberally" (σωφρόνως καὶ ἐλευθερίως).

(4) While equalizing all properties, Socrates fails to provide against an increase of population.

(5) The points of distinction between rulers and subjects are not stated.

(6) As a fivefold increase of a citizen's total property is allowed, why should not a similar increase of his landed estate be allowable?

(7) The proposal to assign each citizen two separate homesteads in different parts of the country would be fatal to Domestic Economy.

The polity of the *Laws* is as a whole neither a Democracy nor an Oligarchy but intermediate, i.e. a Polity in the strict sense. This may be the polity which has most affinity to existing States; but it is not the ideal polity, nor is it so good as the Lacedaemonian or a more aristocratical polity.

It is a gross error to assert, as in the *Laws*, that the best polity is a compound of Democracy and Tyranny, the most debased of all polities, if indeed they deserve the name of polities at all. Nor is there any monarchical element in the polity of the *Laws*; it is a compound of oligarchical and democratical elements with an inclination to Oligarchy, as appears from the method of electing the officers of State and the Council.

It may be added that the election of the officers of State by voting from a body previously elected in the same manner is calculated to place great power in the hands of a small knot of people, if they act in combination.

CHAPTER VII.

Among other projectors of polities, whether statesmen and philosophers or ordinary people, no one has shown such originality as Plato in the *Republic* and *Laws;* no one else e.g. has suggested a community of wives and children.

The polity proposed by Phaleas of Chalcedon.

Phaleas held that, as questions of property are the occasions of civil disturbances, the remedy would lie in an equality of pos. sessions.

But

(1) It is useless to define the amount of a citizen's property without defining also the number of his children.

(2) It is not enough merely to establish an equality of property; the legislator must see that the amount fixed is the right one.

(3) Nor is it enough even to fix the proper moderate amount of property. Men's desires need levelling more than their properties; hence the paramount importance of a true education.

(4) Inequality of property is not the only cause of civil disturbance. Inequality of honours is an equally potent cause ; indeed it is not the desire of the mere necessaries of life which is the motive of the greatest crimes.

(N.B. The objects of human desire are

(1) necessaries of life—food, clothing, &c.

(2) gratifications which are not necessary, but still are desired, e.g. honour.

(3) pleasures which are not preceded by desire and yet afford satisfaction when they are obtained, e.g. intellectual pleasures.)

We conclude then that the equality of property, which is the characteristic of Phaleas's polity, is efficacious only as a preventive of petty crimes.

It may be added that he neglects the external relations of the State, although these affect not only the military system but also the amount of property. Perhaps the true limit of property in a State is that it should not be so large as to afford in itself a sufficient inducement to stronger Powers to declare war.

Further objections to the equality of property proposed by Phaleas :

(5) It will produce a feeling of indignation in the upper classes, who consider themselves entitled to a certain superiority.

(6) The mere institution of an equality will not restrain men's desires. The only true remedy consists in some such social arrangement that the higher natures may be unwilling, and the lower unable, to aggrandize themselves.

(7) Phaleas in his equalization of properties has regard to landed estate alone; of a citizen's personal estate he takes no account.

Finally, the position of the Artisans, who are to be public slaves in Phaleas's polity, is unsatisfactory.

CHAPTER VIII.

The polity proposed by Hippodamus of Miletus.

The State to consist of ten thousand citizens, divided into three classes, viz.

(1) Artisans (τεχνῖται)

(2) Husbandmen (γεωργοί)

(3) The Military Class (τὸ προπολεμοῦν μέρος).

The land to be divided into three parts, viz.

(1) sacred, for the maintenance of religious services,

(2) public, for the support of the Military Class.

(3) private, belonging to the Husbandmen.

Also he held that the subjects of judicial procedure were only three, viz.

(1) Assault (ὕβρις)

(2) Trespass (βλάβη)

(3) Homicide (θάνατος).

Further proposals of Hippodamus :

(1) That there should be a single supreme Court of Appeal, constituted of certain Elders appointed by voting.

(2) That jurors should have the power of returning qualified verdicts.

(3) That public honour should be conferred upon anyone who made a discovery beneficial to the State, and that the children of those who fell in war should be supported at the public expense.

(4) That all the officers of State should be elected by the three classes of citizens, and that the officers elected should be entrusted with the conduct of public affairs and with the protection of foreigners and orphans.

Aristotle's criticisms of the polity.

(1) As the Husbandmen are to possess no arms, and the Artisans are to possess neither land nor arms, they will both be practically slaves of the Military Class. They will therefore be excluded from the highest offices of State. The result will be that they will be ill-disposed to the polity.

(2) The place of the Husbandmen in the State is hard to understand. For they are to possess land of their own and cultivate it for themselves. But if the public land is to be cultivated by the Military Class, there will be no such distinction as Hippodamus intends between the Soldiery and the Husbandmen; if by a class distinct from both, it will be a fourth class in the State destitute of political rights; if by the Husbandmen, who at the same time cultivate their own private land, how is each of them to raise produce enough for the support of two households? and what is the good of this elaborate distinction between public and private land?

(3) The provision for a qualified verdict will have the effect of converting the juror ($\delta\iota\kappa\alpha\sigma\tau\acute{\eta}s$) into an arbitrator ($\delta\iota\alpha\iota\tau\eta\tau\acute{\eta}s$) and of producing inevitable confusion in the verdicts returned.

(4) The proposal to reward the authors of discoveries beneficial to the State will lead to intrigues and even disturbances of the polity.

Question raised—Is it injurious or advantageous to States to alter their ancestral laws and customs, where another better law or custom is possible ?

Arguments in favour of alteration :

(1) Such change has proved beneficial in other sciences.

(2) Ancient customs are generally rude and barbarous.

(3) As a law is necessarily general, it cannot meet all individual cases that occur.

Arguments against alteration :

(1) It is necessary to weigh the good derivable from a change of the laws against the evil of accustoming the citizens lightly to repeal their laws.

(2) There is no true parallel between altering an art and altering a law, as the efficacy of the law is wholly dependent upon the habit of obedience among the citizens, and habit can only be the work of time.

Further, even assuming the propriety of altering the laws, we have still to enquire when and under what conditions and by what agency the alteration should be effected.

CHAPTER IX.

We come now to existing polities.

Every such polity must be considered

(1) relatively to the best possible system,

(2) relatively to the principle of the polity which the citizens propose to themselves.

The Lacedaemonian polity.

Its principal defects :

(1) The condition of the Helots, who have always been hostile to their masters and ready for revolt.

(2) The licence of the women, which is not only indecorous in itself but contributes to produce an avaricious disposition in the citizens.

(N.B. The explanation of this licence is to be found in the long-continued absence of the husbands from home in early times on military expeditions.)

(3) The inequality of property;

for (*a*) although the sale of patrimonial estates is discouraged, yet, as there is absolute liberty of presentation and bequest, the ownership of the soil has fallen into the hands of a few persons.

(*b*) owing to the number of heiresses and the practice of giving large dowries, nearly two-fifths of the whole soil belongs to women. Nor is there any law regulating the betrothal of heiresses.

The result is that the civic population capable of bearing arms has gradually dwindled from fifteen hundred knights and thirty thousand heavy-armed men to less than a thousand soldiers in all.

(There was an ancient practice of conferring the Lacedaemonian citizenship upon foreigners and thereby preventing depopulation; but it has been abandoned.)

The evil is aggravated by the law encouraging the citizens to beget as many children as possible, many of whom, as the landed estates are in the hands of a few persons, are necessarily reduced to poverty.

(4) The institution of the Ephoralty.

It is true that the Ephoral office, as supplying the commons with some sort of representation, tends to the preservation of the polity. But

(*a*) as all classes of citizens are equally eligible to the Ephoralty, it often happens that the Ephors are poor and therefore venal.

(*b*) the high prerogatives of the Ephors degrade and depress the regal authority.

(*c*) the existing method of election to the Ephoralty is puerile.

(*d*) the judicial authority of the Ephors should be exercised, not arbitrarily, as in fact it is, but in accordance with written formulae or laws.

(e) the lax and dissolute life of the Ephors is inconsistent with the spirit of the State.

(5)   The conditions of the Senate.

As the Senators are irresponsible (ἀνεύθυνοι) and hold office for life, they are apt to be corrupt, and their authority remains when they are past the period of intellectual vigour.   Also the method of their election is puerile, and their personal canvass for office highly undesirable.

(6)   The hereditary character of the Kingship.

Kings, if they exist at all, should be appointed on the score of virtue ; whereas the Lacedaemonian legislator clearly distrusts the virtue of the Kings.

(7)   The organization of the common meals (συσσίτια) or Phiditia :

for (a) the expense of them is borne by the individual citizens, and not, as it should be, by the State.

(b) as citizenship depends upon payment of a tax for the maintenance of the common meals, and the poor are unable to pay it, the institution is practically exclusive, instead of being democratical.

(8)   The Admiralty which, being an office held for life, tends to become a second and opposing Kingship.

(9)   The end (τέλος) of the whole polity being military strength, the result has been that the Lacedaemonians were successful, so long as they were engaged in war, but, when their empire was established, came to grief.

(10)   The spirit of the polity is in this respect defective, that Virtue is not regarded as the supreme Good.

(11)   The financial system is bad.   For there is no reserve fund in the Exchequer, and, as all the land is in the hands of the Spartiates, who wink at each other's evasion of the law, the extraordinary taxes (εἰσφοραί) are irregularly paid.

In a word, the Lacedaemonian State as a whole is pauperized, but the individual citizens are avaricious.

CHAPTER X.

The Cretan polity.

It is closely parallel to the Lacedaemonian, although generally less elaborated.

(The story is that Lycurgus lived some time in Crete and afterwards adopted the Cretan polity as the model of his own.)

Comparison of the Cretan and Lacedaemonian polities.

There is in both a subject agricultural class, the Perioeci in Crete, the Helots in Lacedaemon;

and in both the institution of common meals, which in Crete were called Andria and in Lacedaemon Phiditia.

Also the ten Cretan Cosmi correspond to the five Ephors,

and the Council (βουλή) in Crete to the Senate (γερουσία) in Lacedaemon.

Kingship existed formerly in Crete, but was abolished; and military command belongs now to the Cosmi.

Lastly, in Crete as at Lacedaemon all the citizens may attend the Public Assembly (ἐκκλησία), but the power of the Cretan Public Assembly is limited to confirming the resolutions of the Senate and Cosmi.

In the Cretan polity Aristotle eulogizes

(1) the system of the common meals, which are maintained at the cost of the State rather than by the contributions of individuals.

(2) the abstemiousness.

(3) the provision against an excessive increase of population.

He censures

(1) the institution of the Cosmi, which is open to the same objection as the Ephoralty, viz. the eligibility of persons who possess no special qualification, without the same compensating advantage in assuring the goodwill of the commons to the polity; for the Cosmi are elected not from the whole body of citizens, but only from certain privileged families.

(2) the Senate, which, as at Lacedaemon, is an irresponsible body, holding office for life and exercising arbitrary power, and which at the same time consists entirely of ex-Cosmi.

(3) the general tendency to lawlessness, especially among the influential citizens.

The Cretans, despite these causes of weakness, have been hitherto preserved from subjection by their isolation.

CHAPTER XI.

The Carthaginian polity.

The Cretan, Lacedaemonian and Carthaginian polities form a distinct group.

Comparison of the Carthaginian and Lacedaemonian polities :

The common meals of the Clubs ($\tau \grave{a}$ $\sigma \upsilon \sigma \sigma \acute{\iota} \tau \iota a$ $\tau \hat{\omega} \nu$ $\acute{\epsilon} \tau a \iota \rho \iota \hat{\omega} \nu$) answer to the Phiditia ;

the office of the Hundred-and-Four ($\acute{\eta}$ $\tau \hat{\omega} \nu$ $\acute{\epsilon} \kappa a \tau \grave{o} \nu$ $\kappa a \grave{\iota}$ $\tau \epsilon \tau \tau \acute{a} \rho \omega \nu$ $\grave{a} \rho \chi \acute{\eta}$) to the Ephoralty ;

the Kings and Senate to the Kings and Senate.

But there are these two points of superiority at Carthage,

(1) that the Hundred-and-Four are not elected from any ordinary people, but on the score of personal merit,

(2) that the Kings do not belong to a single family, and do not succeed to the throne by seniority.

Aristotle passes the following criticisms upon the Carthaginian polity :

(1) It provides that, if the Kings and Senate agree upon a matter, they need not lay it before the Public Assembly ; if they disagree, they must refer it to the commons. But the Public Assembly has full power of discussing and deciding all such matters as are laid before it—a greater power than any which exists at Lacedaemon or in Crete. This is an error on the side of Democracy.

There are other errors on the side of Oligarchy, e.g.

(2) The authority of the Pentarchies is excessive ; for not only do they enjoy the right of cooption to their own body, but

they elect the highest officers of State, viz. the Hundred, and their tenure of official power both begins before and continues after their actual term of office.

(3) There is practically a disposition in the election of the officers of State to pay regard to wealth as well as to merit.

(4) The highest offices of State, viz. the Kingship and Generalship, are put up to sale.

(5) Several offices are often concentrated in the hands of an individual; the result being that the duties are ill performed.

Despite the oligarchical character of the polity the Carthaginians avoid civil disturbance by a system of emigration. This however is a result that is due to Fortune rather than to the skill of the legislator.

CHAPTER XII.

Notes upon various polities.

(1) Solon is sometimes eulogized as having founded a tempered Democracy in place of an unqualified Oligarchy, by leaving, as he found them, the oligarchical Council of Areopagus and the aristocratical system of election to the offices of State, but establishing the popular Courts of Law ($\delta\iota\kappa\alpha\sigma\tau\acute{\eta}\rho\iota\alpha$) in which all the citizens were allowed to sit.

At other times he is censured for having virtually destroyed the non-democratical element in the State by assigning the supreme judicial power to the Courts of Law, which were chosen by lot.

Aristotle's view is that the progress of Democracy at Athens was due not so much to the policy of Solon as to the importance acquired by the commons in the Persian wars and to the unscrupulous conduct of the demagogues. Solon gave the commons no more than the necessary *minimum* of political power ($\tau\grave{\eta}\nu$ $\dot{\alpha}\nu\alpha\gamma\kappa\alpha\iota\sigma\tau\acute{\alpha}\tau\eta\nu$ $\delta\acute{\upsilon}\nu\alpha\mu\iota\nu$) viz. the right of electing officers of State and holding them responsible ($\tau\grave{o}$ $\tau\grave{\alpha}s$ $\dot{\alpha}\rho\chi\grave{\alpha}s$ $\alpha\acute{\iota}\rho\epsilon\acute{\iota}\sigma\theta\alpha\iota$ $\kappa\alpha\grave{\iota}$ $\epsilon\acute{\upsilon}\theta\acute{\upsilon}\nu\epsilon\iota\nu$); the lowest or Thetic class in his constitution he deliberately excluded from office.

(2) Philolaus, the Theban legislator, is famous for his laws of adoption (νόμοι θετικοί) which were intended to preserve the original number of the allotments.

(3) Charondas instituted the solemn indictment for perjury (ἐπίσκηψις).

(4) In the laws of Phaleas the peculiar feature is the equalization of properties.

(5) Plato alone devised the community of wives, children and property, the common meals of the women, the law regulating convivial meetings, and the law of military exercises intended to make the citizens equally dexterous in the use of both hands.

(6) The laws of Draco, which were made for a polity already existing, are chiefly characterized by their severity.

(7) It was a law of Pittacus that drunken people, if they committed a breach of order, should be punished more severely than sober.

(8) Androdamas of Rhegium, who was the legislator of the Chalcidians in the Thracian peninsula, was the author of laws relating to homicide and to the treatment of heiresses.

BOOK III.

CHAPTER I.

In an inquiry into the nature of particular polities it is necessary to begin by considering the nature of a State,

and, as a State is a whole composed of a number of citizens, it is necessary to inquire the nature of a citizen.

Putting out of sight then persons who acquire the citizenship in some exceptional way, e.g. honorary citizens, we have to determine what it is that constitutes a citizen.

(1) It is not residence; for slaves and aliens (μέτοικοι) are resident in the State as much as the citizens.

(2) Nor is it participation in legal rights; for this is a qualification possessed by members of different States who associate on the basis of commercial treaties (οἱ ἀπὸ συμβόλων κοινωνοῦντες).

It must be participation in judicial power and public office (τὸ μετέχειν κρίσεως καὶ ἀρχῆς) i.e. the right of acting as a member of the Public Assembly and the Courts of Law.

(N.B. The offices of State (ἀρχαί) are either determinate in point of time or perpetual.)

This definition of a citizen is strictly applicable only to Democracies; in polities in which there is no democratical element, or no regular meetings of the Public Assembly, or in which the administration of justice is entrusted to various special boards, it applies, but with a certain limitation.

A State then may be defined as such a number of citizens as is sufficient for independence of life, the word "citizens" being defined as above.

CHAPTER II.

This being the theoretical definition of a citizen,

a citizen is defined for practical purposes as one who is descended from citizens on both sides, although it is sometimes required that his ancestors in the third or a higher degree should have been citizens.

(Parenthetically it is remarked

(1) that in any case the citizenship must in the first instance be dependent upon the qualification stated in Chap. I.

(2) that persons, who obtain political rights in consequence of a revolution, are undoubtedly to be regarded as citizens, even if their title to the citizenship appears to be unjust.)

CHAPTER III.

It is sometimes doubted, especially after a revolution, whether a particular action, performed by the preexisting government, has been the action of the State or only of certain individuals in the State.

W. A.

We are therefore led to inquire: What is it in which the identity of a State consists?

Not (1) in its enclosure within certain walls. The fact of circumvallation does not in itself constitute a State at all; for a State cannot exceed a reasonable magnitude, and yet it would be possible to enclose a whole country within walls.

Nor (2) in the identity of the race inhabiting it.

The identity of a State depends upon the identity of its polity.

CHAPTER IV.

Question raised: Is the virtue of a good man and of a virtuous citizen identical or different?

In order to answer it, we must ascertain what the virtue of a citizen is.

A citizen is a member of a society. But the members of any society have always a common object; and the object of all the citizens is the safety of their association, i.e. of the polity to which they belong. It follows that the virtue of a citizen is necessarily relative to the polity.

If then the virtue of a citizen is relative to his polity, and there are varieties of polity, the virtue of citizens cannot always be one and the same;

therefore the virtue of a good citizen is not always identical with that of a good man, for the virtue of a good man is a uniform perfect virtue.

Or again, Even if all the members of a State are assumed to be virtuous citizens, yet they have different functions to discharge; hence they cannot all be alike, i.e. they cannot all be good men.

Or to put the same argument in another way,

A State consists of dissimilar members, some superior, others subordinate;

therefore they cannot all possess a uniform virtue.

But if it is now clear that the virtue of a virtuous citizen and of a virtuous man is not absolutely ($\dot{\alpha}\pi\lambda\hat{\omega}s$) and in all cases the same, we have yet to ask whether there are certain cases in which the virtue of both is the same.

Let us consider the matter thus:

The virtuous ruler is admitted to combine goodness and prudence;

but prudence (φρόνησις) is not a necessary attribute of the citizen.

Assuming then that the virtue of a good ruler and a good man is identical, we see that, as the subject no less than the ruler is a citizen, it will only be in certain cases, i.e. when the citizen is a ruler, that the virtue of a good citizen and a good man will be identical.

But it may be objected that the capacity for rule and subjection alike is commonly regarded as laudable.

The solution of the difficulty is as follows:

There are two kinds of rule, viz.

(1) despotic, in which the functions of ruler and subject are absolutely distinct.

(2) political or constitutional, in which the ruler learns to rule by being first a subject.

Thus in a State, of which the citizens are free and equal, a good man will be capable alike of rule and subjection. All virtues except prudence he will be able to exercise, although in different degrees, both as ruler and as subject; prudence alone he will exercise only as ruler. Yet, because the time must come when he will be ruler, he will possess prudence, although it be latent, when he is a subject.

CHAPTER V.

The position of mechanics (οἱ βάναυσοι). Are they citizens?

If they are citizens, it follows that, as they are ineligible to office, the ability to hold office cannot be characteristic of all citizens.

If they are not citizens, what is their position?

The truth is that in any State there are classes of people, e.g. slaves and freedmen, who are indispensable to its existence (ὧν ἄνευ οὐκ ἂν εἴη πόλις) and yet are not citizens; and the mechanics constitute such a class.

But their position is variable.

In the best State, and indeed in any aristocratical State, the citizenship will not be conferred upon any mechanic, as mechanics are incapable of a life of virtue. In the extreme Democracy mechanics will be citizens. In an Oligarchy a mechanic, who has acquired great wealth, will obtain the citizenship. For the limits of the citizenship are different in different States.

We conclude then that there are some States in which the virtue of the good man and the virtue of the good citizen are combined in the same individual, and others in which they are distinct, and that in the former they are not combined in every citizen, but only in one who is capable of exercising, whether individually or conjointly with others, an influence upon the conduct of public affairs.

CHAPTER VI.

A polity may be defined as an order of the State in respect of its offices generally and especially of the supreme office.

The nature of the polity is determined by the governing class (πολίτευμά ἐστιν ἡ πολιτεία).

(1) The object for which a State is framed (τίνος χάριν συνέστηκε πόλις).

Man, as has been said, is a political animal; hence independently of personal advantage men are anxious to live together. But life itself, and, still more, the higher life (τὸ ζῆν καλῶς) are also objects of the political association.

(2) The various kinds of rule.

It is possible to rule either for the good of the ruler, as in the government of slaves, or for the good of the subjects, as in the direction of a family.

(3) one who has merely learnt the principles of the medical art (ὁ πεπαιδευμένος περὶ τὴν τέχνην),
and that the right of criticism belongs as much to the third class as to the second. To this third class correspond the Many in political affairs.

It may be added

(1) that the Many, although individually inferior, are collectively superior, as judges, to the select Few; as has been already shown.

(2) that there are some arts of which the artist himself is not so good a judge as the person who uses the product of the art, e.g. the art of building; and Politics, it is implied, is such an art.

We repeat that it is not the individual members of the commons, but the collective body of commons, who are invested with supreme authority in political affairs of the highest moment, such as the election of the officers of State and the scrutiny of their official conduct.

It is clear however that the laws, if enacted on right principles, ought to be supreme, and that the officers of State ought not to enjoy supreme authority except where the laws necessarily fail through their generality. What is the character of right laws is a point we have still to consider.

CHAPTER XII.

(In this and the next Chapter Aristotle resumes and continues several topics which have been already treated.)

As in every science and art the end proposed (τὸ τέλος) is some Good, as in the highest science or art, viz. the political, the end is the highest Good, viz. justice or the interest of the community, and as justice is a species of equality, we have now to ascertain what it is that constitutes personal equality or inequality.

It is clear that the question of superiority must always be considered relatively to the end proposed. For instance, it is the best flute-player, not the person of greatest beauty or highest rank, who is entitled to the best flutes. Similarly a claim to political power can only be justified by the possession of some quality which enters into the constitution of a State.

Accordingly we recognize the claims of birth, freedom and wealth, as these are elements indispensable to a State's existence;

but we recognize also the claims of justice and military virtue, as being essential to its good administration.

CHAPTER XIII.

If then we take a good life as the end or object of a State's existence, it seems that virtue has the strongest claim to political power.

But it will be worth while to consider the case a little more closely.

The title of the rich to political power is that they have a larger interest in the soil, and a higher commercial character.

That of the free population consists in their mere citizenship.

That of the nobles is that they are citizens in a higher sense, and that rank is a certain guarantee of virtue.

That of the virtuous rests upon the primary importance of virtue to a State.

That of the numerical majority consists in their collective superiority of strength and virtue to the select minority.

The question arises then: If all these different classes exist simultaneously in a State, who shall be supreme?

Whichever view we take, a difficulty meets us.

The claim of the wealthy or the noble or the virtuous would logically justify the claim of an individual to absolute power, if he were richer or nobler or more virtuous than all the rest of the citizens.

The claim of the masses to power on the score of superior strength would justify Tyranny or Oligarchy, if the individual or the Few were stronger than all the rest of the citizens.

And lastly, the claim of the Few to power on the score of virtue or wealth may be met by the masses with the reply that they are collectively more virtuous or wealthier than the Few.

The cultivators of the soil should be slaves, although not all of one stock or of spirited temper, or, if not slaves, members of a slavish non-Greek people.

CHAPTER XI.

To revert to the best State:

(6) The site of the city considered relatively to internal purposes.

There are four points to which it is necessary to have regard:

(a) healthiness, which is mainly dependent upon a favourable aspect—an Eastward aspect being the best—and upon a good supply of water.

(b) convenience for military and political purposes.

(It is remarked parenthetically that a citadel is suited to an Oligarchy or Monarchy, level ground to a Democracy, and a number of different strongholds to an Aristocracy.)

(c) the architectural plan of the city, which should be so far regular ($\epsilon \ddot{v} \tau o \mu o s$) as to have a pleasing effect, and yet to some extent irregular, so as to puzzle an invading force.

(d) its walls, which are indispensable as a defence against military attacks.

CHAPTER XII.

Detail arrangements of the city.

(a) Some of the common meals ($\sigma v \sigma \sigma i \tau \iota a$) may conveniently be held in the guard-houses ($\phi v \lambda a \kappa \tau \acute{\eta} \rho \iota a$) which are placed at intervals along the walls.

(b) The buildings appropriated to the worship of the Gods and to the common meals of the priests and the supreme boards of magistrates should be placed close together.

(c) There should be a free market ($\grave{\epsilon} \lambda \epsilon v \theta \acute{\epsilon} \rho a \ \grave{a} \gamma o \rho \acute{a}$) distinct from the market of commerce.

Detail arrangements of the country.

It is well to adopt the same principle of distribution as in the city in regard to the guard-houses and common meals of the commissioners of woods and forests (ὑλωροί) and to the sanctuaries of Gods and heroes.

CHAPTER XIII.

In order to determine the character of the citizens who are proper to compose the best State, it is necessary to begin with a definition of happiness.

Success of any kind (τὸ εὖ) depends upon choosing the right goal and employing the right means to attain it.

All men are evidently desirous of happiness (εὐδαιμονία).

What is then the nature of happiness?

It has been defined in the *Ethics* to be "a complete activity and practice of virtue, and this not conditionally but in an absolute sense" (ἐνέργεια καὶ χρῆσις ἀρετῆς τελεία, καὶ αὕτη οὐκ ἐξ ὑποθέσεως ἀλλ' ἁπλῶς) i.e. the unimpeded practice of such conduct as is virtuous *per se* and not merely necessary owing to certain existing conditions.

Of the elements of happiness some must be preexistent, others must be provided by the legislator. External Goods e.g. which are conditions, although not causes, of happiness are the gifts of Fortune alone. It is the right use of them which constitutes a State virtuous (σπουδαία). But a State cannot be virtuous, unless the citizens composing it are virtuous. We are thus brought face to face with the question, How is virtue produced in an individual? Answer—The means are threefold, nature (φύσις), habit (ἔθος), reason (λόγος).

Nature is necessary; the person must be a human being and must possess certain qualities of body and soul.

Habit is the means by which the ambiguous tendencies of nature are directed to a higher or a lower end.

Reason is the distinctive characteristic of man.

Natural qualities and gifts are beyond our power; we can only pray for them. Habit and reason are formed by education (παιδεία).

CHAPTER XIV.

Education.

The first point to be decided is whether the same persons shall always be rulers, and the same persons always subjects, or the rulers of one time shall be the subjects of another and *vice versa;* for upon this the character of their education will depend.

In default of an absolute and unmistakeable natural preeminence, separating the ruling from the subject class, an alternation of rule and subjection is clearly just. At the same time it is proper that the rulers should be superior to their subjects. Let the same persons then be rulers and subjects, but subjects in their youth and rulers in their later years; so will both conditions be fulfilled.

Hence their education too will be in one sense the same and in another sense will be different. But subjection, unless it is servile, is not incompatible with liberal culture; and as the subject of to-day is destined to be the ruler of to-morrow, it will always be the object of the legislator in his educational system to study the attainment of goodness or a noble life.

The soul (ψυχή) is divided into two parts,

(1) the part which contains reason in itself (τὸ μὲν ἔχει λόγον καθ᾽ αὑτό).

(2) the part which, although not containing reason in itself, is yet capable of obeying it. (τὸ δ᾽ οὐκ ἔχει μὲν καθ᾽ αὑτό, λόγῳ δ᾽ ὑπακούειν δυνάμενον).

Again, reason is (a) speculative (θεωρητικός).

(b) practical (πρακτικός).

According to the universal law by which the lower in Nature or Art always exists for the sake of the higher, it follows that the actions of the rational part of the soul are more estimable than those of the irrational part, and that the actions of the speculative are more estimable than those of the practical reason. Akin to this is the subordination of business to leisure, of war to peace, and of such actions as at best are only indispensable to such as are intrinsically virtuous.

This law of subordination is ignored in many polities, notably in the Lacedaemonian, in which foreign conquest has been regarded as the paramount end of legislation. It is a mistake to consider despotic rule the object of a State. The principles of morality are the same for States as for individuals, and it is these which the legislator should implant in the minds of the citizens.

War is justifiable in three cases only,

(1) if it is defensive.

(2) if the power so acquired is for the good of the subject population.

(3) if the subjects are natural slaves and deserve to be ruled.

History shows that States which have aimed exclusively at military success have collapsed as soon as they had attained their primary object.

CHAPTER XV.

The citizens then must possess all the virtues; not only those e.g. valour and endurance, which are necessary to business or war, but also those which are necessary to leisure, such as intellectual culture (φιλοσοφία), and those which are necessary to both, but especially to leisure, such as temperance and justice.

But how shall they attain these virtues? Shall their education begin with the reason or with the habits! (πότερον παιδευτέοι τῷ λόγῳ πρότερον ἢ τοῖς ἔθεσιν).

Any process of production starts from a beginning and tends to an end. In education, the beginning is nature, the process of production is the training of habits, the end is reason. The training of the habits therefore must precede reason. Similarly, the care of the body must precede that of the soul, and in the soul itself the care of the irrational part must precede that of the rational. Nor must we ever forget the proper subordination of body to soul, and of the irrational part of soul to the rational.

CHAPTER XVI.

The importance of a good physical condition to the citizens necessitates a discussion of marriage.

We have to consider

(1) the proper seasons for marrying,

(2) the proper persons to marry.

It is desirable so to order the ages of the husband and wife that the failure of their generative powers may occur simultaneously, and that the children may be strong and healthy and may be ready in due time to succeed to their parents' places.

Aristotle is strongly opposed to very youthful marriages.

He would have a man marry about 37 and beget children until 50, and a woman marry about 18.

The winter is the best time of year for the matrimonial union.

The best physical condition for men and women alike is one that is neither athletic nor valetudinarian, but intermediate.

The women are to take great care of their health during pregnancy.

It should be forbidden to rear a crippled child; but the exposure of children simply on the ground of their number will be unnecessary in a State in which the number of children a man may beget is limited by law.

Adultery is to be severely punished.

CHAPTER XVII.

The education of the young.

(1) Infancy.

Diet is important in the early days of life; Aristotle recommends plenty of milk and as little wine as possible.

The children should be allowed free movement, and should be gradually inured to cold.

(2) From infancy to the age of five.

No compulsory study or violent exercise, but enough movement in games to prevent a sluggish habit of body. The overseers of youth (παιδονόμοι) are to take care that the children do
not hear any improper tales and legends and to keep them from
associating much with slaves.

All foul language to be prohibited. No indecent pictures to
be exhibited. No one who is not of full age to be present at the
performance of satirical plays or comedies.

(3) From five years to seven.

These years are to be spent by the young in observation of the
lessons which they will be required in future to learn themselves
(θεωροὶ τῶν μαθήσεων ἃς δεήσει μανθάνειν αὐτούς).

The education of the first seven years has now been described.

Education in the strict sense of the word, which does not
begin until after seven years, may be divided into two periods :

(1) from seven years to puberty,

(2) from puberty to twenty-one.

BOOK V.

CHAPTER I.

Three questions proposed :

(1) whether it is desirable to have a definite educational
system.

(2) whether education should be regulated by the State or
committed to the care of private individuals.

(3) if there is to be a system of education, what should be
its nature.

(1) That the education of the young is a matter which has a
paramount claim upon the attention of the legislator is undeni-
able.

For (*a*) as there is a certain character (ἦθος) proper to each polity, the nature of the polity will determine the educational system.

(*b*) virtue, like any art or faculty, can only be acquired by education.

(2) Education must be regulated by the State.

For as the end (τέλος) of the State as a whole is one, the education of all the citizens must be one and the same, and must therefore be an affair of the State.

Every citizen should remember that he is not his own master (αὐτὸς αὑτοῦ) but a part of the State.

CHAPTER II.

(3) The educational system.

At present much uncertainty attaches to the subjects of education.

Are they to be

such studies as are merely useful as means of livelihood (τὰ χρήσιμα πρὸς τὸν βίον),

or, such as tend to the promotion of virtue (τὰ τείνοντα πρὸς ἀρετήν),

or, the higher studies (τὰ περιττά)?

Nor is "virtue" itself an unambiguous term.

According to Aristotle,

(*a*) it is right to teach those useful subjects which are indispensable (τὰ ἀναγκαῖα τῶν χρησίμων), but not such as have a degrading effect upon the learner by reducing him to the level of a mechanic (βάναυσος).

(A mechanical occupation (βάναυσον ἔργον) is defined as one which renders the body or soul or intellect of free persons unfit for the practice of virtue.)

(*b*) there are some sciences which are liberal in themselves but illiberal in their effect upon the mind, if studied with excessive assiduity.

It is not so much the study itself as the object with which it is undertaken which constitutes it liberal or the reverse.

CHAPTER III.

The ordinary branches of education are four, viz.

    (1)   Reading and Writing (γράμματα).

    (2)   Gymnastic (γυμναστική).

    (3)   Music (μουσική).

    (4)   The Art of Design (γραφική).

Of these

    (1)   Reading and Writing and (4) Design are taught for their practical utility.

    (2)   Gymnastic as promoting valour.

    (3)   Music—for a purpose which has not been clearly defined.

What is then the purpose of Music as an educational instrument?

It is generally taught in our own day for no other reason than the pleasure it affords; but it had originally a higher function.

For that men should spend their leisure (σχολή) nobly is in Nature's intention even more important than that they should do their business rightly.

We have to consider then the right employment of leisure.

It should not be spent in amusement; for amusement, far from being the end (τέλος) of human life, is only a resource by which a busy man is enabled to do a greater amount of business.

Amusement is a temporary relaxation of the soul; leisure on the other hand implies happiness (εὐδαιμονία), which is an end or final state.

The conclusion is that there are certain subjects in which education is necessary with a view to leisure, and that these subjects are the highest parts of education.

Thus the true use of Music is that it promotes the rational enjoyment of leisure (ἡ ἐν τῇ σχολῇ διαγωγή). It is an element of the education which should be given not as being indispensable or practically useful but as liberal and noble. Nobility is a better end educationally than mere utility.

(Aristotle remarks that some subjects besides their practical utility possess a higher value, e.g. the Art of design, which not only protects men against imposture in their private purchases but renders them scientific observers of physical beauty.)

The order of natural development suggests that the education of the body should precede that of the intellect, or in other words, that education should begin with Gymnastic.

CHAPTER IV.

Gymnastic (γυμναστική).

The practice of Gymnastic has frequently been carried too far, resulting either in an athletic habit of body to the detriment of natural growth and grace, or, as at Lacedaemon, in a brutality which is supposed to imply and represent valour.

Valour however is neither the sole nor the chief end of education; nor, if it were, would it be produced by severe Gymnastic. Ferocity oftener denotes lack of true courage. The explanation of the Lacedaemonian victories in old days is not that their gymnastic exercises were so severe, but that they were the only people who employed Gymnastic at all; since they have had rivals who have adopted the same discipline, their supremacy has disappeared.

Not brutality, but nobleness should hold the first place in our educational system.

Aristotle's own plan is as follows:

Up to puberty light exercises; no hard diet, lest the growth be injured. For three years after puberty other pursuits; afterwards hard diet and severe exercise.

The principle is that body and mind should not be subjected to severe exertion simultaneously.

CHAPTER V.

Music.

The discussion which was begun in Chap. III. resumed and concluded.

What is the object with which music ought to be studied?

Various answers are given:

(1) For amusement and relaxation (παιδιὰ καὶ ἀνάπαυσις).

(2) For its moral effect (ὡς δυναμένη τὸ ἦθος ποιόν τι ποιεῖν).

(3) As a means of rational enjoyment (διαγωγή).

Aristotle's decision is that Music is capable of all these different effects,

(1) of amusement, as being pleasant and producing relaxation,

(3) of rational enjoyment, because happiness (εὐδαιμονία) can only be attained in rational enjoyment, and happiness implies an element of pleasure as well as of nobleness.

(It is remarked that for two reasons the world often regards its amusements as the end (τέλος) or *summum bonum* of life,

(a) because there is a certain pleasure in the end itself as well as in amusement.

(b) because the end has this in common with amusement, that it is not sought as a means to any future object; for the end is *ex hypothesi* complete in itself, and the reason of amusement lies not in the future but in the past, i.e. amusement is the relief of previous toil.)

But (2) Music has also a moral power.

Of this the proofs are

(a) that Music is able to produce certain moods, e.g. enthusiasm, in our souls,

(b) that Music supplies us with representations of states of mind, such as anger, courage, gentleness &c., and a feeling of sympathy with these representations ensures a sympathy with the actual states so represented.

(N.B. This power of moral imitation or representation is almost peculiar to the sense of hearing; it is not found in the objects of touch and taste, and only to a small extent in the objects of sight.)

Different moods are produced by different harmonies,

e.g. melancholy by the mixed Lydian (ἡ μιξολυδιστί),

sedateness	,,	,,	Dorian (ἡ δωριστί),
enthusiasm	,,	,,	Phrygian (ἡ φρυγιστί).

There is in fact an apparent relationship between the soul on the one hand and harmonies and rhythms on the other.

Music then, having a moral effect, is a subject of instruction appropriate to the young, as they like everything to be sweetened, and there is a natural sweetness in Music.

CHAPTER VI.

The question is started: As it has been shewn that the young ought to receive instruction in Music, are they to be performers themselves or merely to listen to the performances of professionals?

It may be urged

(a) that it is pretty well impossible to become good critics without such practical experience.

(b) that the practice of Music is one way of keeping children occupied.

Yet it is always necessary to remember that the sole object of the musical performances is to enable the young to form a correct musical judgment.

They should perform therefore, but should perform only in youth. Also great care should be taken in the choice of the melodies and rhythms which they practise, and of their musical instruments. Performances of an extraordinary and exceptional kind, suitable only to professional musicians, are to be forbidden. The flute, harp and cithern are undesirable instruments, as de-

W. A. *e*

manding professional skill; the flute too, as strongly exciting (ὀργιαστικόν).

In a word all professional education, whether in regard to the instruments or to the execution, is to be rejected.

CHAPTER VII.

Melodies (μέλη) have been appropriately classified as ethical, practical or enthusiastic, according as they affect the character, incite to action, or produce enthusiasm.

Music (says Aristotle) should be used for three distinct purposes, viz. (1) as a means of education (παιδείας ἕνεκεν), (2) for the purging of the emotions (πρὸς κάθαρσιν), and (3) for the relaxation of the tense condition of the soul (πρὸς τὴν τῆς συντονίας ἀνάπαυσιν).

Also different harmonies are suited to these different purposes, e.g. ethical harmonies to the first, practical and enthusiastic harmonies to the second and third.

(The purging of the emotions (κάθαρσις) is explained as follows:

A person—let us say—is liable to the emotion of enthusiasm. He listens to melodies which rouse the soul to ecstasy. The after-result is that he relapses into his proper normal condition; he has, so to speak, obtained a medical or purgative treatment (ὥσπερ ἰατρείας τυχὼν καὶ καθάρσεως). The same is true of all emotional persons).

Socrates is wrong in admitting the Phrygian harmony into his *Republic*, as it is exciting and emotional in its effects.

The Dorian harmony, being especially staid and valorous, is suited to the education of the young.

The Lydian harmony combines propriety with culture, and may therefore be regarded as fit for the age of childhood.

N.B. Possibility and propriety are the two objects which must be always kept in view in education.

In regard to Music the three canons are that it should be of an intermediate character, within the capacity of the learner, and appropriate to his age.

BOOK VI.

CHAPTER I.

The scientific politician ought to know

(1)   the absolutely best polity (ἡ ἁπλῶς ἀρίστη).

(2)   the best polity under the actual conditions (ἡ ἐκ τῶν ὑποκειμένων ἀρίστη).

(3)   the best polity under certain supposed conditions (ἡ ἐξ ὑποθέσεως ἀρίστη).

(4)   the polity which is most appropriate to the mass of States (ἡ μάλιστα πάσαις ταῖς πόλεσιν ἁρμόττουσα), or which is comparatively easy of attainment and has a closer affinity to the polities of all existing States (ἡ ῥάων καὶ κοινοτέρα ἁπάσαις).

In order to reform existing polities as well as to call new polities into being, he must be familiar with all the different kinds of polity and with all the specific varieties of each kind. It is this knowledge alone which will be his guide in the enactment of laws ; for law is always relative to the polity in which it exists.

N.B.   A polity is defined as the general system of any State in regard to the distribution of the executive offices, the supreme political authority and the end which the citizens propose to themselves ; laws, on the other hand, are only the conditions by which the tenure of office is regulated.

CHAPTER II.

Upon the arrangement of the work.

Polities having been divided (Book iii. Chap. 7) into three normal, viz. Kingship, Aristocracy and Polity in the narrow sense, and three perversions (παρεκβάσεις), viz. Tyranny, Oligarchy and Democracy,

Kingship and Aristocracy have been virtually discussed in the delineation of the best polity ;

There remain then Polity, Oligarchy, Democracy, Tyranny.

Of the perverted forms of polity, Tyranny is the worst, Democracy the least bad.

(Plato's theory in the *Politicus* that there is a good and a bad form of every polity differs from ours, as we hold that the perversions are always vitiated.)

CHAPTER III.

The reason of the existence of a number of polities is that a State necessarily consists of numerous parts ; there are differences of race, character, wealth, &c., and the nature of the polity is determined by the distribution of the offices of state among these parts.

Practically however the different polities may be reduced to two, viz. Democracy, which includes Polity, and Oligarchy, which includes Aristocracy.

Aristotle himself prefers to speak of a single noble or ideal polity, regarding all the rest as the perversions of it.

CHAPTER IV.

Democracy is commonly defined as a polity in which the masses are supreme, Oligarchy as a polity in which the Few are supreme. But these definitions are inadequate. For it may happen that the rich, who are predominant in the State, are a majority, or that the poor, who are predominant, are a minority of the whole population.

The amended definition of Democracy is that it is a polity in which the poor are supreme, being a majority ; that of Oligarchy, that it is a polity in which the rich are supreme, being a minority.

In order to determine the varieties of polity, it is necessary to ascertain all the constituent parts of a State, for the number of

CHAPTER XIII.

The artifices (σοφίσματα), appropriate to particular polities may be ranged under five heads :

   (1) The Public Assembly.

   (2) The offices of State.

   (3) The Courts of Law.

   (4) The possession of arms.

   (5) Gymnastic exercises.

 (A) Oligarchical artifices.

(1) To fine the rich, but not the poor, or to fine the rich heavily and the poor only lightly, for non-attendance in the Public Assembly.

(2) To allow the rich, but not the poor, the privilege of declining public office.

(3) To fine the rich, but not the poor, or to fine the rich heavily and the poor only lightly, for neglect of their judicial duties.

(4) To fine the rich, but not the poor, for being without arms.

(5) To fine the rich, but not the poor, for omitting their gymnastic exercises.

 (B) Democratical artifices.

These will be the opposites of the oligarchical, e.g. to pay the poor for attendance in the Assembly and the Courts of Law, but not to fine the rich for non-attendance.

 (C) Artifices of a fusion of Democracy and Oligarchy.

It will be necessary to combine the characteristics of both polities, e.g. to pay the poor for attendance and fine the rich for non-attendance.

In a Polity it is the heavy-armed class which should be supreme. The property qualification should be fixed as high as possible, provided always that a majority of the population enjoy full political privileges.

In the history of Greece the early Kingships were succeeded by constitutional polities resting upon the military class, upon the cavalry at first and afterwards upon the heavy infantry.

CHAPTER XIV.

Every polity comprises three departments (μόρια), viz.

    (A)   The Deliberative Body.

    (B)   The Executive.

    (C)   The Judicial Body.

(A) The functions of the Deliberative Body are the determination of war and peace, the formation and dissolution of alliances, the enactment of laws, the power of death, exile and confiscation of property, the power of electing officers of State and of holding them responsible for their conduct in office.

But these functions may be variously ordered.

(1) The rule in Democracy is that the power of deliberation upon all subjects is enjoyed and exercised by all the citizens.

Yet the rule admits of four different applications :

(a) When the citizens exercise their deliberative power not collectively but by alternation, and assemble collectively only in order to enact laws, to settle constitutional questions and to receive the reports of the officers of State.

(b) When the citizens assemble collectively only in order to elect officers of State, to enact laws, to determine questions of war and peace, and to conduct the audit of the officers' accounts; upon all other matters the power of deliberation is vested in particular officers.

(c) When the citizens assemble collectively for the election of officers of State, for the audit of their accounts, and for deliberation upon questions of war and alliance; all other matters are administered by the officers of State.

(d) When the citizens meet collectively to deliberate upon all questions, and the officers of State possess only the power of preliminary examination (προανάκρισις). This is the system characteristic of the latest or extreme Democracy.

(2) The principle of Oligarchy is that deliberation upon all matters is confined to certain citizens.

But again there are various applications of the principle :

(a) When the Deliberative Body is large, the property qualification being low, when everyone who acquires the amount of property is admitted to the Deliberative Body, and the law is supreme.

(b) When deliberation is limited to an elected body, and the law is supreme.

(c) When the Deliberative Body has the power of cooption and is superior to the laws.

(d) When the Deliberative Body is hereditary and superior to the laws.

(3) If certain matters, e. g. questions of war and peace and the audit of the officers' accounts, come before the citizens collectively, and everything else is left to executive officers appointed by suffrage, the system is aristocratical.

(4) If the subjects of deliberation come in some cases before persons appointed by suffrage, and in others before persons appointed by lot, or before persons appointed partly by suffrage and partly by lot, the system is a mixture of Aristocracy and Polity.

Expedients appropriate to the extreme Democracy :

(1) To impose a fine upon any citizen for non-attendance in the Public Assembly.

(2) To appoint an equal number of the members of the Deliberative Body from each division of the citizens.

(3) If the Democrats have a vast numerical preponderance, either to pay a certain number only of the citizens, and not all, for attendance in the Public Assembly or to exclude by lot all who are in excess of the proper number.

Expedients appropriate to Oligarchy :

(1) To elect certain representatives of the commons as members of the Deliberative Body, or to allow the commons to consider all such matters as have already passed a board of Preliminary Councillors (πρόβουλοι), or Guardians of the Laws (νομοφύλακες).

(2) To invest the commons with the right of simply confirming the resolutions of the Preliminary Council, or the Guardians of the Laws, or to allow the privilege of giving advice to all the citizens, but an actual vote to none but the officers of State.

(3) To give the commons an absolute power of veto, but not of positive resolution, and to let a bill which has been rejected by the commons be referred back to the executive officers.

CHAPTER XV.

· (B) The Executive.

The offices of State are all positions to which are assigned the functions of deliberation, decision and command, more especially of command.

In large States it is possible and proper to have a separate officer for every function. In small States it is often necessary to concentrate a number of offices in a few hands.

There are certain officers peculiar to particular polities ;

e. g. a Preliminary Council (πρόβουλοι) is oligarchical,

a Council (βουλή) is democratical,

a Censorship of women and children is aristocratical.

In regard to the appointment· of the officers of State generally, three questions arise ;

(1) Who are the persons that appoint ?

(2) Who are eligible to office ?

(3) What is the mode of election ?

(3)   the appointment of officers of State by lot.

(4)   the absence of a property qualification for office or the requirement of as-low a qualification as possible.

(5)   the regulation that the same person shall never or only in exceptional circumstances hold the same office twice.

(6)   short tenure of office.

(7)   the endowment of all the citizens or of a body chosen from all with judicial powers in all or the most important cases.

(8)   the supreme authority of the Public Assembly in all or the most important questions.

(9)   the payment of the members of the Public Assembly and the Courts of Law and of the executive officers.

As birth, wealth and culture are characteristics of Oligarchy, so the characteristics of Democracy are low birth, poverty and intellectual degradation (βαναυσία).

Universal arithmetical equality is the democratical principle of justice; and from it flows the rule of the majority, i.e. of the poor.

CHAPTER III.

That the decision of the majority then is just is the argument of Democrats; that the decision of the wealthier is just, of Oligarchs. But in either case a difficulty arises.

The democratical argument would justify the spoliation of the wealthy minority by the poor; the oligarchical argument on the other hand would justify Tyranny, if there were an individual wealthier than all the other members of his class.

It may be suggested that, as a State is composed of two elements, viz. rich and poor, the decision of the majority of both, if they agree, and, if they disagree, of the absolute majority i.e. of the party, comprising both rich and poor, which has the higher collective property assessment, should be supreme.

W. A.   *f*

CHAPTER IV.

Of the four species of Democracy,

The best is one in which the population lives by agriculture. For an agricultural population, not possessing great wealth, occupies itself in business and takes no large interest in politics; nor is it obliged to seek office as a means of livelihood or to enrich itself by spoliation of the wealthy. Such a population is often content, if it enjoys only the power of electing officers of State and of holding them to account for their conduct in office. Agriculture may be encouraged by law, e.g. by the prohibition of holding more than a certain amount of land or of taking a mortgage upon a certain part of the land belonging to a citizen.

The next best population is one of graziers, as they have many points of resemblance to agriculturists and are well disciplined physically.

A population of mechanics, tradesmen or labourers is morally low, not to say that it is always ready to interfere collectively in political matters.

The latest development of Democracy, which is its worst form, is one in which civic rights are widely extended without regard to legitimacy ($\gamma\nu\eta\sigma\iota\acute{o}\tau\eta s$), and the commons exercise supreme and arbitrary power.

N.B. For a good form of Democracy it is desirable that the country should lie at a considerable distance from the city itself, as the citizens, dwelling then upon the fields, will be unable to meet often in the Public Assembly.

CHAPTER V.

It is not enough for a legislator to establish a polity; he must provide for its continued existence.

Rules for preserving Democracies:

(1) To ordain that all fines imposed shall be devoted to the service of the Gods, in order to prevent unjust condemnations.

(2) To impose heavy penalties upon the authors of wanton and baseless prosecutions, so that the wealthy class may not be rendered inimical to the polity.

(3) If the revenues of the State are small, to allow only few sessions of the Assembly and Courts of Law, lest the citizens be tempted to provide themselves with payment for attendance at the expense of the wealthy class.

(4) To alleviate the poverty of the masses,

(*a*) by affording them out of the public revenues an opportunity of starting in business or agriculture, whether all at once or, if means are insufficient, by tribes or otherwise.

(*b*) by making the rich supply the payment for the necessary meetings of the Public Assembly and the Courts of Law, on condition of being released from useless public burdens.

(*c*) by encouraging wealthy persons to furnish individual members of the poorer class with the means of setting themselves up in business.

(*d*) by opening some at least of the offices of State to the commons through the ballot.

CHAPTER VI.

The forms of Oligarchy.

The primary form of Oligarchy approximates to Polity; in it there are two kinds of property qualification, a lower which is requisite for the ordinary, and a higher which is requisite for the more important, offices of State, and the better elements of the commons are admitted from time to time to political privileges in such number as to ensure the predominance of the enfranchised over the unenfranchised class.

A slight intensification of the oligarchical principle produces the second form of Oligarchy.

The form of Oligarchy, which approximates to Tyranny, is the most corrupt, and requires the strongest precautionary measures.

The best safeguard of Democracy is a large population (πολυανθρωπία), of Oligarchy good discipline (εὐταξία).

f 2

CHAPTER VII.

The military service may be divided into four branches, viz. cavalry, heavy infantry, light-armed troops and marines.

A country suited to cavalry invites a pronounced form of Oligarchy, as it is only the rich who can afford to keep horses.

A country suited to heavy infantry invites a more temperate form of Oligarchy, but still an Oligarchy, as heavy infantry service is appropriate to the rich rather than to the poor.

Light-armed soldiers or marines are suited to Democracy.

(N.B. As Oligarchies have often been overthrown by means of light-armed soldiers, it is advisable that the Oligarchs should allow their children, while they are young, to be instructed in light-armed exercises.)

Admission to the governing class in an Oligarchy should be open either to all who acquire the requisite amount of property, or to all such persons after a stated period of abstinence from mechanical occupations, or to selected individuals who deserve the honour.

In order to prevent dissatisfaction among the commons at their exclusion from the most important offices of State, the officers should be liable to heavy public burdens.

CHAPTER VIII.

The offices of State ($\dot{a}\rho\chi a\dot{\iota}$) may be classified as (A) political, (B) religious, (C) extraordinary.

(A) Political officers.

    (1) controllers of the market ($\dot{a}\gamma o\rho a\nu\dot{o}\mu o\iota$).

    (2) commissioners of the city ($\dot{a}\sigma\tau\nu\nu\dot{o}\mu o\iota$).

    (3) commissioners of public lands ($\dot{a}\gamma\rho o\nu\dot{o}\mu o\iota$), or of woods and forests ($\dot{\nu}\lambda\omega\rho o\dot{\iota}$).

    (4) receivers ($\dot{a}\pi o\delta\dot{\epsilon}\kappa\tau a\iota$) or treasurers ($\tau a\mu\dot{\iota}a\iota$).

    (5) recorders ($\dot{\iota}\epsilon\rho o\mu\nu\dot{\eta}\mu o\nu\epsilon\varsigma$), presidents ($\dot{\epsilon}\pi\iota\sigma\tau\dot{a}\tau a\iota$), or remembrancers ($\mu\nu\dot{\eta}\mu o\nu\epsilon\varsigma$), who register contracts, legal decisions &c.

(6) persons who levy the fines imposed by the Courts of Law (πράκτορες),

(7) the police.

Officers of less importance are

(8) warders of the city gates and walls (ἐπιμελ ηταὶ πυλῶν τε καὶ τειχῶν φυλακῆς),

(9) generals (στρατηγοί) or members of the Council of War (πολέμαρχοι), &c.

(10) auditors (εὔθυνοι), accountants (λογισταί), inspectors of accounts (ἐξετασταί) or public prosecutors (συνήγοροι),

(11) the supreme legislative office, whether called a Preliminary Council (πρόβουλοι) or a Council (βουλή).

(B) Religious officers,

(1) priests.

(2) superintendents of the ordinances of religion (ἐπιμελη-ταὶ τῶν περὶ τὰ ἱερά) whose duty it is to maintain the temples in good repair, &c.

(3) directors of public sacrifices, whether called archons, kings or presidents (πρυτάνεις).

(C) Extraordinary officers, not found in all States.

(1) censors of women (γυναικονόμοι),

(2) guardians of the laws (νομοφύλακες),

(3) censors of boys (παιδονόμοι),

(4) presidents of gymnastic exercises (γυμνασίαρχοι),

(5) superintendents of gymnastic and Dionysiac contests, &c.

N.B. The office of Guardians of the Laws is aristocratical,

a Preliminary Council is oligarchical,

a Council is democratical.

BOOK VIII.

CHAPTER 1.

Political revolutions.

The general cause of sedition (στάσις) is inequality. The Many raise sedition in an Oligarchy, if they consider themselves to be deprived of the equality which is their right. The upper classes raise sedition in a Democracy, if they consider themselves to be merely equals despite their natural superiority.

But a revolution may take various forms ;

it may be either a complete revolution of polity, or a change of the holders of political power, the polity itself remaining the same, or an intensification or mitigation of the existing polity, or an innovation in some single department of the polity.

As inequality is the productive cause of seditions, it is to be noticed that equality is of two kinds, arithmetical (ἀριθμῷ), and proportional (κατ' ἀξίαν), or in other words equality determined by numbers and by merit.

Numbers and wealth being facts of universal occurrence, whereas virtue, e. g. which is the characteristic of Aristocracy, is rarely found, it follows that the only common polities are Democracy and Oligarchy.

But neither of these polities is sound or permanent, although Democracy is more stable than Oligarchy. For an Oligarchy may be destroyed by disturbances arising either within the oligarchical body itself or between the Oligarchs and the commons ; whereas Democracy is liable only to attacks of the commons upon the Oligarchs who aspire to exclusive power, not to say that it is nearer to the polity which rests upon the middle class.

CHAPTER II.

In the investigation of seditions and political revolutions, it is necessary to ascertain

(A) The conditions which lead to sedition (πῶς ἔχοντες στασιάζουσι).

(B). The objects or final causes of sedition (τίνων ἕνεκεν στασιάζουσι).

(C). The predisposing occasions (τίνες ἀρχαί).

(A). The principal condition favourable to sedition is the aspiration after equality in the Many or after superiority in the Few.

(B). The objects of sedition are gain, honour, or the desire to avoid their opposites, loss and dishonour.

(C). The predisposing occasions are

(1) gain.

(2) honour.

not however, as before, from the desire of acquiring them for ourselves, but from indignation at the larger share of them possessed by others.

CHAPTER III.

(3) insolence on the part of persons holding an official status.

(4) fear among persons who have committed crimes and are afraid of punishment, or who expect to be the victims of injustice and seek to anticipate it.

(5) predominant influence (ὑπεροχή), i.e. the excessive and intolerable power of some individual or party in the State.

(6) contempt of the subordinate class for its masters.

(7) the disproportionate increase of one class in the State (αὔξησις ἡ παρὰ τὸ ἀνάλογον).

(8) party-spirit (ἐριθεία).

(9) neglect (ὀλιγωρία) in allowing persons disloyal to the polity to be admitted to the supreme offices of State.

(10) insignificant changes (τὸ παρὰ μικρόν).

(11) diversity of race (τὸ μὴ ὁμόφυλον) among the citizens.

(12) locality, when the natural divisions of the country divide the citizens into parties.

CHAPTER IV.

It is not the objects of sedition that are unimportant but the occasions (γίγνονται αἱ στάσεις οὐ περὶ μικρῶν, ἀλλ' ἐκ μικρῶν, στασιάζουσι δὲ περὶ μεγάλων).

Further predisposing occasions :

(13) quarrels arising among influential persons, as is shewn by many instances.

(14) the accession of high repute or power to some one office or class in the State, which is also exemplified.

(15) an even balance of the two antagonistic classes, the rich and the poor, and the weakness of the middle class.

Political disturbance may be effected either by force or by fraud, and, if in the first way, by force employed either at the initial or at a later stage.

Having thus considered the causes of revolution in polities generally, we come now to consider them in regard to particular polities.

CHAPTER V.

Revolutions in Democracies.

The main cause of revolutions in Democracies is the intemperate and unprincipled conduct of demagogues, compelling the propertied class to combine.

A Democracy may be revolutionized

(1) into an Oligarchy, from the cause already mentioned.

(2) into a Tyranny, as in ancient times, when the functions of demagogue and general were united in the same hands, when official positions of immense importance were entrusted to in_dividuals, and when the commons being busily engaged in their occupations did not keep a sharp eye upon the ambition of their leaders.

(3) from a moderate to an extreme form of Democracy.

CHAPTER VI.

Revolutions in Oligarchies.

There are two general causes of revolution :

(1) Oppression of the masses by the Oligarchs.

(2) Dissension among the Oligarchs themselves, which may take various forms,

(a) when the limitation of the honours of State to a narrow clique inspires persons who are members of the propertied class, although not of the official body, with revolutionary ideas.

(b) when personal rivalry among th'. Oligarchs induces some of them to play the part of demagogues, whether it is to the mob or to other members of the oligarchical body that they pay court.

(c) when an attempt is made to narrow the Oligarchy still further than has been the rule.

(d) when some of the Oligarchs have wasted their fortunes in dissipation and are consequently eager for change.

(e) when some members of the oligarchical body are subjected to a repulse or affront at the hands of others.

(f) in consequence of the over-despotic character of the Oligarchy.

(g) when there is a smaller Oligarchy enjoying exceptional privileges, within the Oligarchy itself.

(h) in time of war, if the Oligarchs from fear of the commons are obliged to employ mercenary troops, and the commander of these troops establishes himself as tyrant.

(*i*) in time of peace, if the mutual distrustfulness of the Oligarchs leads them to put the police of the city into the hands of mercenary troops and an arbiter between the two factions, who succeeds in making himself master of both.

(*j*) from accidental circumstances, e. g. if the value of landed estates rises so much that nearly the whole population comes to possess the property qualification for office.

N.B. It is to be observed that both Democracies and Oligarchies are sometimes revolutionized not to the antagonistic polities but to other polities, whether more or less pronounced, of the same kind.

CHAPTER VII.

Revolutions in Aristocracies.

The causes are as follows :

(1) the limitation in the number of persons admitted to the honours of State.

(2) the discontent or ambition of some powerful individual.

(3) great inequality of wealth.

(4) self-aggrandisement on the part of the nobles.

(5) gradual and almost imperceptible innovation.

But the main cause of revolution both in Aristocracies and in Polities is a departure from their proper principles of justice, i. e. the unsuccessful fusion of virtue, wealth and numbers in Aristocracies, of wealth and numbers in Polities.

The comparative stability of Polities as contrasted with Aristocracies arises from the greater importance of the numerical majority in Polities.

A polity is usually revolutionized in the direction of its own bias, i. e. a Polity to Democracy and an Aristocracy to Oligarchy, but may also be revolutionized to its opposite.

The only conditions of permanence are proportionate equality (τὸ κατ' ἀξίαν ἴσον), and security of rights (τὸ ἔχειν τὰ αὑτῶν).

N.B.　Polities in general are liable to dissolution,

(a)　from within, as has been shewn.

(b)　from without, i. e. by the influence of another antagonistic polity.

CHAPTER VIII.

Having described the causes of revolutions and seditious, we come now to the preservatives of polities both generally and individually.

The means of preservation will be clearly the opposites of the means of destruction.

In order to preserve a polity, it is advisable

(1)　to take strict precautions against illegality, especially in matters insignificant.

(2)　in an Oligarchy to have no faith in artifices ($\sigma o \phi i \sigma-\mu a \tau a$) intended to impose upon the masses.

(3)　in an Aristocracy or Oligarchy to cultivate a good understanding between the persons who hold official positions and the non-privileged or partly privileged classes.

(4)　to prevent abuse of power on the part of the officers of State, e. g. by establishing short tenure of office.

(5)　to live in constant fear of such influences as corrupt the polity.

(6)　to check the feuds and rivalries arising in the upper classes.

(7)　in an Oligarchy or Polity to revise the census frequently and adapt the property qualification to the circumstances of the State.

(8)　to avoid investing any individual with disproportionate authority.

(9)　to institute a censorship of the manners and morals of the citizens.

(10)　to prevent a monopoly of power in the hands of a single class or order..

(11) in all polities, and especially in an Oligarchy, to afford the officers of State no opportunity of personal gain.

(12) in a Democracy to abstain from oppression of the rich.

(13) in an Oligarchy to treat the poor with signal consideration.

(14) to allow equality or even precedence in many respects to the classes debarred from supreme political power.

CHAPTER IX.

Three qualifications are requisite in the holders of the supreme officers of State, viz.

(1) loyalty to the polity.

(2) capacity for their offices.

(3) virtue and justice in the sense appropriate to the polity.

Where these three qualifications are not found in the same individual, it is the qualification which is rarer and more important to the office in question that should carry the day.

One rule of great value, as preservative of polities, is the observance of the proper mean, i. e. the avoidance of extreme measures whether democratical or oligarchical.

But the best of all preservatives is the education of the citizens in the spirit of the polity (τὸ παιδεύεσθαι πρὸς τὰς πολιτείας). Without this education the wisest laws are futile.

CHAPTER X.

The natural destructives and preservatives of Monarchy.

Monarchy is, as we have seen, the generic name, including Kingship and Tyranny as its species. The king is generally chosen from the better classes (οἱ ἐπιεικεῖς), to protect them against the commons; the tyrant from the commons to act against the nobles. But a tyrant may have been

  either a successful demagogue,

  or an encroaching hereditary king,

  or a high officer of State,

  or the nominee of an Oligarchy.

Kingship, on the other hand, may be based

  either upon the personal virtue of the king,

  or upon the virtue of his family,

  or upon eminent public services,

  or upon the combination of these with power.

Further, the king is in theory the protector of the propertied class from spoliation, and of the commons from insolence ; but the tyrant pays no regard to the public weal. The object of the tyrant is his personal pleasure ($\tau\grave{o}$ $\acute{\eta}\delta\acute{\upsilon}$), that of the king moral elevation ($\tau\grave{o}$ $\kappa\alpha\lambda\acute{o}\nu$). The tyrant is ambitious of gain, and his body-guard consists of mercenaries; the king is ambitious of distinction, and his body-guard consists of citizens.

Tyranny combines in itself the evils of Oligarchy and Democracy ; for from the former it borrows the pursuit of wealth and the absolute distrust of the masses, from the latter the hostility to the upper classes.

In Monarchies then as in constitutional polities—for Aristotle here distinguishes the two—the predisposing causes of revolution are injustice (which oftenest shews itself in insolence), fear and contempt, the object is the acquisition of wealth and honour.

But an insurrection may take the form of an attack (*a*) upon the person, (*b*) upon the authority of the rulers.

It takes the first form, when it is occasioned by insolence ($\H{\upsilon}\beta\rho\iota\varsigma$), as is shewn by numerous examples.

Instances are also given of conspiracies arising from fear and contempt.

Also of these three predisposing causes, two or more may exist in combination.

Lastly, the mere desire of notoriety is itself, although only in rare cases, a motive of insurrection.

A Tyranny like any other polity is liable to destruction,

(a) from without, by contact with an antagonistic polity of superior strength

(b) from within, by a feud among the associates of the tyrant.

Contempt is more frequently a cause of the destruction of Tyrannies than hatred.

A Tyranny in short may be destroyed by any of the causes of destruction which exist in the extreme form of Oligarchy or of Democracy.

A Kingship is seldom destroyed from without. It is liable to destruction from within,

(a) if sedition arises among the members of the royal family.

(b) if the king arrogates to himself unconstitutional and tyrannical powers.

Monarchy is comparatively rare in modern times, and, if it exists at all, it generally takes the form not of Kingship but of Tyranny. For the characteristics of Kingship, viz., the voluntary obedience of the subjects, and the high authority of the ruler, are incompatible with the existing social condition, which produces a large number of similar persons rather than an individual of preeminent distinction.

Hereditary Kingship is exposed to an additional peril owing to the frequent incapacity of the kings.

CHAPTER XI.

The preservatives of Monarchy.

(1) of Kingship,

Moderation in the exercise of power.

(2) of Tyranny,

(a) The repressive method, e. g. by removing eminent individuals, prohibiting clubs, creating mutual distrust among the citizens, establishing a system of espionage, keeping the citizens poor and always occupied, taxing them heavily, &c. It is characteristic too of a tyrant that he regards his friends with suspicion, encourages the influence of women and the licence of slaves, treats sycophants with honour, likes low companions, and prefers the society of foreigners to that of citizens.

There are in fact three objects of Tyranny, viz. :

(1) to degrade and reduce the spirit of the subjects.

(2) to prevent them from placing confidence in each other.

(3) to produce in them an incapacity for affairs ($\dot{a}\delta\nu\nu a\mu ia$ $\tau\hat{\omega}\nu$ $\pi\rho a\gamma\mu\dot{a}\tau\omega\nu$).

(b) the conciliatory method, by imitating the temper and conduct of a king. Such a tyrant will be economical in his management of the public revenues, will be dignified ($\sigma\epsilon\mu\nu\dot{o}s$), but not stern ($\chi a\lambda\epsilon\pi\dot{o}s$) in his address, will be, or affect to be, virtuous and moderate in life, will shew a zeal for religious ordinances, will pay especial honour to distinguished citizens, will dispense rewards himself, while he inflicts punishments by the agency of subordinates, will not humiliate a powerful subject except in rare instances and by gradual measures, and, while abstaining from all forms of insolence, will abstain most carefully from the infliction of corporal punishment and from indecency. Lastly, as there are two elements in every State, viz. the rich and the poor, it is desirable that both, if possible, should see the basis of their security in the exercise of the tyrant's power, or at least that the stronger party of the two should be his creature.

CHAPTER XII.

The duration of polities.

Of all polities none have so short a life as Oligarchy and Tyranny. The most permanent Tyrannies were those of the Orthagoridae at Sicyon, which lasted 100 years, of the Cypselidae at Corinth which lasted 73 years and 6 months, of the Pisistratidae at Athens which lasted 35 years.

Conclusion.—A criticism of the theory of revolutions put forward by Socrates in the *Republic*.

(1) He omits to treat particularly the form of revolution which is incident to his best or primary polity.

(2) His account of the sequence of polities is incomplete.

(3) He does not consider the liability of Tyranny to revolution or the nature of its revolutions.

(4) His explanation of the cause of revolutions in Oligarchy, which he defines to be avarice, is insufficient.

(5) It is not more true that Oligarchy, as he alleges, than any other polity contains in itself two different States, one of the rich and another of the poor.

(6) Without the impoverishment of any citizen a polity may be revolutionized from Oligarchy to Democracy, or from Democracy to Oligarchy.

(7) Socrates mentions one only out of many causes of revolutions in Oligarchies, viz. the impoverishment of the citizens by profligacy and usurious interest.

(8) Although there are various forms of Oligarchy and Democracy, Socrates in describing the revolutions of each speaks as though there were only one.

THE POLITICS OF ARISTOTLE.

BOOK I.

SEEING that every State is a sort of association and
every association is formed for the attainment of
some Good—for some presumed Good is the end of
all action—it is evident that, as some Good is the
object of all associations, so in the highest degree
is the supreme Good the object of that association
which is supreme and embraces all the rest, in other ✗
words, of the State or political association.

Now it is wrong to confound, as some[1] do, the
functions of the constitutional statesman, king,
householder and slavemaster. They hold that the
difference between them is not one of kind, but
depends simply upon the number of persons ruled,
i.e. that a man is a slavemaster, if he has but few
subjects ; if he has more, a householder ; if still
more, a constitutional statesman or king, there being
no distinction between a large household and a small

---

[1] The reference is to Plato *Politicus*, pp. 258 sqq.

State; also that a man is either a king or a constitutional statesman according as he governs absolutely or in conformity to the laws of political science, being alternately ruler and subject. Such an opinion is erroneous. Our meaning will be clear, however, if we follow our usual method of investigation. For as in other cases we have to analyse a compound whole into the uncompounded elements which are its least parts, so in examining the constituents of a State we shall incidentally best ascertain the points of difference between the abovementioned forms of government and the possibility of arriving at a scientific conclusion in regard to each of them.

CHAP. II.   Here, as elsewhere, the best system of examination will be to begin at the beginning and observe things in their growth.

Genesis of the State.   There are certain primary essential combinations of those who cannot exist independently one of another. Thus male and female must combine in order to the procreation of children, nor is there anything deliberate or arbitrary in their so doing; on the contrary, the desire of leaving an offspring like oneself is natural to man as to the whole animal and vegetable world. Again, natural rulers and subjects combine for safety—*and when I say* "*natural*," I mean that there are some persons qualified intellectually to form projects, and these are natural rulers or natural masters; while there are others qualified physically to carry them out, and these are subjects or natural slaves, so that the interests of master and slave are coincident.

Now Nature has differentiated females from slaves. None of Nature's products wears a poverty-stricken look like the Delphian[1] knife as it is called that cutlers make; each has a single definite object on the principle that any instrument admits of the highest finish, only if it subserves a single purpose rather than several. Among non-Greek peoples on the other hand females and slaves stand on one and the same footing. The reason is that natural rulers do not exist among them, and the association they form consists of none but slaves male and female; hence the poets say[2]

"'Tis meet Greeks rule barbarians,"

implying the natural identity of barbarians or non-Greeks and slaves.

But to resume: the associations of male and female, master and slave constitute the primary form of household, and Hesiod was right when he[3] wrote

"Get thee
First house and wife and ox to plough withal,"

for an ox is to the poor what a servant is to the rich.

Thus the association naturally formed for the supply of everyday wants is a household; its members, according to Charondas, are "those who eat of

---

[1] The Δελφικὴ μάχαιρα was evidently a knife intended to serve more purposes than one, and therefore not especially suited to any, as the ὀβελισκολύχνιον mentioned below, p. 173, l. 19, and περὶ ζώων μορίων, p. 683 A22, seems to have been a spit which could on occasion be used as a candlestick.

[2] Euripides, *Iph. in Aul.* 1400.

[3] Ἔργα καὶ Ἡμέραι, 403.

1—2

the same store," or, according to the Cretan Epimenides[1] "those who sit around the same hearth."——

The Village. Again, the simplest association of several households for something more than ephemeral purposes is a village. It seems that the village in its most natural form is[2] derived from the household, including all the children of certain parents and the children's children, or, as the phrase sometimes is, "all who are suckled upon the same milk."

This is the reason why States were originally governed by kings as is still the case with uncivilized peoples; they were composed of units accustomed to this form of government. For as each household is under the kingly government of its eldest member, so were also the offshoot-households as comprising none but blood-relations. It is this condition of things that Homer means when he describes *the Cyclopes* as

"law-givers each
Of his own wives and children,"

in allusion to their want of corporate life. This patriarchal government was universal in primitive times; in fact the reason why all nations represent the polity of the Gods as monarchical is that such originally was, if it is not still, their own polity, and men assimilate the lives no less than the bodily forms of the Gods to their own.

The State. Lastly, the association composed of several villages

---

[1] Reading ὁμοκάπνους.

[2] I have adopted —although not without hesitation—Mr Heitland's ingenious suggestion, ἀπ' οἰκίας for ἀποικία οἰκίας.

to live happily or indeed to live at all. Nor can
the[1] art of the householder any more than any definite
art dispense with its proper instruments, if its work is
to be adequately performed. Instruments however
may be animate or inanimate. In the case e.g. of a
pilot, the tiller is an inanimate instrument, the "look-
out" an animate one; in fact in every art an assistant
is virtually an instrument. Thus we conclude that
any given property is an instrument conducing to
life, property as a whole is a mass of instruments; a
slave is an animate property, and every assistant
may be described as a single instrument doing the
work of several. For suppose that every instrument
could obey a person's orders or anticipate his wishes
and so fulfil its proper function like[2] the legendary
figures of Daedalus or[3] the tripods of Hephaestus
which, if we may believe the poet,

"Entered self-moved the conclave of the Gods,"

suppose, I say, that in like manner combs were in the
habit of combing and quills of playing the cithern of
themselves, mastercraftsmen would have no need of
assistants nor masters of slaves. While then instruments in the common use of the term are instruments
of production, a property is an instrument of action;
that is to say, while a comb is not only used but
produces something else, a coat or a bed can only be
used. And as there is this difference of kind between

1 Reading ὥσπερ δὲ ταῖς ὡρισμέναις τέχναις, and below, τῷ οἰ-
κονομικῷ.
2 See Plato, *Menon*, p. 97. *Euthyphron*, p. 11.
3 *Iliad* XVIII. 369 sqq.

production and action and instruments are necessary
to both, it follows that there must be a corresponding
difference in the instruments. Now life consists not
in production but in action; and as *every property is*
an instrument conducing to existence, and a slave is
an animate property, it follows that a slave is an
assistant in the sphere of action.

The term 'property' may be compared to the
term 'member,' in that a member is not only a member of something else but belongs wholly to that
something, and the same is true of a property. Thus
while a master is master of his slave but in no sense
belongs to him, a slave[1] is not only the slave of a
certain master but belongs wholly to his master.

These facts clearly prove the nature and faculty
of the slave. A natural slave is one who, although a
human being, is naturally not his own master but
belongs to someone else. Now this is the case with a
human being when he is nothing more than a property[2], and a property means any instrument of
action which has a separate existence, *i.e. is not a*
mere part of the person who uses it.

CHAP. V.
Natural
Slavery.

We have now to consider whether there are any
persons naturally answering to this description, persons for whom a life of slavery is advantageous and
just or on the contrary all slavery is a violation of
Nature. Nor is the truth hard to discover theoreti-

Its justifi-
cation in
Nature.

cally or to infer from actual experience. The principle
of rule and subjection is equally inevitable and bene-
ficent; indeed there are some things which from

---

[1] ἡ δὲ δοῦλος in Bekker's text is a misprint for ὁ δὲ δοῦλος.
[2] Omitting ἄνθρωπος ὤν.

their very birth take different lines and tend either to a position of rule or the reverse. Also rulers and subjects are both of various kinds, and the superiority of the rule corresponds in all cases to the superiority of the subjects, e.g. the rule of one man over another is superior to the rule of a man over a beast. For the relation of ruler and subject always implies a common work to be performed, and the excellence of the work is proportionate to that of the person performing it. *That there are various kinds of subjects and rulers is evident,* because wherever several parts combine to form one common whole, whether they are connected *like the limbs of the human body* or separate *like the citizens of a State,* the relation of ruler and subject invariably manifests itself. And this fact which is characteristic of animate things is true of Nature generally; for even in inanimate things there is a sort of rule *and subordination,* e.g. in harmony, although perhaps this subject is proper to a less scientific investigation than the present.

But to confine ourselves to the case of animals : an animal consists primarily of soul and body, of which the former is natural master and the latter natural subject. Observe however that in order to discover the law of Nature we must choose instances in a natural and not a corrupt condition. Thus we must examine a man whose body and soul are both in a perfectly healthy state, and in his case the natural supremacy of the soul is evident enough ; for in depraved persons or persons whose condition at the time is depraved the soul will often appear to be under the rule of the body, but the reason is that their condition is corrupt and unnatural. However it is possible, as we say, in the first place to observe in an animal the two forms of rule, despotic and constitutional ; for the soul rules the body like a slavemaster, while the intellect rules the appetite like a constitutional statesman or king. Nor can we doubt in these instances that it is natural and expedient for the body to be ruled by the soul and for the emotional part of the soul to be ruled by the intellect or the part in which the reason resides, and that if the two are put on an equality, or the relations are reversed, the consequence is injurious to both. Again, the same is true in regard to man and the other animals. Domestic animals are superior in nature to wild ones, and for all domestic animals subjection to man is advantageous, as their safety is thereby secured. Also a comparison of males and females shows that the former are naturally stronger and dominant, the latter naturally weaker and subject. And the same law *of subordination* must hold good in respect of human beings generally.

Hence wherever there are two classes of persons, and the one are as far inferior to the other as the body to the soul or a beast to a man—and this is the condition of all whose function is mere physical service and who are incapable of anything better—these persons are natural slaves and for them as truly as for the body or for beasts a life of slavish subjection is advantageous. For the natural slave is one who is qualified to be and therefore in fact is the property of another, or who is only so far a rational being as to understand reason without himself possessing it. *And herein the slave is different from other animals,* as

they neither understand reason[1] nor obey it but
obey their instincts only. As for the uses to which
they are put there is little distinction; for slaves and
domestic animals alike render us physical help towards acquiring the necessaries of life.

Now in accordance with these facts it is Nature's *Its practical limitation.*
purpose to differentiate the bodies as well as the souls
of slaves and free persons, making the former sturdy
for the satisfaction of our necessary wants, and the
latter upright and suited not to employments of this
kind but to political life in both its departments civil
and military. But it frequently results contrary to
the intention of Nature that those who possess the
bodies do not possess the souls of free men and vice
versa. For assuredly were there to be found certain
persons as superior even physically to the rest as are
the images of the Gods to ordinary men, it would be
universally admitted that their inferiors deserved to
be their slaves. But if this is true of mere physical
superiority, with far more justice may it be determined of the soul; only it is not so easy to discern
beauty of soul as physical beauty.

It is evident then that there is a class of persons,
some of whom are naturally free and the others
naturally slaves, persons for whom the condition of
slavery is alike expedient and just. Yet it is easy to *Chap. VI.*
see that there is some truth also in the opposite
theory. The fact is that the terms "slavery" and
"slave" are used in two distinct senses. There are
not only natural but also legal slaves, or persons in a *Legal slavery.*
state of legal slavery, the law being a sort of convention

[1] Reading λόγῳ.

according[1] to which all conquests in war are the property of the conqueror.. It is this principle of legal justice that many jurists impeach as if they were impeaching a statesman for illegality, insisting on the monstrous nature of the doctrine that anyone who has been the victim of force is to be the slave or subject of anyone who is able to employ force, in other

Theories of slavery.

words of the stronger party. Upon this point there is a difference of opinion even among philosophic thinkers. Now the ground of this disagreement, the reason why the two theories overlap each other *so to say* is *firstly* that in a certain sense nothing is so well able to employ force as virtue, if possessed of external means, and *secondly* that the conqueror is always superior in respect of some Good or other ; hence it appears as though force were never dissociated from virtue, and the only question at issue were the principle of justice. Accordingly one school identifies justice with benevolence, *thereby excluding slavery altogether ;* the other defines it simply as the rule of the stronger. Whereas if only we take these theories by themselves, and contrast them, *viz.* (1) *that some slavery is natural,* (2) *that slavery based on mere force is unjust,* there is no strength or plausibility in the latter as against the right of the superior in virtue to exercise rule and mastery. Other thinkers there are, who while they keep absolutely, as they suppose, to a certain principle of justice— for such is the law—lay it down that all slavery which is the result of war, *as having the sanction of*

---

[1] Reading ἐφ' ᾧ for ἐν ᾧ and omitting φασίν.

law, is therefore just, although in the same breath
they contradict themselves. For wars may be unjust
in their origin, and if a man is not deserving of slavery,
↖ nobody would call him slave; else persons who are
esteemed the noblest of mankind will turn out to be but
slaves and children of slaves, if they or their parents
chance to be taken prisoners and sold into servitude.
Accordingly the advocates of this opinion do not mean
to apply the term "slaves" to themselves *or other
Greeks*, but only to non-Greeks. Yet herein what
they have in view is simply the class of natural slaves
as we described it at the beginning of our remarks ; p. 10.
for they are constrained to admit the existence of
people, some of whom are slaves universally and the
rest are not slaves in any circumstances. So too as
regards nobility, they consider themselves *and other
Greeks* to be noble not in Greece alone but universally, whereas non-Greeks are noble nowhere but at
home, implying the existence of a class of persons,
some only conditionally or relatively noble and free,
and others absolutely, as when Helen in the play of
Theodectes says

> "Who should presume to term me serf,
> The offspring of a twofold stock divine ?"

Now to use this language is to make the distinction of slave and free, noble and ignoble depend on
virtue and vice alone. It is assumed that, as the offspring of men are men and of beasts beasts, so the
offspring of good men are good. And indeed[1] it is

---

[1] Reading ἡ δὲ φύσις βούλεται μὲν τοῦτο ποιεῖν, πολλάκις μέντοι
οὐ δύναται.

Nature's object to bring about this result, although not infrequently she fails.

Thus we see that there is some reason in the controversy and that in[1] some cases actual slaves or free persons are not so naturally, yet on the other hand that there are cases where this distinction does exist, where the relation of master and slave is mutually advantageous and just and where the form of rule natural to the circumstances i.e. despotic rule is right both for ruler and subject. Any abuse of this rule is prejudicial to both parties, inasmuch as the interests of part and whole, body and soul are coincident, and the slave is a part of his master, a sort of animate and self-existent part of his body.

Thus there is a mutual helpfulness and friendship of master and slave wherever the relation is in accordance with Nature's ordinance ; just the contrary is the case where it is unnatural and depends upon law or force.

CHAP. VII.
The govern-
ment of
slaves.

These facts taken by themselves clearly prove that the government of slaves and of a constitutional State is not the same, nor are all the forms of rule the same, as[2] is sometimes said. For in the case of the State the subjects are naturally free, while in the other they are naturally slaves ; also the government of a household is a Monarchy, all households being monarchically ruled, whereas in constitutional government the subjects are free and equal to their rulers.

Now when we use the term "slavemaster," we do not mean that a person has learnt a certain science but that he possesses certain qualities, and the same

[1] Omitting εἰσὶ καί.
[2] The reference is again to the *Politicus* of Plato. See Chap. I.

such articles as are necessary to life or useful to persons associated in a State or household and at the same time are not incapable of accumulation. It may be said that these and these alone constitute genuine wealth. For the amount of such possessions which is enough for independence and a good life is not unlimited like the wealth described by Solon in the line

"No bound is set to riches i' the world."

To these there is a definite limit as much as in any other art; for in none are there any instruments limitless in number or size, and true wealth consists simply in a number of instruments suited to the purposes of a household or a State.

The fact then that there is a certain Art of Acquisitiou which falls naturally within the sphere of the householder or statesman, as well as its reason, are now evident. But there is another kind of Art of *Chap. IX* Acquisition which is in an especial sense known as *Unnatural* Finance, as it rightly may be ; and it is this which gives rise to the opinion that there is no limit to wealth or property. This second kind is so nearly allied to the first as to be often considered one and the same with it. It is not the same however, although on the other hand it is not widely different; but whereas the first has a natural existence, it has not, but is rather the product of what may be termed experience or art.

In coming to the discussion of it the first remark to be made is that every article of property admits of two uses, both of which are inherent in it though not inherent in the same degree, one being proper to the *The Art of* article and the other not. To take e.g. a shoe, there *Exchange.*

is its use as a covering of the foot, and also its use as
an article of exchange ; both are uses of a shoe, for if
you barter it to someone who wants a shoe in exchange for money or food, you use the shoe *qua* shoe
just as much as if you wear it, but the use you make
of it in this case is not its proper use, inasmuch as
barter is not the object of its production.   The same is
true of all other articles of property ; there is none
that does not admit of use in exchange.   This use arose
in the first instance from natural circumstances, as
people had more of some things and fewer of others
than they required.   And *as the true Art of Exchange
was the outcome of natural wants*, so conversely it is

Retail
Trade.

plain that Retail Trading is no natural part of Finance ; else the barter would not be carried beyond
the point of satisfying mere requirements.   Now it
is obvious that in the primary association, viz. the
household, there is no room for the Art of Exchange ;
it is not possible until the association is already
enlarged.   For in the household the members shared
everything alike, while in the larger associations, *viz.
the village or the State*, where they lived separately[1],
they experienced various wants and having these wants
were forced to interchange their properties by barter,
as is still the common way of non-Greek nations, who
never go beyond bartering actual commodities one
against another, e.g. giving or receiving wine in exchange for corn and so on.   Accordingly the Art of
Exchange when thus limited is not unnatural, nor is it a
species of Finance *in the bad sense*, as its object is no
more than the completion of that independence which

---

[1] Reading οἱ δὲ κεχωρισμένοι πολλῶν πάλιν καὶ ἐδέοντο.

Nature herself requires. However the bad Art of The origin of a cur-
Finance was a logical outcome from it. For as the rency.
benefits of commerce were more widely extended by
importing commodities of which there was a deficiency
and exporting those of which there was an excess, the
use of a currency was an indispensable device. As
the necessaries of Nature were not all easily por-
table, people agreed for purposes of barter mutually
to give and receive some article which, while it was
itself a commodity, was practically easy to handle in
the business of life, some such article as iron or silver,
which was at first defined simply by size and weight;
although finally they went further and set a stamp
upon every coin to relieve them from the trouble of
weighing it, as the stamp impressed upon the coin
was an indication of quantity. Thus it was after
the invention of a currency as the result of necessary barter that the second species of Finance, viz.
Retail Trading, came into existence, at first probably as a simple process, and afterwards, as experience progressed, more and more as a scientific
system of the most profitable means and manner of
monetary exchange. Hence it is a common opinion
that Finance has to do almost exclusively with the
currency, and that its function consists in the ability
to discover the means of getting a quantity of money—
an opinion resting on the assumption that it is productive of wealth or in other words of money. For
wealth is often defined as a quantity of current coin,
as it is with the currency that Finance *in the bad
sense* or the Art of Retail Trading has to do. Sometimes on the other hand the currency is regarded as

mere trash and as having only a current or conventional and not in any sense a natural value, because,
if the people by whom it is used give it up and
adopt another, it is wholly valueless, it does not serve
to supply any want, and a person may have abundance
of this currency and yet lack the means of bare subsistence; although it is a paradox to identify wealth
with anything of such a nature that one may have
plenty of it and yet perish with hunger, like Midas
in the old story when his insatiable prayer had been
granted and everything which was set before him
turned to gold. Accordingly people look for another
definition of true wealth and of true Finance, and they

Character-
istics of
natural and
unnatural
Finance.

are right. Finance in the natural sense, like natural
wealth, is something different and belongs to the
sphere of Domestic Economy, whereas the[1] other is a
part of Trade and produces money not indiscriminately but exclusively by means of exchange. It is
this last which may be said to be occupied solely with
current coin, for the currency is the alpha and omega
of such barter. Also it is wealth of this kind, viz.
wealth produced by unnatural Finance, which is unlimited. As in the medical art there is no limit to
the degree of health it seeks to produce, nor in any
other art to the end it has in view—for they all endeavour to realize their end to the fullest possible
extent—whereas the reverse is true of the means
which in every art are limited by the end, so in the
case of unnatural Finance there is no limit to the end
proposed which is the wealth appropriate to it or the

[1] Reading ἡ δὲ καπηλική, ποιητικὴ χρημάτων οὐ πάντως ἀλλ᾽ ἡ
διὰ μεταβολῆς.

acquisition of money. [1] On the other hand in that
species of Finance which belongs to Domestic Economy
there is a limit; for the mere acquisition of money is
not its function. Hence from this point of view there
appears to be necessarily a limit to wealth of every
kind, although in experience the actual fact is quite
the contrary, as all financiers seek to accumulate an
unlimited amount of current coin. The explanation is
to be found in the close connexion of the two species
of Finance. As they both [2] make use of the same material, *viz.* money, the uses practically overlap; for the
property [3] which they use is the same, although they
use it in different ways, one finding its end in something
beyond mere accumulation and the other in accumulation alone. Consequently there are some people who
take the accumulation of money to be the function of
the economical Finance, *i.e. the Finance which is proper to Domestic Economy,* and are always under the
impression that they ought either to preserve or infinitely augment their property in money. This disposition of mind arises from their anxiety about mere
living rather than about living well. The consequence
is that, as their desire of life is infinitely great, they
desire an infinite amount of all that is conducive to life;
nay even people who do aspire to live well set their
minds solely on the means of sensual gratification, and,
as these like other things are apparently bound up
with the possession of property, all their efforts are
directed to moneymaking, and thus the bad species of

---

[1] Reading τῆς δ' οἰκονομικῆς αὖ χρηματιστικῆς.

[2] Reading ἑκατέρας τῆς χρηματιστικῆς.

[3] Reading κτήσεως χρῆσις.

Finance has come into vogue. For as sensual gratification implies superfluity, they are eager to find an art productive of the superfluity indispensable to gratification, and, if they fail to attain their object by means of Finance, they try to compass it by other means, putting all their faculties to an unnatural use. Thus although it is the function of valour to produce not money but intrepid action and of strategy or medicine to produce not money but victory or health, they convert all these arts into arts of Finance, assuming that money is the one end to be attained, and to this end everything else is bound to conspire.

We have now considered both the species of Finance, the unnecessary and the indispensable; we have described the nature of the first and the ground of its necessity and have shown that the second which is concerned with the supply of food is distinct from the first, that it is in its nature economic, and that it is not unlimited like the[1] first but strictly bounded *in respect of the wealth it seeks to produce.*

CHAP. X.

Answer to the question: What is the relation of Finance to Domestic Economy? p. 18.

We see also the answer to the question propounded at the outset: does Finance fall within the province of the householder or statesman or are financial means on the contrary pre-requisites to the exercise of his functions? *According to the latter view,* as statesmanship does not create men but receives them from Nature's hand and makes use of them, so it is Nature's business to supply the means of sustenance in the shape of land or sea or anything else; while the householder or statesman starting with these means has merely to dispose of the produce aright. Simi-

---

[1] Reading αὕτη.

difficulties, adopt this expedient of establishing a
monopoly of commodities. *There was a case similar to
that of Thales* in Sicily where a person with whom a
sum of money had been deposited bought up all the
iron in the manufactories, and upon the arrival of
the merchants from the centres of commerce his monopoly enabled him without raising the price much
to realize 200 per cent. on all his outlay. Dionysius
hearing of the circumstance bade him take his
money with him but not stay another day in Syracuse, on the ground that he was the inventor of
financial expedients prejudicial to Dionysius's own
interests. However that may be, his device and that
of Thales are identical; both contrived to secure
themselves a monopoly. These are facts which deserve the attention even of statesmen; for States like
households, although in a higher degree, often require
financial expedients and similar sources of revenue.
That is why there are some statesmen whose whole
statesmanship is limited to Finance.

There are, as we have seen, three branches of CHAP. XII.
Domestic Economy, viz. the relations of a slavemaster Marital and
parental
to his slaves, which have been discussed already, the rule.
p. 8.
relations of a father to his children, and thirdly
the relations of a husband to his wife. *I distinguish the paternal from the marital form of rule;*
for[1] although the head of the family rules both his
wife and children and rules them in both cases as
free persons, yet the kind of rule is different, being
constitutional in the wife's case, while in the children's
it is regal. *The justification of these forms of rule*

[1] Reading ἄρχει.

lies in the fact that males are by Nature better qualified to command than females, wherever the union is
not unnaturally constituted, and those who are elder
and more mature than those who are younger and
immature. It is true that in most cases of political
or constitutional rule there is an interchange of the
functions of rulers and subject, as it is assumed that
they are naturally equal and indistinguishable. Nevertheless at any particular time an effort is made to
distinguish the rulers from the subjects by insignia of
office, forms of address and acts of respect according
to the remark[1] Amasis made about his footpan. Now
the relation *which rulers in a constitutional country
bear during their term of office to their subjects* is
the relation which the male at all times bears to the
female. The rule of a father over his children on the
other hand is like that of a king over his subjects; for
the parental rule rests upon affection and respect,
and this is precisely the character of kingly rule.
Hence Homer was right in giving Zeus the title[2]
"Father of Gods and men," Zeus who is the king of
all. For the ideal of a king is that he should be
distinct from his subjects in nature but one with
them in race; and this is exactly the relation of a
senior to a junior or of a parent to his child.

CHAP. XIII. It appears then that in Domestic Economy more
attention is devoted to human beings than to inanimate
property, more to their virtue or excellence than to
that of property, or as we term it to wealth, and more
to the virtue of free persons than to that of slaves.

[1] Herodotus II. 172.
[2] *Iliad* I. 544.

As to slaves the first question which arises is The capacity of slaves for virtue, whether a slave is capable of any virtue beyond that of a mere instrument or menial, i.e. of any more honourable virtue, such as temperance, courage, justice or any similar moral habit; or on the contrary there is no virtue of which he is capable apart from acts of bodily service. Whichever view we take we are met by a difficulty. If we affirm the capacity of the slave for the higher virtues, we may be asked wherein the difference between slaves and free persons will consist; if we deny it, the denial is a paradox in the case of human and rational beings as slaves are. The same question or one very similar is and of women and children. raised in regard to women and children. Are they capable like men of virtues? is a woman bound to be temperate, brave and just? may a child be called licentious or temperate? Indeed it is a general question The virtue of natural rulers and natural subjects generally. worthy of consideration whether the virtue of natural rulers and natural subjects is identical or different. For if we say that both are to possess high moral qualities, why should there be this absolute distinction of ruler and subject? It cannot be answered that the difference lies in the more or less *of moral nobleness that they possess;* for the difference between rule and subjection is one of kind—not so the difference between more or less *which is one of degree.* On the other hand the theory that moral nobleness is necessary to the one and not to the other is a strange one. Unless he is temperate and just, how shall a ruler be a good ruler or a subject a good subject? for if he is licentious and cowardly, he will fail to perform any of his duties. It seems clear then that they must both

possess virtue but that there must be different kinds
of virtue corresponding to the difference between
natural rulers and natural subjects. In fact, to take
an obvious illustration, this relation of rule and subjection is shewn in the soul. There is one part of
the soul which naturally rules and another which
naturally obeys ; and the virtue we ascribe to them,
i.e. to the rational part and the irrational, is different.
We see clearly then the same is true of the other
cases. [1]Hence, as there are naturally various kinds of
rulers and subjects—the rule of a free person over a
slave is one kind, that of male over female another
and that of a man over a child a third—and as the
parts of the soul are innate in all, although in different
manners (for the slave is wholly destitute of the deliberative part, whereas it exists in the female and
child but in the former has no authority and in the
latter is imperfectly developed) ; on the same principle, if we take the moral virtues, the right view is
that they must be possessed by all, not however in
the same manner but by each in the degree essential
to the discharge of his function. It follows that the
ruler must possess moral virtue in its full development. For *in any handicraft* the work to be

[1] It seems necessary to make some alteration of the text.
The reading which I have translated is as follows : ὥστ᾽ ἐπεὶ
φύσει πλείω τὰ ἄρχοντα καὶ ἀρχόμενα (ἄλλον γὰρ τρόπον τὸ ἐλεύ-
θερον τοῦ δούλου ἄρχει καὶ τὸ ἄρρεν τοῦ θήλεος καὶ ἀνὴρ παιδός)
καὶ πᾶσιν ἐνυπάρχει μὲν τὰ μόρια τῆς ψυχῆς, ἀλλ᾽ ἐνυπάρχει διαφε-
ρόντως (ὁ μὲν γὰρ δοῦλος ὅλως οὐκ ἔχει τὸ βουλευτικόν, τὸ δὲ θῆλυ
ἔχει μὲν ἀλλ᾽ ἄκυρον, ὁ δὲ παῖς ἔχει μὲν ἀλλ᾽ ἀτελές) ὁμοίως τοίνυν καὶ
περὶ τὰς ἠθικὰς ἀρετὰς ὑποληπτέον δεῖν μὲν μετέχειν πάντας, ἀλλ᾽ οὐ τὸν
αὐτὸν τρόπον ἀλλ᾽ ὅσον ἀναγκαῖον ἔχειν ἑκάστῳ πρὸς τὸ αὐτοῦ ἔργον.

performed depends altogether upon the mastercraftsman, and reason is the mastercraftsman *of the soul;*
therefore in order to perform his work the ruler
must needs possess perfect reason which implies fully-
developed moral virtue. The various classes of subjects
on the other hand require only such a degree of virtue
as is proper to the part they have to play.

These considerations shew clearly (1) that all the
persons mentioned above are capable of moral virtue;
(2) that *this virtue is not the same in all cases, e.g.*
the temperance of a man and a woman is not the
same nor their courage and justice, as Socrates[1]
supposed, but a man's courage is of a ruling and a
woman's of a subordinate kind, and so with all the
other virtues. We shall discover the same truth by
examining the subject more in detail. For people
merely deceive themselves by such general definitions
of virtue as "a good condition of the soul," "upright-
ness of conduct," and so forth; it is far more sensible
to follow Gorgias in drawing up catalogues of the
virtues *appropriate to each class.* Thus we must
suppose that what the poet[2] says of woman,

"Silence is woman's crown,"

is applicable to all the subject classes ; but the truth
does not extend to men. Also, as a child is not yet
completely developed, it is clear that his virtue is not
the virtue of an independent being but has reference
to one [3]in whom he finds complete development and

[1] The reference is to Plato *Menon,* p. 73 A sqq.
[2] Sophocles *Ajax,* 293.
[3] Reading πρὸς τὸ τέλος.

guidance, *viz. his father.* So too the virtue of a slave has reference to his master. And further, from the principle we laid down, viz. that a slave is useful merely in providing us with the bare necessaries of life, it is evident that he needs no high degree of virtue but only just so much as will prevent his failing in his duties from licentiousness or timidity.

The capacity of artisans for virtue.

And here the question may be raised, If our present statement is true, will it be necessary for artisans also to possess a certain virtue, as licentiousness often leads them to fail in their duties? It seems however that there is a wide difference between the cases. The slave and his master have a common existence; whereas the artisan stands to his master in a relation far less close and participates in virtue only so far as he participates in slavery. For the mechanical artisan lives in a condition of what may be called limited slavery. *Another reason why virtue is impossible or hardly possible to the artisan* is that cobblers and all other artisans, unlike slaves, are in no sense creations of Nature.

The means of producing virtue in slaves.

It is evident therefore that the virtue appropriate to a slave must be produced in him by his master and not by [1]anyone who is acquainted with that art of slaveowning which merely gives a slave instruction in his duties. [2]They are wrong therefore who deny reason to slaves and affect to employ commands only *in dealing with them;* for advice is more suitable to slaves than to children.

But this discussion of the whole subject must

---

[1] Reading οὐ τὸν τὴν διδασκαλικὴν ἔχοντα.
[2] The reference is to Plato *Laws,* p. 777 E.

suffice. As regards husband and wife, father and children, the moral laws determining the virtue of each and their intercourse one with another and the true method of following the good and eschewing the bad, all this it will be necessary to consider when we come to treat of the different forms of polity. For as every household is a part of a State, and man and wife, father and children are parts of a household, and the excellence of any part must have reference to that of the whole, it is essential to educate our women and children with constant reference to the polity, if indeed the virtue of the women and children is of any importance in its bearing upon the virtue of the State. Nor indeed can this be doubtful, when we consider that women form half the free population and the children grow up to be the citizens of the State.

Having fully discussed then one part of the subject and deferred for the present our consideration of the rest, we may leave our present arguments as complete and start afresh upon a new topic. We will begin by examining the theories of those authors who have put forward their views of the best polity.

BOOK II.

AS our purpose is to investigate what[1] is the best of all forms of political association for persons whose life is capable of approximating most nearly to an ideal, we are bound to examine all other forms of polity, not only such as exist in states which are reputed to be well-ordered but such others also as have been proposed by individual thinkers and are popularly considered to be successful. In this way we shall be likely to discover what is right and what is expedient; and instead of our endeavour to find some new form of polity seeming to indicate a desire to display our own cleverness at any cost, the inquiry we undertake will seem to be due to the imperfection of all polities now existing or proposed.

We must begin with the natural beginning of an investigation like the present. The collective citizens of a State must of necessity either have everything in common or nothing in common or some things in common and not others. It is plainly impossible that they should have nothing in common. For the polity is a species of association; and, if we go no further,

---

[1] Reading τίς κρατίστη.

its members must live in a common locality, as the locality of a single State is necessarily single, and *from the nature of the case* the fellow-citizens are members of a single State. Is it desirable however that in a State which is to be rightly ordered they should have the greatest possible number of things in common or only some things and not others? It is possible for the citizens to have children, wives and property in common, as is proposed in the *Republic* of Plato where Socrates argues for a community of all three. *The Republic of Plato.* Is it better to follow the existing system in this respect or the order of things described in the *Republic?*

Not to speak of many difficulties inherent in a *CHAP II.* general community of wives, the reason alleged by Socrates in behalf of such an institution is clearly not a legitimate consequence of his arguments. Nor again is the institution as portrayed in the *Republic* effectual as a means to the end which according to him ought to be realized in the State. And, *thirdly*, he has wholly omitted to lay down its proper limitations. By the end I mean the doctrine that it is best for the whole State to be as nearly as possible a unit; for this is the fundamental position assumed by Socrates.

It is evident however that as a State advances and *(1) Objections to the* becomes more a unit it will cease to be a State at all. *proposed unification of the State.* A State essentially implies a number of people; and as it becomes more and more a unit it will cease to be a State and be a household and will cease to be a household and be an individual, for it will be admitted that a household is more a unit than a State and an individual than a household. Hence even if one were able to effect this unification it would not be right

to do so, as it would mean the destruction of the
State.

Again, not only does a State consist of a number
of individuals but the individuals are different in
kind. It is impossible to form a State all the members of which are alike. This is just the distinction
between a State and a confederation. [1]A confederation, the object of which is military strength, derives
its efficiency from its size, even if all the constituent
parts are of one kind, just as if one weight is heavier
than another, *it turns the scale.* There will be much
the same difference between a State and a tribe in all
cases where the members of the tribe are not scattered
in different villages but *have a collective organization*
like [2]the Arcadians. On the other hand the parts
which are to constitute a single organic whole must
be different in kind. And thus it is the principle of
reciprocal equality which is the preservative of States,
as [3]I have already stated in the *Ethics;* for this principle necessarily obtains even in a society of free and
equal persons. In this case they cannot all rule
simultaneously but must follow a system of yearly
rotation or some other order of succession or period
of office ; and in this way all become rulers *in turn,*
just as if cobblers and carpenters changed places
instead of the same people being always one or

---

[1] Reading τὸ μὲν γὰρ τῷ ποσῷ χρήσιμον, κἂν ᾖ τὸ αὐτὸ τῷ εἴδει
(βοηθείας γὰρ χάριν ἡ συμμαχία πέφυκεν) ὥσπερ ἂν εἰ σταθμὸς
πλεῖον ἑλκύσῃ.

[2] "Like the Arcadians," i.e. since the foundation of Mega-
lopolis.

[3] *Nicom. Eth.* v. ch. 5.

the other. But[1] as it is best that this should be the
case, *i.e. that a man who is a cobbler or carpenter
should be so always*, so too in the political association
it is obviously best that the same persons should, if
possible, be perpetual rulers. Where however this is
impossible owing to the natural equality of all *the
members of the State*, and at the same time justice
demands that rule, whether it be a privilege or a
burden, should be shared by all alike, [2]in these cases
an attempt is made to imitate the condition of original
dissimilarity by the alternate *rule and* submission of
those who are equals. Here there are always some
persons in a position of rule and others of subjection ; [3]*but the rulers of one time are the subjects of
another and vice versâ*, as though their actual personality had been changed. The same principle *of
alternation* during the period of their rule regulates
the distribution of the different offices among different
persons. It is clear then from these facts that the
kind of unification proposed by some thinkers is not
the natural condition of a State, and that what has
been described as the highest good of which States
are capable means their destruction; *it cannot there-*

---

[1] Reading ἐπεὶ δὲ βέλτιον οὕτως ἔχειν, καὶ τὰ περὶ τὴν κοι-
νωνίαν τὴν πολιτικὴν δῆλον ὡς τοὺς αὐτοὺς ἀεὶ βέλτιον ἄρχειν, εἰ
δυνατόν.

[2] Reading οὕτω δὴ μιμεῖται τὸ ἐν μέρει τοὺς ἴσους εἴκειν τὸ ἀνο-
μοίους εἶναι ἐξ ἀρχῆς.

[3] The words παρὰ μέρος or κατὰ μέρος do not seem to have the
support of the best MSS.; in their absence it is necessary to
supply some clause from the context to explain the meaning of
ὥσπερ ἂν ἄλλοι γενόμενοι.

fore be a Good, for the Good of anything acts as its preservative.

But it may be demonstrated also in another way that the endeavour after an excessive unification of the State is no advantage. A household is a more independent body than an individual and a State than a household ; in fact the true conception of a State is not realized until the association of people composing it has attained independence. Assuming then that a condition of more independence is preferable to one of less, we must conclude that a condition of less is preferable to one of greater unification.

CHAP. III.
(2) Objec-
tions to the
test and
means of
unification. *But to come to the second point.* Even granting that it is best to reduce the association as far as possible to a unit, the existence of this unity does not appear to be proved by the formula "'where all simultaneously term the same object *mine* or not *mine*," which Socrates takes to be an evidence of the complete unification of a State. The word "all" is ambiguous. If it means "each individually," it is possible that the result which Socrates seeks to compass would be in a fair way to be realized, i.e. each individual will call the same child his son and even the same woman his wife, and so with his property and every casual incident of life. But in the case supposed this will not be the sense in which the word will be used by persons who have a community of wives and children ; *they will all call the wives and children theirs,* but it will be " all " in the sense of "all collectively," not of "each individually." So too with the

---

[1] Plato, *Republic,* v. p. 462 c.

property; it will belong to all collectively, not to each
as an individual.

It appears then that the formula "All call the
same thing *mine*" is virtually a quibble. The fact is
that words like *all, both, odd, even,* by their ambiguity
give rise to fallacious reasonings even in regular dis-
putations; and our conclusion must be that "All call
the same thing *mine,*" if it means "each individually,"
is specious but chimerical, whereas if it means "all
collectively," it is very far from conducive to harmony.

But besides this the formula involves a further Community
evil. The more numerous the joint-owners of any- of wives and children.
thing, the less it is cared for. People pay most
attention to their own private property and less to
that in which they have but a part interest, or at the
best they only attend to it so far as it concerns them
personally; for, apart from other reasons, they are
disposed to neglect it by the idea that somebody
else is looking after it, as in domestic service a
number of attendants sometimes do their work less
efficiently than a few. Now *in the Republic of Plato*
every citizen is supposed to have a thousand sons,
not in the sense of sons who are his and no one
else's; on the contrary, any child is equally the son
of any parent, and the result will be that all the
parents will be equally neglectful of all the children.
Again, *in the Republic* when any citizen is prosperous
or unsuccessful everybody speaks of him as "mine"
in a restricted sense corresponding to the fraction he
himself is of the whole population, i.e. *when he calls
him "mine"* he means "mine or so-and-so's," the "so-

and-so" being each of the thousand citizens or however many the State includes. Nay even here he is
in doubt, as it is impossible to tell who had a son born
to him or whose son, if he were born, was spared to
grow up. But I ask, which is the better state of things,
that the term 'mine' should be used [1]without any
distinctive appellation by each of two thousand or
ten thousand persons as the case may be or should
be used as it actually is in existing States, where the
same person is called by A his son, by B his brother,
by C his cousin or whatever the relationship may be,
whether one of consanguinity or connexion and
affinity direct or indirect, and [2]by others again fel-
low-clansman or fellow-tribesman? Surely it is better
to be a person's own cousin than his son in Plato's
sense.

At the same time, *even where there is a community of wives and children*, it is impossible to
prevent persons suspecting their own brothers,
children, fathers and mothers; they are sure to derive
their proofs of mutual relationship from the likenesses
which the children bear to their parents. Indeed
some authors of Voyages round the world assert that
this is actually the case, as in some tribes of [3]Upper
Libya there exists community of wives, but the
children born are assigned to different parents according to their personal likenesses. So too there
are also some females among the lower animals, e.g.

---

[1] Reading τὸ ἐμὸν λέγειν ἕκαστον, τὸ αὐτὸ μὲν προσαγορεύοντας,
δισχιλίων καὶ μυρίων.

[2] Reading ἕτεροι.

[3] See e. g. Herodotus IV. 180.

mares and cows, which naturally produce an offspring closely resembling their parents, as in the case of the Pharsalian mare called Dicæa.

Further, if we establish this community *of wives* CHAP. IV. *and children,* it is difficult to provide against the untoward events which naturally follow, such as cases of outrage, involuntary or even voluntary homicide, assault and vituperation which are innocent perhaps in the case of strangers but involve pollution in the case of parents or near relations. Nay such proceedings will inevitably be more frequent if the relationships are unknown than if they are known; and upon their occurrence, if this knowledge exists, it is possible to make the proper atonements, whereas otherwise it is quite out of the question.

It is strange too that after introducing a community of sons the only thing which Socrates prohibits should be the actual intercourse of lovers, while he does not prohibit the passion of love itself or those other kinds of intimacy which cannot exist between father and son or between two brothers without the grossest breach of decency, as in fact is true even of the passion of love itself. Another remarkable point is that the sole reason assigned by Socrates for prohibiting this intercourse is the vehemence of the pleasure it affords, while the fact that the parties to it are father and son or two brothers is in his opinion of no importance whatsoever.

Again, it would seem to be more expedient *for the State* that this community of wives and children should exist among the Husbandmen *or subjects in Plato's Republic* than among his "Guardians" *or rulers;* for such a community will tend to weaken mutual affection, and the affection existing among the members of the subject class ought to be weak, if they are to be obedient and not revolutionary.

Speaking generally too we may say that this institution will necessarily result in the very opposite of that state of things which should be produced by a wisely-ordered legislation and of the object which Socrates has in view in so regulating the status of the children and wives. Mutual affection, as we hold, is the greatest of all blessings in a State, as it affords the best guarantee against sedition; and it is the unity of a State that Socrates eulogizes so highly. But according to the general opinion of men as well as the doctrine of Socrates himself this unity is the result of mutual affection; witness Aristophanes's description in the [1]Erotic Dialogue of lovers in their strong affection desiring to be united and to be no longer two but one flesh. In the case of these lovers such a union necessarily involves the destruction of one, if not of both. In the State, on the other hand, the result of a community of wives and children is that the affection is inevitably reduced to a watery kind, and it is only in an extremely feeble sense that a son terms a father or a father a son *mine.* Just as when a little sugar is melted in a quantity of water the admixture is imperceptible, so [2]will it be with

---

[1] The reference is to Plato *Symposium*, p. 191 c, d.

[2] Reading οὕτω συμβαίνει καὶ τὴν οἰκειότητα τὴν πρὸς ἀλλήλους τὴν ἀπὸ τῶν ὀνομάτων τούτων, διαφροντίζειν ἥκιστα ἀναγκαῖον ὂν ἐν τῇ πολιτείᾳ τῇ τοιαύτῃ ἢ πατέρα ὡς υἱοῦ ἢ υἱὸν ὡς πατρὸς ἢ ὡς ἀδελφοὺς ἀλλήλων.

the mutual relationships implied in these names ; for
in a polity so constructed there is no reason why a
parent should devote himself to any child as his son
or a son to any parent as a father or any citizens to
each other as brothers. For there are two principal
causes of attachment and affection in the world, viz.
the exclusive possession of anything and its precious-
ness, neither of which can be found among the citizens
in the Socratic polity.

Again, as regards the transference of the children
that are born, whether from the class of Husbandmen
or Artisans to that of Guardians or *vice versâ*, one
has much difficulty in seeing how it is to be carried
out, not to say that the persons engaged in the work
of consignment and transference will of course know
to whom they consign particular children, *and hence
a child cannot be absolutely separated from the class
to which he belongs.* Also the evils specified before,
viz. instances of outrage or sensual love or homicide,
will be more likely to occur in the case of the children
so transferred. For the Guardians cease *ex hypothesi*
to be addressed as brothers, children, fathers or
mothers by the members of their class who are
consigned to the rank of ordinary citizens, and the
ordinary citizens by those who are placed in the
Guardian class ; hence it is impossible for them to
be on their guard against actions of the kind described,
as a sense of their relationship would suggest. ✗

Having thus settled the question of a community CHAP. V.
of wives and children we proceed to the consideration Community
of property. What is the right system of property for of property.
people who are to live as citizens of the best polity ?

is it to be held in common or not? This is a question
which may be considered quite irrespectively of the
legislative enactments in regard to wives and children.
I mean that, even assuming the separate possession of
wives and children as is now the universal rule, we may
still inquire respecting property ¹whether the best
state of things is a community of produce or of landèd
property or of both, i.e. whether it is best that the
estates should be held separately, while the fruits are
brought into the common store to be consumed, as is
the manner of some uncivilized tribes, or conversely
that the land should be common property and cultivated in common, while the produce is divided for
the use of individuals—a sort of community which is
reported to obtain among some non-Greek peoples—
or, thirdly, that both the estates and the produce
should be common.

Where the agricultural population forms a class
distinct from the citizens, a different and less complex
system is possible ; but where the citizens live altogether by their own labour, the conditions of property
will involve various difficulties. Thus if the shares of
enjoyment or labour are unequal, those who get less
and work more are sure to raise complaints against
those who enjoy or get much and labour little. In
fact as a general rule it is no easy matter for people
to live together and enjoy any worldly goods in
common, more especially such things as land and
landed produce. This is evident from the case of
people who travel together and keep a common purse ;

¹ Reading τὰς χρήσεις ἢ τὰς κτήσεις ἢ τάς τε κτήσεις κοινὰς εἶναι
βέλτιον καὶ τὰς χρήσεις.

they almost invariably come to quarrels and collisions
arising from common and unimportant causes. So
too we are most likely to come into collision with
those servants with whom we have most to do, as
they wait upon us in the affairs of everyday life.

There are then these and other similar incon-
veniences inherent in a community of property. The
existing system, if embellished by the moral tone
of those who live under it and by a code of wise
laws, would be far superior, as it would combine the
advantages of both principles, viz. of common and
individual possession. For property ought to be
common in a certain sense, although in its general
character it should be private. Thus the division of
superintendence will prevent mutual recriminations;
and all will succeed better, as each devotes himself to
his own private possessions, while in practice virtue
will render "friends' goods common goods" according
to the proverb. The outlines of such a system are
actually found in some states, so that it is not wholly
chimerical, and in well-ordered states especially it is in
some respects already realized and in others easily
attainable. For every citizen, although he holds his
property in private possession, uses part of it for the
benefit of his friends and shares part of it with them,
as e.g. in Lacedaemon the citizens use each other's
slaves as virtually their own and so too their horses,
dogs and provisions, if they require them in their
[1] hunting expeditions through the country. Plainly
then it is desirable that the tenure of property should
be private but that practically it should be made

[1] Reading ἐν ταῖς ἄγραις.

common. To produce in the citizens a disposition to make this use of their property is a task proper to the legislator.

Again, if we take account of personal gratification, there is an unspeakable advantage in the sense of private property. No doubt the love each individual bears to himself is not purposeless ; it is a natural feeling. Self-love on the contrary is justly censured ; but self-love does not mean loving oneself but loving oneself more than is right, just as the love of money *means an excessive love of money*, for a certain love of all such things is pretty well universal. On the other hand there is nothing pleasanter than to afford gratification or help to friends, guests or companions, and this is impossible unless our property is ours exclusively.

Such are the [1]ill results of the endeavour after an undue unification of the State. I may add that it undoubtedly does away with the exercise of two virtues, viz. of continence in regard to women—for it is a noble act to abstain from adultery in virtue of continence—and of liberality in regard to property ; for *where property is held in common* nobody will shew a liberal spirit or perform any liberal action, as the exercise of liberality consists in the use a person makes of his own possessions.

Legislation then of the kind proposed in Plato's *Republic* has a specious and philanthropic appearance ; it is eagerly embraced by people at the first hearing under the impression that a sort of marvellous universal love will be its result, especially if one

[1] Omitting οὐ.

inveighs against the actual evils of existing polities as
arising from the want of a community of property—
such evils, I mean, as civil law-suits, trials for false
witness and the habit of toadying to the rich. All
these evils however are due not to the want of community of property but to the depravity of human
nature. For experience teaches that disputes are far
more likely to occur among people who possess
property in common and live as partners than among
those who hold their estates in separate tenure,
although the instances we observe of litigants among
whom this community exists are few absolutely as
compared with the number of those among whom the
private tenure of property is the rule. And further
it is fair to state the benefits as well as the evils
we shall lose by establishing such a community. But
life appears wholly impossible *on such principles.*

The cause of Socrates's mistake is to be found in
the falsity of his fundamental position. It is true
that in a certain sense both the household and the
State ought to be units, but not absolutely. For a
State as it progresses towards unity may altogether
cease to be a State or, although it remains a State,
may nearly cease to be one and so become a worse
State ; just as you would spoil a harmony or a rhythm
by reducing it to unison or to a single metrical foot.
The right course, as has been already remarked, is to p. 40.
retain the essential plurality of the State and to make
it a community or a unit by education ; and we may
well be surprised that Socrates, of all persons, whose
purpose was to introduce education and who looked
upon education as the means of making the State

virtuous, should think to order it aright by such means as he proposes rather than by moral discipline, intellectual culture and legislation, after the example of the legislators who in Lacedaemon and Crete effected a certain community of property by the institution of common meals.

Nor again can we rightly shut our eyes to the duty of paying regard to history, to all the ages of the past in which the system proposed by Socrates, were it a wise one, would not have failed to be discovered; for it may be said that all discoveries have been already made, although in some cases they have not been combined and in others when made are not acted upon.

However *the impossibility of complete unification* would be most conspicuous, could we once see a polity of the Socratic type in actual process of construction. It will be found impossible to create the State without [1]immediately making divisions and separations whether into common tables, *as at Sparta,* or into clans and tribes, *as at Athens.* Hence the sole result of the legislation *proposed in the Republic* will be the prohibition of an agricultural life to the Guardians, a result which the Lacedaemonians even under existing conditions try to effect.

(3) Incompleteness of the polity proposed in the *Republic.* But *to come to the third main objection:* Socrates has not stated, nor is it easy to state what is to be the character of his polity as a whole in respect of its members. Yet it may be said that certainly the main body of the State consists *not in the Guardians but* in the mass of other citizens, about whom nothing is

[1] Reading μερίζων αὐτίκα καὶ χωρίζων.

determined, e.g. whether property is to be held in common by the Husbandmen as well as by the Guardians or to be separate and individual, and again whether their wives and children are to belong to them separately or in common. —If there is a general community of everything as in the first case, how will they differ from the Guardians as above described? [1] and what is to induce them to submit to the rule of the Guardian class, unless some such artifice is devised as by the Cretans who, while they allow all other rights to their slaves as much as to freemen, have merely denied them gymnastic exercises and the possession of arms? If on the other hand the system of property and of the family relations among the Husbandmen is to be the same as exists in ordinary States, how is the association of the two classes to be constituted? The necessary consequence is that there will be two States in one and these States mutually hostile. For Socrates divides his State into the Guardians on the one hand who form a sort of military garrison and on the other the Husbandmen, Artisans, and the rest of the population who constitute the ordinary citizens; and among these two classes recriminations, lawsuits and all the other evils he describes as existing in States will be just as prevalent as elsewhere. Yet according to Socrates his citizens will be so educated as to require but few legal regulations, such as police regulations of the city and market or the like, although he assigns the education to the Guardian class alone.

Again Socrates gives his Husbandmen an absolute ownership of their estates on condition of paying a

---

[1] Omitting ἢ τί πλεῖον τοῖς ὑπομένουσι τὴν ἀρχὴν αὐτῶν;

fixed rent to the Guardians. But *if they are absolute owners*, they are likely to be far more intractable and arrogant than the classes of Helots, Penestae or Serfs which exist in some countries.

However, whether ordinances *as to the conditions of property and of the family* among the Husbandmen are as important as among the Guardians or not, certain it is that no definite statement on the subject has been actually made by Socrates. [1]Nor again has he said anything about the questions which next suggest themselves, viz., the political constitution, education and laws of the Husbandmen. Yet these are points of considerable difficulty, and at the same time the character of the Husbandmen is highly important to the maintenance of the association existing among the Guardians. Again if it is the intention of Socrates to establish community of wives and individual possession of property *among the Husbandmen, it is natural to raise the objection*, Where will be the women to devote the same attention to domestic as their husbands to agricultural affairs?[2]

(1) Minor objections.

...It is strange too that Socrates, when he is arguing that the pursuits of women should be the same as those of men, should draw his illustration from the

---

[1] Reading νῦν γ᾽ οὐδὲν διώρισται, καὶ περὶ τῶν ἐχομένων, κ.τ.λ.

[2] The imperfect sentence κἂν εἰ κοιναὶ αἱ κτήσεις καὶ αἱ τῶν γεωργῶν γυναῖκες is necessarily omitted in translation. It seems probable that some words have dropped out of the text after γυναῖκες, as Aristotle having considered the case where there is community of wives and separateness of property would naturally proceed to the case where both wives and property are common.

lower animals, among whom no such thing as Domestic Economy exists.

There is a danger also in the system of rulers proposed by Socrates. He would have the same persons rulers in perpetuity. But this perpetuity of rule is the cause of political disturbance even among people who possess no sense of self-respect and *à fortiori* among men of spirit and martial temper *like his Warriors*[1]. Yet we see at once that he could not help creating perpetual rulers. For [2]the divine gold is not infused into the souls now of some and again of others but of the same persons for ever. His theory is that at the moment of birth God infused gold into some people, silver into others and brass or iron into those who should be Artisans or Husbandmen.

Finally, while denying happiness to the Guardians, Socrates teaches that it is the legislator's duty to make the State as a whole happy. Yet how can the whole State be happy unless [3] if not all its parts, yet most or at least some enjoy happiness? Happiness is not like evenness in numbers; it cannot belong to the whole without belonging to either of the parts, as evenness can. But if the Guardians are not happy, who else will be? certainly not the Artisans and the multitude of mere Mechanics.

In the polity described by Socrates *in the Republic* these difficulties and others not less serious are inherent. The same or nearly the same is true of Plato's later work, the *Laws*. It is worth while then to devote

---

[1] It is the ἐπίκουροι of the *Republic* who are here meant.

[2] See Plato *Republic*, III. p. 415.

[3] Reading μὴ τῶν πλείστων εἰ μὴ πάντων.

a brief consideration to the polity delineated in the *Laws*. For the points determined by Socrates in the *Republic* are extremely few, viz. the right conditions of the community of wives and children and of property and the general system of the polity. The mass of the population he divides into two parts, the Husbandmen and the military class, with a third class formed from members of the second, viz. the deliberative class which is supreme in the State. As to the Husbandmen and Artisans, whether they are not to be eligible to any offices or only to particular offices, whether they are to possess arms like the Guardians and fight in the wars with them or not, Socrates has left wholly undetermined; he merely lays it down that the wives of the Guardians ought to fight in the wars and receive the same education as the Guardians themselves, while for the rest he has filled his discourse with extraneous topics and with a discussion of the education to be given to the Guardian class.

Comparison of the *Republic* and the *Laws*.
The *Laws* consists mainly of legislative enactments with but few remarks on the subject of the polity. And although the purpose of Plato *in the Laws* is to create such a polity as shall have more affinity to existing States, he gradually brings it round again to the old polity *described in the Republic*. For if we except the community of wives and property, all his regulations are the same for both ; there is the same education, the same rule of abstinence from menial labours, the same institution of common meals. The only points of difference are that in the polity of the *Laws* he insists upon common meals for women as well as men and that the number of citizens possess-

ing arms is supposed to be five thousand instead of
one thousand, as in the *Republic*.

Now although all the Socratic dialogues are
characterized by brilliancy, grace, originality and
research, it is perhaps difficult to succeed in every
detail. Thus if we take e.g. the number just mentioned,
we must not conceal from ourselves that a country
as large as the Babylonian or some other of bound-
less extent will be required, if it is to support five
thousand citizens in idleness and ¹with them a host
of women and attendants many times as numerous as
themselves. Impossible assumptions *of this kind*
however are inadmissible *in constructing an ideal
State*, although arbitrary ones are allowable.

Further it is the duty of the legislator according
to Socrates in enacting his laws to have regard to
two things, viz. the country and the people. He
might properly have added " to neighbouring lands
also," ²especially if the State is to lead a social life
as a member of the family of States; for in that case
it will need to use such means of offence and defence
in war as are serviceable in dealing with foreign lands
no less than within the country itself. In fact even if
we do not accept this social life either for the individual
or for the State as a body, it is none the less necessary
to inspire our enemies with fear not only when they
have invaded the country but even after their retreat.

Again, it is a question whether it would not be

Criticism of the polity of the Laws.

---

¹ Reading παρὰ τούτοις.

² Reading πρὸς τοὺς γειτνιῶντας τύπους, πρῶτον μὲν εἰ δεῖ τὴν
πόλιν, κ.τ.λ., and substituting a colon for the full stop after τοὺς
ἔξω τόπους.

better to adopt a different, i.e. a less ambiguous definition, of the amount of property the citizens are to
hold. Socrates *in the Laws* says it should be "large
enough for living temperately," which is like saying
"large enough for living well." The definition is too
vague, not to say that a person may "live temperately"
when he is living penuriously. A better definition
would be "temperately and liberally"; for if the
two are separated, liberality of life may be compatible
with luxury and temperance with hardship. *The
reason for naming liberality and temperance is* that
these are the only moral habits[1] which have to do
with the use of property. It is impossible, I mean,
to make a mild or valorous use of property but
possible to make a temperate or liberal use of it,
and consequently temperance and liberality must be
the [2]moral habits which have to do with property.

One may well be surprised too that, while equalizing all properties, Socrates should omit to regulate
the number of citizens and should set no limit to the
procreation of children, assuming that, however large
the number of children born, it [3]will be sufficiently
reduced to the original standard of population by
cases of unfruitful marriage, because this seems to be
actually the case in existing States. Greater exactness however will be necessary in States where the
Socratic polity exists than at present. At present
there is no destitution, as the estates are subdivided
according to the number of citizens, however large it

---

[1] Omitting αἱρεταί.

[2] Reading ὥστε καὶ τὰς ἕξεις.

[3] Reading ὡς ἱκανῶς ἀνομαλισθησομένην.

Accordingly Phaleas of Chalcedon set the example by advocating equality in the possessions of the citizens. This he thought although easily attainable by States at the time of their foundation was more difficult in the case of States already organized; still the equalization of properties would be soonest effected, if dowries were given but not received by the rich and received but not given by the poor. Plato, when he wrote the *Laws,* held that inequality of property up to a certain point should be allowed, but that no citizen should be permitted to acquire more than five times the minimum, as has been already p. 59. remarked. But it ought not to escape the attention of legislators who adopt these principles, as in fact it does, that, if they define the amount of property, it is incumbent upon them also to define the number of children. For if the quantity of children becomes too great for the total amount of the property, the law will inevitably be broken; and not only is it broken but there is an evil in reducing a number of people from affluence to poverty, as they are almost certain to display a revolutionary temper. The importance of an equality of property to the political association is a truth which seems to have been fully discerned by some of the ancients, as may be inferred from the legislation of Solon and the fact that in some countries there exists a law prohibiting the indefinite acquisition of property at pleasure. It is on the same principle that the laws *in some States* forbid the sale of property—among the Locrians, e.g. a man may not legally sell his property unless he has proved himself to have been the victim of a notorious

misfortune[1]—and in others enjoin the perpetual maintenance of the original allotments. It was the violation
of this last rule which at Leucas e. g. gave a democratical bias to the polity ; for the result *of splitting
up the patrimonies* was that the offices of State
ceased to be filled exclusively by persons possessing
the legal property qualification.

However this equality of property may exist and
yet the amount of property be too large, so as to
occasion luxury, or too small, so as to be a cause of
penurious living. We see then that it is not enough
for the legislator to equalize properties ; he must
aim at the right mean *in the amount fixed.* Nor
again is it any good merely to fix the proper moderate
amount of property for all the citizens. Men's desires need to be levelled more than their properties,
and this is impossible unless they are adequately
educated by the laws. Perhaps however Phaleas
would rejoin that this is precisely his own point ;
for his theory is that there are two things which
ought to be equalized in all States, viz. property and
education. But it is necessary to define the education. The mere fact that it is one and the same for all
is no good ; it may be one and the same, and yet of
such a kind as to dispose people to seek an undue
share of money or honour or both. Again inequality
of honours is as much a cause of civil disturbance as
inequality of property, although the cases are just
reversed ; for the commons *are moved to disturb the
peace* by inequality of property, and the upper

---

[1] There should be only a comma after συμβεβηκυῖαν.

without a struggle." His words induced Autophra-
dates to reflect and eventually abandon the blockade.

No doubt there is a certain advantage in an *Inadequacy of the system of property.* equality of properties among the citizens as a safeguard against civil discord; but it is not in fact very
great. For *in the first place* it will produce a feeling
of indignation among the upper classes, as they consider themselves entitled to more than mere equality,
and consequently, as experience teaches, often become
the authors of conspiracies and seditions. And
secondly there is no satisfying men's depravity: they
are content at first with two obols *as an allowance
for the theatre,* but no sooner is this the constitutional
sum than they crave a larger one and so on *ad infini-
tum.* For desire is in its nature limitless; and the
satisfaction of desire is the sole object of most men's
lives. The [1]remedy of these evils lies not so much
in reducing all properties to the same level as in so
disposing the higher natures that they are unwilling
and the lower that they are unable to aggrandize
themselves. But this last result can only be attained
where the lower classes are weaker and are not the
victims of injustice.

But even the equality of property proposed by
Phaleas is open to objection. It is in the landed
estate alone that he makes an equality, whereas there
is also such a thing as wealth which consists in slaves,
cattle and money or a large stock of what is called
household furniture. It is right then either to aim at
an equalization or a moderate fixed maximum of all
such goods or else to put no restriction upon any.

[1] Reading ἄκη.

Position of the Artisan class.

Lastly it is evident from the legislation of Phaleas that the State he proposes to construct is a small one, since the Artisans *according to his theory* are all to be public slaves and not to contribute to the complement of the State. [1] If however there are to be public slaves, the slavery ought to be confined to the persons engaged upon public works, as is the case at Epidamnus and in the system which Diophantus once tried to establish at Athens.

These considerations will enable us to form a tolerable judgment how far Phaleas has been successful or unsuccessful in his proposals for a polity.

Chap. VIII.

The polity proposed by Hippodamus.

The first person, not being a practical politician, who set himself to make a statement of the best polity, was Hippodamus the son of Euryphon of Miletus, the same who invented the method of partitioning cities and laid out the Piraeus with intersecting streets—a man who in his love of ostentation made himself rather eccentric in his general life, so that to some people his manner of living appeared extravagant from his thick flowing locks and the [2] adornments of his dress, which although simple was warm not only in winter but in the summer months as well, yet who at the same time aspired to be a man of learning in all the domain of physical science. His projected State comprised ten thousand citizens and was divided into three parts, the first consisting of Artisans, the second of Husbandmen, and the third of the Military or

---

[1] Reading ἀλλ᾽ εἴπερ δεῖ δημοσίους εἶναι, τοὺς τὰ κοινὰ ἐργαζομένους δεῖ, καθάπερ ἐν Ἐπιδάμνῳ τε καὶ Διόφαντός ποτε κατεσκεύαζεν Ἀθήνῃσι, τοῦτον ἔχειν τὸν τρόπον.

[2] Reading τριχῶν τε πλήθει καὶ κοσμήσεσιν ἐσθῆτος.

Armed Class. The land too he wished to divide into three parts, viz., sacred, public and private; the sacred being that which was to supply the cost of the customary religious services, the public all that was devoted to the support of the Military Class, and the private the land of the Husbandmen. Further he held that there were but three kinds of laws, as the possible subjects of judicial procedure were but three, viz., assault, trespass and homicide. He proposed to institute also one supreme Court of Appeal for all cases in which there seemed to have been a failure of justice, and to constitute the court of certain Elders appointed by voting. Judicial verdicts according to him ought not to be returned by balloting; but each juryman should bring a tablet on which to inscribe his verdict, if it were one of simple condemnation[1], while, if it were one of simple acquittal, he was to leave the tablet blank, and, if it were a qualified one, he was to specify the fact. For he disapproved of the system at present established by law on the ground that the jurors are compelled to perjure themselves by returning an absolute verdict one way or the other. Also he proposed a law to confer honour upon anyone who made a discovery beneficial to the State and to provide support at the public expense for the children of those who fell in war—a fact from which we may infer that no such custom had as yet been legally instituted in other countries, although at the present time this law exists both at Athens and in other States as well. He proposed too that all the officers of State should be elected by the commons, meaning by

---

[1] Omitting $\tau\grave{\eta}\nu$ $\delta\acute{\iota}\kappa\eta\nu$.

the commons the three classes in the State, and that the officers elected should undertake the conduct of affairs of State and the protection of foreigners and orphans.

Criticism of (1) the classification of the citizens, Such are the most numerous and important features of the system proposed by Hippodamus. The first difficulty which might be raised is as to the division of the civic population. The Artisans, the Husbandmen and the Military Class are all alike members of the polity; but the Husbandmen do not possess arms, and the Artisans possess neither land nor arms, so that they both become practically slaves of the Military Class. Hence it is impossible that they should be eligible to all the honours of State, as generals, guardians of the citizens and, I may say, the supreme officers generally will necessarily be taken from the Military Class. But if they do not enjoy full civic rights, how can they cherish a friendly disposition to the polity? It may be answered that the Military Class ought certainly to be stronger than the other two together. But this cannot well be the case, unless it is numerous, and, if so, why should the other classes enjoy civic rights and have the appointment of the officers of State in their control? Again, what is the use of the Husbandmen in this State? An Artisan population is of course indispensable, as no State can do without Artisans, and they can support themselves *in the State of Hippodamus* as in any other State by their art. But the case of the Husbandmen is different. There would be good reason why they should form a separate class in the State, if they *merely* supplied the military class with their sustenance; but in the polity of Hippodamus they possess land of their own and cultivate it for their own private interest. And as to the public land from which the military defenders of the State are to derive their sustenance, if they cultivate it themselves, there will be no distinction between the Soldiery and the Husbandmen, although it is the intention of the legislator to create one; while if the cultivators of it are distinct from the class which cultivates the private estates and from the Soldiery, instead of two classes coinciding there will be here a fourth class in the State not enjoying civic rights but alien to the polity. On the other hand, if Hippodamus makes the same persons cultivators both of the private and the public land, how is each of them to raise produce enough ¹for the support of two households? and why in the world should they not simply get their own sustenance and supply the soldiery ²from the same allotments of land *without distinguishing the land at all as public or private?* All these are points which involve much confusion.

Again, there is a defect in the proposed law of (2) the judicial procedure ³by which a divided verdict is cial procedure, required, whereas the terms of the suit are simple, and the juror is converted into an arbitrator. Although in arbitration this is possible, even where there are several arbitrators, as they consult together on the verdict to be returned, it is impossible in Courts of Law ; on the contrary, most legislators ex-

---

¹ Reading ὑπουργήσει δύο οἰκίαις.

² Reading ἀπὸ τῆς γῆς τῶν αὐτῶν κλήρων.

³ Reading τὸ κρίνειν ἀξιοῦν διαιροῦντας τῆς δίκης ἁπλῶς γεγραμμένης.

pressly provide against consultation among the jurors.
Further will there not be inevitable confusion in the
verdict whenever it is the opinion of the juror that
the defendant is liable but not to the full amount
alleged by the plaintiff? Suppose e.g. the plaintiff
demands twenty minae, whereas the juror awards[1]
him ten, or one juror rather more than ten, a
second rather less, a third five, and another four; it
is evident that they will fix various fractions in this
way, while some again will mulct him in the full sum
demanded and others will let him off scot-free. What is
to be the method of reckoning these votes? And
further no one compels a juror to perjure himself if
he returns a verdict of simple acquittal or condemnation, where the accusation is duly preferred in simple
terms. For a juror who votes acquittal decides not
that the defendant owes nothing but that he does not
owe the twenty minae claimed; and the only person
guilty of perjury is a juror who returns a verdict for
the plaintiff, when he does not believe that the defendant owes the twenty minae.

(3) the re-
wards con-
ferred upon
public bene-
factors.
Again, as to the propriety of conferring some distinction upon persons who make a discovery beneficial
to the State, such legislation is not free from peril
and has merely a specious sound, involving as it does
intrigues and possibly disturbances of the polity. But
this is a question which merges itself in a different
problem and a distinct inquiry. It is a difficult
question to some people whether it is injurious or
advantageous to States to alter their ancestral laws
and customs where another better law or custom is

[1] Reading κρίνει.

possible. Hence it is not easy to yield an offhand
assent to the proposal of Hippodamus, if we assume
the inexpediency of such alteration. People may
move the abolition of old laws and customs or of the
political constitution as a public benefit.

But as we have alluded to the subject, it will be
worth while to discuss it a little more fully. There is
room, as we said, for a difference of opinion. At first
sight there would seem to be an advantage in alteration, as it has certainly proved beneficial in the other
Sciences. Thus there has been a benefit in the departure from ancestral rules in Medicine, Gymnastic
and the arts and faculties generally; and as Politics
deserves to be placed in this category, it is evident
that the same must be true also of Politics. It may
be said that there is an indication of this truth in the
facts of History, as ancient customs are exceedingly
rude and barbarous. For instance, the Greeks always
carried daggers and purchased their wives from one
another; in fact all such primitive institutions as
survive in the world are quite absurd, as e.g. the
law at Cumae in cases of homicide that the defendant
is held to have been guilty of the murder, if the
prosecutor produces a certain number of his own
kinsmen as witnesses. As a general rule it is not
what is ancient but what is good that the world
wants. Nor is it likely that our first parents, whether
they were the children of earth or the survivors of
some catastrophe, were any better than ordinary or
unwise people, as in fact is the common notion of
the Earth-children *or Giants*. It is absurd therefore
to abide by their decrees. We may add that it is

Arguments for and against the alteration of ancestral laws and customs.

not desirable to leave even the written laws unaltered. For as in the arts generally, so in the political system it is impossible that everything should be precisely specified in writing. The terms of the written law are necessarily general, whereas its practical application is to individual cases. It is evident then that an alteration is right in the case of certain laws and on particular occasions. From another point of view however such alterations seem to require no little caution. Where the improvement is but slight compared with the evil of accustoming the citizens lightly to repeal the laws, it is undoubtedly our duty to pass over some mistakes whether of the legislature or the executive, as the benefit we shall derive from the alteration will not be equal to the harm we shall get by accustoming ourselves to disobey authority. The illustration from the arts is fallacious. There is no parallel between altering an art and altering a law. For all the potency of the law to secure obedience depends upon habit, and habit can only be formed by lapse of time ; so that the ready transition from the existing laws to others that are new is a weakening of the efficacy of law itself. And further even if we assume that it is right to alter laws, we have still to ask whether this is true of all laws and in every form of polity, and whether the alteration should be the work of any one who chooses or only of certain definite people. These are points of great importance, and in view of them we may now abandon this inquiry as being rather suited to another occasion.

Chap. IX.   In the polity of Lacedaemon or Crete, and indeed, we may say, in any polity whatever there are two

points to be considered, viz. firstly, how far it is successful or the reverse in its legislative enactments
considered relatively to the best system, and secondly,
how far it runs counter to the general principle or
plan of the polity which the citizens propose to
themselves.

Now it is allowed on all hands that in a State The Lacedaemonian
which is to enjoy a noble polity the citizens must be polity.
relieved from anxiety about the bare necessaries of
life. But the means of securing this relief are not
easy to apprehend. *The natural suggestion is that
there should be a large subject population, but it is*
one which is not free from danger. For the Penestae in The Helots.
Thessaly made frequent attacks upon the Thessalians,
as did also the Helots upon the Lacedaemonians; indeed they may be described as perpetually lying in
wait to take advantage of their masters' misfortunes.
And if the same result has not yet occurred in the
case of the Cretans, the reason is probably that,
although the neighbouring States are at war among
themselves, none has allied itself with the revolted
serfs of another; for to do so would be prejudicial to
their own interests, as they are themselves too the
masters of a surrounding subject populace. Whereas,
if we look at the Lacedaemonians, we find that their
neighbours without exception were their enemies,
Argives, Messenians and Arcadians, *so that the Helots*
were encouraged to revolt. For the reason why the
Thessalians themselves originally suffered from such
revolts was that they were still at war with the
nations upon their frontiers, viz. the Achaeans, Per-
rhaebians and Magnesians. And even apart from

further trouble the mere supervision *of a subject populace* in itself seems to be troublesome enough. What is the right way of dealing with them? If they are left without restraint, they grow insolent and claim equality with their masters; while, if they are harshly treated, they are in a state of conspiracy and bitter illwill. It is evident then that the Lacedaemonians, whose experience in respect of the Helots is such as I have described, are not the discoverers of the best system *of governing subjects.*

The licence of the women. Again, the licence of the women *at Lacedaemon* is equally fatal to the spirit of the polity and to the happiness of the State. For as husband and wife are constituent elements of a household, it is evidently right to regard a State also as divided nearly equally into the male and female population; and accordingly in any polity where the condition of the women is unsatisfactory, one-half of the State must be regarded as destitute of legislative regulations. And this is actually the case at Lacedaemon. For the legislator in his desire to impart a character of hardiness to the State as a whole, although[1] true to his principle as regards the men, has been guilty of serious oversights in his treatment of the women, as their life is one of unrestrained and indiscriminate licence and luxury. A necessary result then in a polity so constituted is the worship of wealth, especially if the citizens are under the thumb of the women, as is generally the case with military and warlike races, if we except the Celts and any others who have openly attached themselves to men. It was in fact with good reason, as it

[1] Reading κατὰ μὲν τοὺς ἄνδρας τοιοῦτός ἐστιν.

appears, that the author of the myth made Ares tho paramour of Aphrodite ; for experience shews that military nations are all strongly inclined to the passion of love. Accordingly the influence of women prevailed at Lacedaemon ; and while the Lacedaemonian empire lasted a great deal of business passed through their hands. But what difference does it make whether women actually hold office or the officers of State are ruled by the women? The result is in either case the same. And whereas bravery is of no use in any of the routine duties of life [1]but at the best is useful only in the conduct of war, tho Lacedaemonian women were the greatest nuisance even in military matters, as they proved at the time of the Theban invasion, when not only were they wholly useless like the women in other States but they were the cause of more confusion than tho enemy. There seems to have been originally a reason for the licence of the women at Lacedaemon. Living always beyond the borders, as their military expeditions required, the Lacedaemonians were long strangers to their own land during their wars with the Argives and afterwards with the Arcadians and Messenians. And when the turmoil of war was over, the legislator, into whose hands they put themselves, found them already disciplined by their military life—for a soldier's life has many elements of virtue—whereas Lycurgus, as the story goes, made an effort to reduce the women to conformity with the laws, but they resisted so stoutly that he abandoned the at-

---

[1] Reading ἀλλ᾽ εἴπερ, πρὸς τὸν πόλεμον.

tempt. These considerations will account for the actual events and therefore no doubt for the de- fective discipline of the women. But the point we are investigating is not what is or is not excusable, but what is or is not right. And the unsatisfactory condition of the women seems, as was before re- marked, not only to create a certain indecorum in ¹the polity itself but to contribute something to the avarice of the citizens.

Property.   *And this brings me to another point;* for it is a natural sequel of these remarks to take exception to the inequality of property. Things have come to this, that there are some Lacedaemonians who possess vast estates and others who possess extremely little; so that the ownership of the soil has fallen gradually into the hands of a few persons. This is a point upon which the legal regulations too are unsatisfactory. For the legislature, while setting and rightly setting a stigma upon the purchase or sale of patrimonies, allowed absolute liberty of presentation or bequest. Yet the result will of course be the same in the one case as in the other. *Another defect is that* owing to the number of heiresses and the practice of giving large dowries nearly two-fifths of the whole soil belongs to women². *But rather than this should be the case* it were better that dowries should be prohibited alto- gether, or a small or at most a moderate dowry permitted by law. ³*Again there ought to be laws*

¹ Reading τῆς πολιτείας αὐτῆς καθ' αὑτήν.

² Omitting καὶ before τῶν γυναικῶν.

³ The sequence of thought shows that there is a lacuna in the text, probably after τετάχθαι. Perhaps the true reading

regulating the betrothal of heiresses; whereas now *a father* is at liberty to give his daughter and heiress in marriage to any one he chooses, and if he dies without disposing of her by his will, whoever is left heir *to the residue of his property* gives her in marriage to anyone he likes. The result is that, although the country is capable of maintaining fifteen hundred knights and thirty thousand heavy-armed troops, the total number came to be less than one thousand. The evil of this system at Lacedaemon has been proved by actual experience; for the State could not sustain a single blow[1] but perished from the paucity of its population. It is said that under the earlier kings the Lacedaemonians were in the habit of admitting non-citizens to civic rights, thereby preventing de-population in those days despite the long wars in which they were engaged, and that the Spartiates[2] themselves were at one time as many as ten thousand. However, whether this is true or false, it is better that the State should have a large population secured to it by an equalization of property *than by an extension of civic rights.* But the law relating to the procreation of children is also an obstacle in the way of this reform. The legislator in his desire to multiply as much as possible the number of Spartiates encourages the citizens to beget the largest possible number of children. There is a law

was something like the following: νῦν δ' ἔξεστι δοῦναι ὁπόσην ἄν τις θέλῃ· καὶ τῷ πατρὶ ἔξεστι δοῦναι τὴν ἐπίκληρον ὅτῳ ἂν βούληται, κἂν ἀποθάνῃ μὴ διαθέμενος, κ.τ.λ.

[1] The "single blow" is the battle of Leuctra.

[2] Reading τοὺς Σπαρτιάτας.

at Lacedaemon that the parent of three sons is relieved of military service and the parent of four sons enjoys an immunity from all public burdens. But it is evident that if population increases greatly, while the soil remains divided in the way I have described, there will inevitably be a large body of poor.

The Ephoralty. Again the conditions of the Ephoralty are unsatisfactory. [1]Although it is an office which controls issues of the highest importance to the Lacedaemonian State, all the Ephors are elected from the commons, and the result is that very poor people often find their way into the Ephoral College, and their impecuniousness, as experience teaches, makes them venal. Their venality was displayed as on many previous occasions, so quite recently in the Andrian[2] case, where a certain number of the Ephors were corrupted by bribes and did all that in them lay to work the ruin of the State. *Nor is this all;* the dignity, the almost despotic nature of the office compelled the kings themselves to pay court to the Ephors and in this among other ways tended to injure the polity, as it gradually ceased to be an Aristocracy and became a Democracy. It is true that the Ephoral College is the keystone of the polity. For the commons are kept quiet by their eligibility to the highest office of State; and thus, whether the result is due to the legislator or to fortune, *the institution of the Ephoralty* is practically

---

[1] κυρίαν is a mere misprint for κυρία, and αὐτή should be omitted from the text.

[2] Nothing is known of the circumstances here referred to; but νῦν is in favour of Ἀνδρίοις rather than ἀνδρίοις (cp. p. 51, l. 12) as the true reading.

beneficial. For if a polity is to be preserved, all the elements of the State must desire that it should exist and [1]continue permanently the same. Thus *at Lacedaemon* this is the case with the Kings owing to their royal dignity, with the upper classes owing to the Senate, as the senatorial office is a prize proposed to their virtue, and with the commons owing to the Ephoralty, as it is open to the whole body of citizens. But, although it is right that all the citizens should be eligible to this office, the election ought not to be conducted in the present fashion which is absolutely puerile. And further, as the Ephors, being persons of no special qualifications, are supreme judges in cases of high importance, it is desirable that they should not pass judgments according to their own arbitrary discretion but should be guided by written formulae, i.e. by the laws. Also the manner of life of the Ephors is not consistent with the spirit of the State, [2]as it is one of inordinate licence, whereas among the citizens generally the error is rather on the side of excessive austerity, so that their power of endurance fails, and by secret evasions of the law they enjoy the pleasure of sensual gratifications.

Nor again are the conditions of the Senate unexceptionable. It might perhaps be said that they were advantageous to the State, if the Senators were men of virtuous character and adequate discipline in true manly excellence; although even then it would be a question whether they ought to be supreme judges in important cases during the whole period of

The Senate.

---

[1] Reading διαμένειν τὴν αὐτήν.
[2] Reading αὕτη.

their natural life, as there is an old age of the intellect as well as of the body. But when their discipline has been such that the legislator himself is distrustful of their virtue, the state of things is full of danger. Experience shows that the occupants of this office frequently sacrifice the public interest to corruption or personal favouritism. It is desirable therefore that they should not be, as now in fact they are, irresponsible. It may be thought that all the officers of State are responsible to the Ephors. But *in the first place* the prerogative so conferred upon the Ephoralty is too great, and *secondly* this general responsibility to the Ephors is not what we mean, when we say that the officers of State ought to be responsible. Further, the election of the Senators is puerile as regards the means of deciding *between the candidates;* nor is it right that anyone who is to be found worthy of the office should be obliged to make a [1]personal canvass, as the right man ought to fill the office whether he wishes or not. But in the present instance it is evident that the legislator is acting upon the same principle as in the other arrangements of the polity. It is because his object is to render the citizens ambitious that he has introduced [2]this personal canvass in the election of Senators; for nobody but an ambitious man would personally solicit office. Yet it may be said that nearly all the deliberate crimes which are done in the world are the results of ambition and avarice.

The Kings. But to come to the Kings: the question whether

---

[1] τὸν αὐτὸν is a misprint for τὸ αὐτὸν.

[2] Reading τούτῳ.

Kingship is or is not a desirable institution in States may be discussed at another time. Assuredly however it is desirable to depart from the system which now exists *at Lacedaemon* and select each King in virtue solely of his own life. It is clear that the legislator himself despairs of making the Kings noble and good; at all events he distrusts them, as not being men of sufficient goodness, and it was accordingly the custom of the Lacedaemonians to associate the enemies of the Kings with them in their missions beyond the borders and [1]to look upon the dissensions of the Kings as constituting a safeguard of the State.

Again the institution of common meals, the so-called Phiditia, as regulated by its author, is open to objection. The expenses of these meetings ought rather to be borne by the State Exchequer as in Crete; whereas at Lacedaemon every one is bound to contribute, although some of the citizens are extremely poor and unable to afford the outlay. The result is therefore just the opposite of the legislator's intention; while he means the institution of common meals to be a democratical one, as at present regulated it turns out anything but democratical. For the very poor cannot well take part in it; and yet the constitutional limit of the citizenship at Lacedaemon is that any one who cannot pay this tax should not enjoy the rights of a citizen. *The Phiditia or common meals.*

The law relating to the Admirals has already been attacked by others; and rightly so, as it is a cause of civil discord. For the Admiralty is little less than *The Admiralty.*

---

[1] Omitting the full stop after ἐχθροῖς.

a second Kingship established as a counterpoise to
the Kings who are [1]perpetual generals.

Military
spirit.

There is yet another criticism which may be advanced against the fundamental principle of the legislator, as indeed it has been advanced by Plato himself
in the *Laws*[2]. It is that the whole system of the
Lacedaemonian legislation is intended to produce one
element of virtue, viz. military virtue, as conducing to
a career of conquest. The result was that, so long as
the Lacedaemonians were at war, all was well with
them; but no sooner had they made the empire their
own than their power began to decay, because they
had not learnt to live a life of leisure nor acquired
any more valuable discipline than that of war. And
they make another mistake not less serious. They
hold that those Goods which are the supreme objects
of human desire are to be obtained by virtue rather
than by vice, and so far they are right; but when
they regard these Goods as preferable to Virtue itself,
they are wrong.

Finance.

Lastly the system of public Finance among the
Spartiates is bad. There is no reserve fund in the
State Exchequer against the necessity of great wars,
and they are slow to pay extraordinary taxes; for as
nearly all the land is in the hand of the Spartiates,
they are not careful to examine each other's pay-
ments. In fact the issue of the Lacedaemonian
legislation has been just the opposite of such a state
of things as would be expedient. For while the legislator has reduced the State to poverty, he has in-
spired the individual citizens with a love of money.

[1] Reading αἰδίοις.   [2] *Laws* i. pp. 625, sqq.

We must now leave our survey of the Lacedaemonian polity, as these are the features in it which
most invite criticism.

The Cretan polity is closely parallel to the Lacedaemonian; but although in some small respects
it is rather superior, its general character is one of
less fiuish. One might suspect, even if History did
not relate, that the Lacedaemonian polity has been in
most of its features modelled upon the Cretan; and
as a general rule ancient institutions are not so finely
elaborated as more modern ones. The story runs
that Lycurgus, when he gave up his guardianship
of King Charillus and went abroad, spent his time
chiefly in Crete, being led to do so by the relationship
existing between the Lacedaemonians and the Cretans.
For the Lyctians were Laconian colonists, and the
founders of the colony discovered the system of laws
in question already existing among the inhabitants of
that day. Accordingly the same laws prevail to the
present time among the Perioeci *or subject peoples
in Crete*, the theory being that this legislative system
was introduced in the first instance by Minos. It
may be said that the island is naturally adapted by
the advantages of its situation to be the imperial
State of the Greeks; for it commands the whole
Mediterranean, upon which all or nearly all Greek
States are situated, being but a short distance from
Peloponnesus on the one hand and from the parts of
Asia about Triopium and Rhodes on the other. It
was thus that Minos acquired the empire of the sea,
reduced or colonized all the islands and eventually in
an invasion of Sicily lost his life near Camicus in
that island.

CHAP. X.
The polity
of Crete.

Relation of
the Lace-
daemonian
polity to
the Cretan.

There is a certain analogy between the Cretan
polity and the Lacedaemonian. There is in both a
subject agricultural class, the Helots at Lacedaemon
and the Perioeci in Crete ; and in both there is the
institution of common meals which were originally
called by the Lacedaemonians not Phiditia but Andria
as by the Cretans—a clear proof that they have been
introduced from Crete. And further the political
systems are analogous. The Ephors have the same
authority as the so-called Cosmi in Crete, although
the Ephors are five in number and the Cosmi ten ;
so too the Senate in Lacedaemon is equivalent to the
Senate, or, as it is called, the Council, in Crete.
There were Kings at one time in Crete ; but subsequently the Kingship was done away, and the
command in war belongs now to the Cosmi. All
the citizens may attend the Public Assembly ; but
its power is limited to confirming the resolutions of
the Senate and Cosmi.

Common
meals.

The common meals are better regulated in Crete
than at Lacedaemon. At Lacedaemon every citizen
pays his quota as a poll-tax ; and, if he fails, there is

p. 83.

a law which disfranchises him, as I said before. In
Crete, on the other hand, the expense is more an
affair of the State. [1]Of the entire landed produce and
live stock belonging to the State as well as of the
taxes paid by the Perioeci one portion is set apart
for the worship of the Gods and the public services and the other for the common meals, so
that all alike, women, children and men, are sup-

[1] Reading ἀπὸ πάντων γὰρ τῶν γινομένων καρπῶν τε καὶ βόσκη-
μάτων τῶν δημοσίων καὶ ἐκ τῶν φόρων.

whenever they submit business to the Commons, the
popular assembly is thereby empowered not merely
to listen to all the resolutions of the government, but
it has authority also to pronounce judgment upon
them, and anyone who chooses is at liberty to object
to the proposals—which is not the case in the Lacedac-
monian and Cretan polities. *So far the polity of
Carthage is democratical.* But there is an oligarchical
element in the power of cooption enjoyed by the
Pentarchies, which are boards of high and various
authority, in their right of electing the Hundred who
are the highest officers of State and in their tenure
of official power for a longer period than any other
board of officers, as their power begins before they actually enter upon office and continues after they have
actually gone out of it. The unpaid character of the
Pentarchies, their appointment by other means than
by lot, and other similar features of the polity may
be regarded as aristocratical ; so too is the rule by
which all cases alike are tried by [1] certain fixed boards
of magistrates, instead of being divided among different
boards as at Lacedaemon. The point in which the
Carthaginian system departs most widely from Aristocracy on the side of Oligarchy is in the popular
idea that wealth as well as merit deserves to be considered in the election of officers of State, as it is
impossible for a poor man to enjoy the leisure necessary for the proper performance of official duties.
Assuming then that election by wealth is oligarchical
and election by merit aristocratical, we may reckon
as a third method the one which obtains in the con-

---

[1] Reading ὑπὸ τινῶν ἀρχείων.

stitutional system of the Carthaginians who in the election of officers of State generally and especially of the highest officers, viz. the Kings and the Generals, pay regard *not to wealth only nor to merit only but* to both. This departure from the principles of Aristocracy must be regarded as an error of the legislator. It is a point of primary importance to provide in the first instance that the best citizens, not only during their period of office but in all their private life, may be able to enjoy leisure and be free from degrading duties. But granting that it is right to have regard *not only to merit but* also to affluence as a means of securing leisure, we may still censure the arrangement by which at Carthage the highest offices of State, viz. the Kingship and Generalship, are put up to sale. The effect of such a law is that wealth is more highly esteemed than virtue, and the whole State is avaricious. [1]Whenever the ruling class regards a thing as honourable, the opinion of the citizens generally is sure to follow suit. No polity however can be permanently aristocratical where merit is not held in supreme honour. Nor is it unreasonable that people, [2]if they pay for the privilege, should get the habit of making their official status a source of pecuniary profit, when they have been put to heavy expenses in order to hold it. If a poor man of good character will aspire to be the gainer *by his office*, the same will be true, *à fortiori*, of one whose character stands lower, *as is the case with the purchaser of official power,* when he has already been put to great expense. It follows that the offices of State ought

---

[1] Reading ὅ τι δ' ἂν ὑπολάβῃ.   [2] Reading τοῦτ' ὠνουμένους.

There is no legislative enactment peculiar to Charondas. Charondas, except the procedure in cases of false witness ; he was the author of the solemn indictment for perjury. In point of [1]detail however he is more exact even than legislators of our own time.

The peculiar feature in the laws of Phaleas is the Phaleas. equalization of properties ; and in those of Plato the community of women, children and property, the common meals of the women, the law relating to convivial meetings, that the sober people are to be presidents of the banquet, and the law of military exercises intended to make the citizens by practice equally dexterous with both hands, as it is not right *according to Plato* that one hand should be useful and the other useless.

There are also laws of Draco; but he made Draco. them for a polity already existing, nor is there any special feature in them which deserves to be mentioned, except their severity as shown in the heavy penalties.

Pittacus too was the framer of a code and not of Pittacus. a polity. It is a law peculiar to him that drunken people, [2]if they commit a breach of order, are to be punished more severely than sober. For as outrages are more frequently committed by people in a drunken than in a sober state, Pittacus disregarded the idea that an allowance should be more readily made for drunken people, and looked solely to the public interest.

[1] Omitting τῶν νόμων.
[2] Reading ἄν τι πταίσωσι.

Androda-
mas.

Lastly, Androdamas of Rhegium acted as lawgiver to the Chalcidians in the Thracian peninsula ; he is the author of laws about cases of homicide and about heiresses, although there is no peculiar law of his to be mentioned.

Our survey of polities, whether actually realized or merely proposed by certain thinkers, may now be regarded as complete.

BOOK III.

In any inquiry into the nature and character of particular polities we may say that the first point to be considered is the nature of the State. At present there is often a difference of opinion, as one party asserts that it is the State which has done a certain action, and another that it is not the State but the Oligarchy or the Tyrant *by whom it was governed.* Also *it is necessary to settle this point, as* a State is the sphere in which all the activity of a statesman or legislator is displayed, and the polity itself is nothing more than a certain order of the inhabitants of the State. But as the State belongs to the category of compound things, like anything else which is a whole but composed of many parts, it is clear that we must first investigate the conception of the citizen ; for the State is composed of a number of citizens. We have to inquire then to whom the title "citizen" belongs, or, in other words, what is the nature of a citizen. For the conception of the citizen as of the State is often disputed, nor is the world agreed in recognizing the same person as a citizen. Thus it often happens that one who is a citizen in a Democracy is not a citizen in an Oligarchy.

7—2

Now putting out of sight persons who acquire the title of citizen in some exceptional way, e.g. honorary citizens, we may lay it down that it is not residence which constitutes a citizen, as the qualification of residence belongs equally to aliens settled in the country and to slaves. Nor again does citizenship consist simply in the participation in legal rights to the extent of being party to an action as defendant or plaintiff, for this is a qualification possessed equally by the members of different States who associate on the basis of commercial treaties[1]. (It may be observed that in many places resident aliens are not admitted to the full enjoyment even of these legal rights, but are obliged to put themselves under the protection of a patron. It is only in a certain imperfect sense then that they are members of an association so constituted[2].) Such persons on the contrary are much in the same position as children who are too young to be entered upon the register of the deme or old men who are exempted from civil duties ; for although these classes are to be called citizens in a certain sense, it is not in a sense quite absolute and unlimited, but with

---

[1] The clause καὶ γὰρ ταῦτα τούτοις ὑπάρχει is not found in the best MSS. and should probably be omitted from the text. If it is retained, the meaning is "as these rights among others are enjoyed by them."

[2] I have enclosed these two sentences within brackets, not meaning that they are spurious but that they are parenthetical and interrupt the argument of the passage. In an English work they would naturally appear as a foot-note. Aristotle wishes to explain that the qualification described in the words οἱ τῶν δικαίων μετέχοντες κ.τ.λ. does not necessarily belong to μέτοικοι as well as to οἱ ἀπὸ συμβόλων κοινωνοῦντες.

some such qualifying word as "immature" or "super-annuated" or the like, it does not matter what. Our meaning at least is plain; we want a definition of the citizen in the absolute sense, one to whom no such exception can be taken as makes it necessary to correct our definition. For difficulties of a similar kind may be discussed and settled respecting persons who have been disfranchised or exiled. There is nothing whereby a citizen in the absolute sense is so well defined as by participation in judicial power and public ✕ office. But the offices of State are of two kinds. Some are determinate in point of time; thus there are certain offices which may never in any circumstances or may only after certain definite intervals be held a second time by the same person. Other officers again are perpetual, e.g. jurors and members of the public Assembly. It will be objected perhaps that jurors and members of the public Assembly are not officers of State at all and that their functions do not invest them with an official status; although it is ridiculous to deny the title of "officers" to the supreme authorities in the State. But this matter we may regard as unimportant; it is a mere question of name. The fact is that there is no word to express rightly the common function of a juror and a member of the public Assembly. Let us call it for distinction's sake a perpetual office. Citizens then we may define as those who participate in judicial and deliberative office.

This is perhaps the definition of a citizen which is most appropriate to all who are so called. It is to be observed however that, where things included under a general head are specifically different and one is con-

ceived of as first, another as second and another as
third, there is either no characteristic whatever common
to them all as such, or the common characteristic exists
only in a slight degree[1]. But polities, as we see, differ
specifically from each other, some are later and others
earlier; for the corrupt or perverted forms are necessarily later than the uncorrupted. What we mean by
p. 118 perverted forms will appear hereafter. It follows then
that the citizen in each polity must also be different.
Accordingly it is principally to the citizen in a Democracy that our definition applies; it is possibly true in
the other polities, but not necessarily. For in some
there is no democratical element, nor are there any
regular public assemblies but only extraordinary ones,
and the administration of justice is divided among
various boards, as e.g. at Lacedaemon, where different
civil cases are decided by different Ephors, cases of
homicide by the Senate and no doubt other cases by
some other magistracy. It is the same at Carthage,
where all suits are tried by certain magistrates. However, *we need not give up* our definition of a citizen,
as it admits of correction. For in all polities except
Democracy the right of voting in the Assembly and of
acting as jurors belongs not to perpetual officers but
to persons whose term of office is strictly defined; as
it is either to such officers collectively or to some of
them that judicial and deliberative functions, whether
upon all or upon certain matters only, are assigned.

[1] Aristotle's meaning becomes clearer if the present passage
is compared with Κατηγορίαι ch. 1. τὰ ὁμώνυμα there are the
same as τὰ πράγματα ἐν οἷς τὰ ὑποκείμενα διαφέρει τῷ εἴδει
here.

Thus we see clearly the nature of the citizen. One who enjoys the privilege of participation in deliberative or judicial office—he and he only is, according to our definition, a citizen of the State in question, and a State is in general terms such a number of persons thus qualified as is sufficient for an independent life.

¹But for practical purposes a citizen is usually de- CHAP. II. fined as one who is descended from citizens on both sides and not on one side only, whether the father's or mother's, although this requirement itself is sometimes extended, e.g. to ancestors in the second or third or a higher degree. ²But in view of this offhand definition, which is suited only to practical politics, a difficulty is sometimes raised as to the qualification of the original citizen in the third or fourth degree of ancestry. Gorgias of Leontini, partly perhaps in serious doubt, and partly in irony, ³said that as it only wanted mortar-makers to make mortars, so it only wanted mayors to make Larisæans, as there were certain persons who might be called Larisan-

---

¹ Reading ὁρίζονται δέ.

² Reading οὕτω δέ.

³ The point of the joke, such as it is, seems to be that λάρισα or λάρισσα would mean either the town of that name or a kettle, and δημιουργός either a civic magistrate or an artisan. "The reply is much the same," says Mr Cope, "as if some one being asked, What makes a citizen of the town of Sandwich? were to answer, 'A cook, for he is a sandwich-maker'." The conjectural reading λαρισαιοποιούς in place of λαρισοποιούς has much to recommend it. It is well known that Gorgias, who spent a long time in Thessaly, made a boast of his ability to answer any question that might be put to him.

makers (λαρισοποιούς). But the case is simple enough. If the ancestors in the third or fourth degree satisfied our definition of citizenship, [1] they were citizens ; for descent from a citizen on the father's or mother's side is a condition which cannot be applied to the original inhabitants or colonists. It may be supposed however that [2] there is more difficulty in the case of persons who obtained political rights in consequence of a revolution of polity, as at Athens when Cleisthenes, after the expulsion of the Tyrants, enrolled a number of foreigners, slaves and resident aliens in the tribes. The difficulty here is not so much to decide who is a citizen as whether he is so unjustly or justly. At the same time it is possible to raise the further question whether, if he is not a citizen justly, he does not cease to be a citizen at all, as the words "unjust" and "false" are virtually the same. But as indisputably there are rulers in the world who have no just title, and we shall recognize them as ruling, although not justly ruling, and as further it is a particular rule or office which constitutes our definition of a citizen—for it is one who participates in such and such an office who is a citizen, as we said—it is clear that the persons supposed, viz. *persons who have obtained political rights after a revolution,* are to be regarded as citizens of the State, but that the question whether they are justly or unjustly citizens is closely connected with the controversy already referred to. Some people feel a certain difficulty in determining when a particular

CHAP. III.

p. 99.

---

[1] Omitting ἄν.

[2] Reading ἐκεῖνο μᾶλλον ἔχει ἀπορίαν.

action has been the action of the State or not of
the State *but of some individuals,* e.g. in the case
of a revolution from an Oligarchy or Tyranny to a
Democracy. In such circumstances there is sometimes an indisposition to discharge contracts, the
argument being that it is not the State but the tyrant
who has had the benefit of them, or to meet various
other obligations of a similar nature, on the ground
that there are some polities which depend wholly
upon superior force and do not subserve the interests
of the community. On the same principle, as there
are in some States democratical polities also which
rest upon force, the actions of such a polity ought
[1]no more to be regarded as actions of the State in
question than those performed under the Oligarchy
or Tyranny.

But this is a subject which seems to be cognate
to the difficult question: What are the general
conditions under which a State is to be described as
the same, or as not the same but different? The
most obvious point to be considered in this question
is one which touches the site and the inhabitants.
For it is possible that the inhabitants should be
divorced from the site and should come to dwell in
different sites. The difficulty *as to the identity of the
State in such a case* is one which need not be regarded as so serious ; it is a question admitting of
easy settlement, if we remember the various senses of
the term "State." *For the State in the sense of "an
organized body" remains the same, but in the sense
of "the city" it is different.* Similarly in the case

The identity
of a State.

---

[1] Reading ὁμοίως οὐ τῆς πόλεως.

where the same inhabitants occupy the same site *it is a question* when the State is to be considered one and the same. The identity obviously does not depend upon its enclosure within certain walls; *indeed the mere fact of circumvallation does not constitute a State at all.* For it would be possible to enclose all Peloponnesus within a single wall; and in fact Peloponnesus is probably not much larger than Babylon or any other city which includes within its circumference the territory of a tribe rather than of a State, if the story[1] is true that at the time of the capture of Babylon it was three days before a part of the city was aware of the fact. However the investigation of this difficulty is one which may be usefully entered upon at another time; for it is a Statesman's business to know what is the right size for the State, and whether it is expedient that its inhabitants should be all of one race or of several. But *for the present the question before us is this:* Assuming that the inhabitants and the site they occupy are the same, are we to describe the State as the same, so long as the race of inhabitants is unaltered, in spite of the fact that some persons are dying at every moment and others coming into life, as we habitually speak of rivers and fountains as the same, although some water is continually flowing up and other passing away, or on the contrary are we to say that, although the inhabitants are for a similar reason the same, the State is different, *if there is a change of polity?* Since the State is a species of association,

---

[1] See Herod. i. ch. 191; but if Herodotus is Aristotle's authority, he has somewhat exaggerated the story.

and ¹an association of citizens implies a polity, it
would seem a necessary consequence that, when the
polity changes its character and becomes different,
the State too remains no longer the same, as a chorus
e.g. is called different, if it appears at one time in
Comedy and at another in Tragedy, although the ✓
members composing it are often the same, ²and similarly any other association or combination is called
different, if the kind of combination is different, as
when we term a harmony composed of the same notes
different, if at one time it is Dorian and at another ✓
Phrygian. And if the same principle holds *in regard
to States*, it is evident that in predicating the identity
of a State we must look at the polity, whereas its✓
name may be changed while the inhabitants remain
the same or be the same while the inhabitants are
wholly changed. The justice of fulfilling engage- ✗
ments or not, when the State exchanges one polity
for another, is a different question.

As a sequel to these remarks, we have now to consider whether the virtue of a good man and of a
virtuous citizen is to be regarded as identical or
different.

But if we are to investigate this point, we must
first ascertain roughly the virtue of a citizen. A
citizen then like a sailor may be described as a member of a society. And although the sailors have
different faculties, one being an oarsman, another a
pilot, a third a "look-out" man, and a fourth having

CHAP. IV.
The virtue
of a good
man and of
a good
citizen.

---

¹ Reading ἔστι δὲ κοινωνία πολιτῶν πολιτεία, γινομένης ἐτέρας
τῷ εἴδει καὶ διαφερούσης τῆς πολιτείας.
² Changing the full stop after ἀνθρώπων ὄντων to a comma.

some other similar title, it is evident that, while the
most exact definition of the virtue or excellence of
each will be exclusively appropriate to the individual,
there will at the same time be a common definition
applicable to all. For safety in navigation is the
object they all have in view; it is this that every
sailor strives for. Similarly then in the case of the
citizens, although they are different, yet it is the
safety of the association or in other words of the
polity which is their object; and hence the virtue of
the citizen is necessarily relative to the polity.

Assuming then that there are several kinds of
polity, we see that the virtuous citizen *in all polities*
cannot have a uniform perfect virtue, whereas [1]it
is a uniform perfect virtue which in our theory is
characteristic of the good man. It is therefore clearly
possible to be a virtuous citizen without possessing
the virtue characteristic of a virtuous man. However we may investigate and discuss the same question in a different way by taking the case of the
best polity. [2]If we assume the possibility of a
State consisting solely of virtuous members, still
each of them is bound to perform his own work well,
and this is itself a result implying virtue; but as all
the citizens cannot be alike, it follows that *in this
case as in others* the virtue of a good citizen and a
good man cannot be one and the same. For the
virtue of the virtuous citizen must be possessed by
all the citizens of this State, as otherwise it cannot be
the best possible; but it is impossible that they

---

[1] Reading κατὰ μίαν ἀρετὴν εἶναι τὴν τελείαν.
[2] Reading εἰ γὰρ δυνατόν.

specting the definition of a citizen. Is it really the case that no one is a citizen who is not eligible to public office, or are mechanics to be included in the roll of citizens? If we are to include mechanics, it follows that, as they are not eligible to office, the virtue above described, *viz. virtue suited alike to rule and to subjection,* cannot be characteristic of all citizens, for here are persons who *never hold a position of rule and yet ex hypothesi* are citizens. If on the other hand no mechanic is a citizen, it may be asked to what class any particular mechanic is to be assigned, as certainly he is not a resident alien or a foreigner. It would seem however that this is not a case which causes any difficulty; for neither slaves nor freedmen belong to any of the classes named, *and yet they are not citizens.* The fact is that we cannot regard all who are indispensable to the existence of a State as being citizens. For instance, children, *although a State cannot exist without them,* are not citizens in the same sense as men; they are citizens not absolutely, as men are, but only conditionally, or in other words they are citizens but immature ones. In ancient days there were some States where the mechanic population was composed of slaves and foreigners, and accordingly the majority of mechanics still belong to these classes. Nor will citizenship in the best State be conferred upon any mechanic, or, if it is, the definition we gave of a citizen's virtue must be held to apply not to all citizens nor to all who are merely free persons, but only to such as are exempt from the occupations necessary to bare

existence. The rest¹, if they render these services to
an individual, are slaves; if ²to the State, they are
mechanics or hired labourers.

Their actual position becomes plain on a little
reflexion from the following facts; for the remark
already made *respecting polities* makes it clear. at
the first glance. As there are varieties of polity,
there will necessarily also be various kinds of citizens
and especially of citizens who are subjects. Hence
there is a particular polity, *viz. the extreme Democracy,*
in which the mechanic and hired labourer must
needs be citizens, while there are others in which this
is impossible, e.g. wherever there exists a polity of
the kind commonly called aristocratical, in which
virtue and desert constitute the sole claim to the
honours of State; for it is impossible to live the life
of a mechanic or labourer and at the same time devote oneself to the practice of virtue. In an Oligarchy,
on the other hand, although it is impossible for a
hired labourer to be a citizen, as the elections to
office are dependent on a high property qualification,
it is not impossible for a mechanic; for artisans are
generally persons of great wealth. There was a law at
Thebes that nobody should be eligible to office who
had not abstained for ten years from business in the
market. But there are many polities, on the contrary, in which the law admits even foreigners to the
citizenship. Thus any one whose mother was a
citizen is a citizen in some Democracies, and the
same is the case in many places with the bastard
children *of citizens.* However, as it is only the de-

¹ Reading τῶν δ' ἄλλων.　　² Reading κοινῇ.

p 102.

ficiency of genuine citizens which leads to the en-
franchisement of these classes, the danger of depopulation being the sole reason of these provisions in the
laws, so with the increase of population the citizenship
is gradually withdrawn, first from those whose father
or mother was a slave, then from those who are citizens
only on the mother's side, and eventually is. confined
to those whose parents were both citizens of the State.

It is clear then from these facts that there are
various kinds of citizens, and that eligibility to the
honours of State is the most exact definition of
citizenship. Thus Homer puts *into Achilles's mouth
the complaint that Agamemnon had treated him*

"Like some poor honourless vagabond[1],"

applying the epithet "honourless" to a vagabond, as
one who is ineligible to the honours of State is no
better than an alien resident in the land. [2]But there
are some States in which the exclusion of certain
classes from office is carefully veiled, the object being
to delude this portion of the population.

As to the question whether the [3]virtue characteristic of a good man and a virtuous citizen is to be
regarded as identical or different, our remarks have
served to prove that there are certain States in which
they are combined in the same individual and others
'in which they are distinct, and that in the former

---

[1] *Iliad* IX. 644. It is strange that Aristotle should interpret
the Homeric ἀτίμητος to mean "a person living in a state of
political ἀτιμία."

[2] Reading ἀλλ' ἔστιν ὅπου τὸ τοιοῦτον κ.τ.λ. and omitting ἐστίν
at the end of the sentence.

[3] Reading τὴν αὐτὴν ἀρετὴν θετέον.

they are not found together in every one but only in the practical statesman who exercises or is capable of exercising, whether individually or conjointly with others, an influence in the conduct of public affairs.

CHAP. VI.   This being determined, we have next to consider whether it is right to assume a single polity or several, and, if several, what is the nature of each, and how many there are, and what are the points of distinction between them. A polity may be defined as an order of the State in respect of its offices generally and especially of the supreme office. For the governing class is everywhere supreme in the State, and the nature of the polity is determined by the governing class. I mean e.g. that it is the commons who are supreme in a Democracy and the Few on the other hand in an Oligarchy, and *accordingly* we call their polities distinct. The same remark may be extended to all the rest; *if the governing class is different, so is the polity.*

We must begin by laying down (1) the object for which a State is framed and (2) the various kinds of rule which may be exercised over man in his social existence.

The object of political association. p. 5.   It has been stated at the very outset of our treatise in the discussion of Domestic Economy and the government of slaves that Man is naturally a political animal, and consequently, even where there is no need of mutual service, men are none the less anxious to live together. Still it cannot be denied that the common advantage of all is also a motive of union, *more or less operative* according to the degree in which each individual is capable of the higher life. Although to the citizens, both collectively and in-

dividually, this higher life is emphatically the end ✗
proposed, [1]yet life itself is also an object for which
they unite and maintain the corporate political association; for it is probable that some degree of the
higher life is necessarily implied in merely living, ✗
unless there is a great preponderance of hardship in
the life. Certain it is that the majority of men endure
much suffering without ceasing to cling to life—a
proof that a certain happiness or natural sweetness
resides in it.

But *to proceed to the second point:* it is not difficult Different
to distinguish the forms of rule which are generally forms of rule.
recognized; for even in our unscientific discourses we
often discuss and determine their character. In the
government of slaves, although the interests of natural
slave and natural master are really identical, yet the ᴧ
object of the rule is nevertheless the interest of the
master and is that of the slave only incidentally, because, if the slave is destroyed, it is impossible that
the master's government should be maintained. On
the other hand, in the rule of children or a wife
or a whole household, which in our terminology
is economic rule, the end is either the good of
the subjects or some common good of rulers and
subjects alike, i.e. it is essentially the good of the ⼂
subjects, as we see in the other arts such as Medicine   PLA⼂
and Gymnastic, although it may perhaps incidentally
be also the good of the rulers themselves. For there
is no reason why the gymnastic trainer should not

---

[1] Reading συνέρχονται δὲ καὶ τοῦ ζῆν ἕνεκεν αὐτοῦ καὶ συνέχουσι
τὴν πολιτικὴν κοινωνίαν· ἴσως γὰρ ἔνεστί τι τοῦ καλοῦ μόριον καὶ
κατὰ τὸ ζῆν αὐτὸ κ.τ.λ.

himself be occasionally one of the gymnasts, as the pilot is invariably one of the crew. And thus while the trainer or pilot has in view *not his own interest but* the interest of those who are under him, yet in any case where he himself shares their position he enjoys incidentally the same benefit as they do ; for the one becomes a sailor and the other one of the gymnasts, although he is a trainer. *It is because the object of political rule is the benefit of the subjects* that in any State framed on the principle of equality and similarity among the citizens a claim is put forward for an alternation of rule. It was originally claimed, as is natural enough, that all should serve the State in turn, and that, as each citizen during his period of rule or office had already paid regard to the interest of another, so that other should in turn pay regard to his. But nowadays the profits derivable from the public service and an official status create a desire for perpetuity of office ; it is as though the officers of State, being invalids, were to enjoy good health *during all their term of power*, in which case it is probable that they would be equally eager for office.

It is evident then that all such polities as regard the good of the community are really normal according to the principle of abstract justice, while such as regard the private good of the rulers are all corruptions or perversions of the normal polities ; for the relations of rulers to the subjects in them are like the relations of a master to his slaves, whereas the State is *properly* a society of free persons.

CHAP. VII.   Having now settled these points, we have next to consider the number of different polities and their nature. We will begin with the normal polities; for when they are determined the perverted forms will be evident at once.

As in any State [1] the polity and the governing class are virtually the same, *i.e. the polity is determined by the governing class*, as the governing class is the supreme authority in a State, and as supreme power must be vested either in an individual or in a Few or in the Many, it follows that, when the rule of the individual or the Few or the Many is exercised for the benefit of the community at large, the polities are normal, whereas the polities which subserve the private interest either of the individual or the Few or the masses are perversions; for either the members of the State do not deserve the name of citizens, or they ought to have a share in its advantages. The form of Monarchy in which regard is paid to the interest of the community is commonly known as Kingship, and the government of the Few, although of a number exceeding one, for the good of all, as Aristocracy, whether because the rule is in the hands of the best citizens (οἱ ἄριστοι) or because they exercise it for the best interests (τὸ ἄριστον) of the State and all its members; while when it is the masses who direct public affairs for the interest of the community, the government is called by the name which is common to all the polities, viz. a Polity. The result in this case is such as might have been expected. For although it is possible to find an individual or a few

Classifica- tion of polities.

---

[1] Reading ἐπεὶ δ' ἡ πολιτεία μὲν καὶ τὸ πολίτευμα κ.τ.λ.

persons of eminent virtue, it can hardly be the case
that a larger number are perfectly accomplished in
every form of virtue; at the best they will be accomplished only in military virtue, as it is the only one
of which the masses are capable. The consequence
is that in this polity, *viz. the Polity proper*, the military
class is supreme, and all who bear arms enjoy full
political privileges.

As perverted forms of the polities just mentioned
we have Tyranny by the side of Kingship, Oligarchy
of Aristocracy and Democracy of Polity. For Tyranny
is monarchical rule for the good of the monarch,
Oligarchy *the rule of a Few* for the good of the
wealthy, and Democracy *the rule of the Many* for
the good of the poor; none of them subserves the
interest of the community at large.

CHAP. VIII.   But we ought to describe at rather greater length
the nature of these several polities, as the matter is
one which presents certain difficulties, and it is proper
that a philosophical inquirer in any subject, who
looks at something more than the merely practical
side, should not ignore or omit any point but should
bring to light the actual truth in all.

Tyranny is, as has been said, a form of Monarchy
corresponding in the political association to the rule
of a master over his slaves; Oligarchy a government
where the supreme power in the polity is vested in
the propertied classes; Democracy, on the contrary,
a government where it is vested in those who possess no considerable property, i.e. the poor. But
Definition
of Demo-
cracy and
Oligarchy.   there is an initial difficulty in this definition. Democracy being defined as a polity in which the

of the State, i.e. that it promotes the virtue of its citizens. For if one were to combine different localities in one, so that e.g. the walls of Megara and Corinth were contiguous, yet the result would not be a single State. Nor again does the practice of inter- X marriage *necessarily imply a single State,* although intermarriage is one of the forms of association which are especially characteristic of States. So too if we suppose the case of certain persons living separately, although not so far apart as to prevent association, but under laws prohibitive of mutual injury in the exchange of goods, if we suppose e.g. *A* to be a carpenter, *B* a husbandman, *C* a cobbler, *D* something else, and the total to amount to ten thousand, but their association to be absolutely confined to such things as barter and military alliance, here [1]again there would certainly not be a State. What then is the reason? It is assuredly not the absence of local contiguity in the association. For suppose the members were actually to form a union upon such terms of association as we have described, suppose at the same time that each individual were to use his own household as a separate State, and their intercourse were limited as under the conditions of a defensive alliance to rendering mutual assistance against aggression, still the conception of a State in the strict view would not even then be realized, if their manner of social dealings after the union were to be precisely the same as when they lived apart.

It is clear then that the State is not merely a local association or an association existing to

[1] Reading οὐδ' οὕτω που.

prevent mutual injury and to promote commercial exchange. So far is this from being the case that, although these are indispensable conditions, if a State is to exist, yet all these conditions do not necessarily imply a State. *A State on the contrary is first realized when there is* an association of households and families in well living with a view to a complete and independent existence. (This will not be the case, however, unless the members inhabit one and the same locality and have the practice of inter-marriage[1].) It is for this reason that there were established in the different States matrimonial con-nexions, clanships, common sacrifices and such amuse-ments as promote a common life. But all this is the work of friendship, for the choice of a common life implies *no more than* friendship. And thus while the end of a State is living well, these are only means to the end. A State on the contrary is the association of families and villages in a complete and independent existence or in other words, according to our defini-tion[2], in a life of felicity and nobleness. We must assume then that the object of the political association is not merely a common life but noble action. And from this it follows that they who contribute most to the association, as so conceived, possess a larger in-terest in the State than they who are equal or superior in personal liberty or birth but inferior in political virtue, or than they who have the superiority in wealth but the inferiority in virtue.

[1] The brackets are meant to show that the sentence is paren-thetical.

[2] See *e.g. Nicom. Eth.* x. p. 1176 B_{30}—p. 1177 A_{11}.

It is evident then from our observations that in the controversy respecting the different polities each party is the representative of a certain partial justice. It is difficult however to decide what ought to be the supreme authority in the State. It must be either the masses or the rich or the respectable classes or an individual of preeminent merit or a tyrant. But all these suppositions appear to involve awkward consequences. For suppose the poor, as being a majority, distribute among themselves the property of the rich, is such action not unjust? *No*, it may be said, for it was decreed by the supreme authority in the State and *therefore* justly decreed. What then are we to describe as the height of injustice, *if not this?* Or again, take the whole body of citizens and suppose that the majority distribute among themselves the property of the minority, it is evident that they thereby destroy the State. But it is certainly not the virtue of anything which destroys its possessor, nor can justice be destructive to a State. It is evident then that such a law as we have supposed cannot be just. Again, the same hypothesis would inevitably justify all the actions of a tyrant, as his oppression depends upon superior strength, like the oppression of the wealthy by the masses. Well then, is it just that rule should be in the hands of the minority or the propertied class? But on that hypothesis, if the minority adopt the same line of action, if they plunder the masses and despoil them of their possessions, is such action just? If it is, so was the action of the majority in the former case. That all such conduct then is wrong and unjust

CHAP. X.
Difficulties as to the supreme authority in the State.

is indisputable. Ought then the respectable classes
to enjoy rule and supreme power? But if so, it is a
necessary consequence that all the rest of the citizens
are excluded from honours, as they do not enjoy the
honour of political office. For we regard the offices
of State as public honours; and if they are always in
the hands of the same persons, it follows that all
others are excluded from honour. Is then the rule of
the most virtuous individual to be preferred? It may
be objected that this is a system still more oligarchical than the last, as it involves the exclusion of a still
larger number from honour.

Perhaps however it will be urged [1] that there is an
evil in the supremacy of any human being with his
liability to the emotions incident to the soul, and that
the law ought rather to be supreme. But on that
hypothesis, if the law is oligarchical or democratical,
what difference will it make to the difficulties we have
raised? The difficulties already described will still
meet us.

CHAP. XI.   We may defer for the present the discussion of all
Ought the
Many or the these cases except one. But the theory that supreme
best Few to
be supreme? power should be vested in the masses rather than in a
few persons, although they are the best, [2] is one which
would seem to be refuted by the remarks we have
made; and indeed there is a certain difficulty involved in it, although there is probably also a certain
degree of truth. For it is possible that the Many, of

---

[1] Reading ἄνθρωπον εἶναι ἔχοντά γε τὰ συμβαίνοντα πάθη περὶ
τὴν ψυχὴν ἀλλὰ μὴ νόμον φαῦλον.

[2] Reading δόξειεν ἂν λύεσθαι· καί τιν' ἔχει ἀπορίαν, τάχα δὲ κἂν
ἀλήθειαν.

or of suitable age, whereas a [1]higher property qualification is required for lords of the treasury, generals
and the highest officers of State. Yet[2] this difficulty
admits of a similar solution. It may reasonably be
argued that the existing state of things is right. For
it is not the individual juror or the individual member
of the Council or Assembly who exercises official
power but the whole Court or Council or body of
commons, of which the individuals specified are but
fractions. It is as a mere fraction *of the whole and so
deriving all importance from the whole* that I conceive of the individual member of the Council, Assembly or Law-court. Hence it is right that the
masses should control greater interests *than the Few*,
as there are many members of the commons, the Council or the Law-court, and the actual collective property
of them all exceeds the property of those who hold
high offices of State as individuals or in limited bodies.

With this discussion of these points we must be
content. But the initial difficulty we mentioned *as to
the supreme authority in the State* brings out nothing
so clearly as that it is the laws, if rightly enacted,
which should be supreme, and that the officers of
State, whether one or many, should have supreme
authority only in those matters upon which it is wholly
impossible for the laws to pronounce exactly because
of the difficulty of providing in a general statement
for all cases. What should be the character of the
laws if rightly enacted has not yet been ascertained;
on the contrary our old difficulty still remains. [3]This

*The supre-
macy of the
laws.*

p. 128.

---

[1] Reading ἀπὸ μειζόνων.   [2] Reading ὁμοίως δὲ.

[3] It seems clear that two equivalent sentences have both

only is indisputable, that the laws enacted are necessarily relative to the polity in which they exist. But if
this is the case, it is evident that the laws adapted to
the normal polities are necessarily just, whereas those
adapted to the perverted polities are unjust.-

CHAP. XII. · We have seen that in all sciences and arts the end
proposed is some Good, that in the supreme of all
sciences and arts, i.e. the political faculty, the end is
preeminently the highest Good and that justice or in
other words the interest of the community is the political Good. We have seen too that justice is universally regarded as a species of equality, and that up to
a certain point, if not further, the conclusions of the
philosophical arguments, [1] in which ethical questions
have been discussed and determined, are accepted on
all hands, in so far as it is admitted that the notion of
justice implies a thing to be given and persons to
receive it, and that equals ought to receive an equal

Political
equality
and ine-
quality.
share. [2] We have therefore to ascertain the characteristics which constitute personal equality or inequality—
a difficult question which can be settled only by the
aid of political philosophy.

It may perhaps be urged that superiority in respect of any and every Good should be a ground for an
unequal distribution of public offices, if the persons
were absolutely alike in all other respects, as any difference in the persons constitutes a difference in their

found their way into the text. One of them, ἀλλὰ γὰρ καὶ ὁμοίως
......ἢ ἀδίκους, is therefore omitted in the translation.

[1] It can hardly be doubted that Aristotle is again referring to
the doctrine of *Nicom. Eth.* especially Bk. v. ch. 6. See p. 71, l. 30.

[2] It would be better to put a colon instead of a comma after
.φασίν, as the apodosis of the sentence begins at ποίων δ' ἰσότης ἐστὶ.

rights and deserts. Yet, if this is true, complexion, stature or any other Good will equally entitle persons to a preference in political rights. But the falsity of this position is apparent on the surface, as may be seen in any other science or faculty. For instance, if there are several flute-players of equal skill, it is not right to give the persons of higher birth a preference in the flutes, for their birth will not make them better flute-players, and the superior instruments ought to be given to the superior performers. If our point is still obscure, it will be plain if we carry the illustration a little further. Suppose there is a person superior to others in the art of flute-playing, but far inferior in nobility of birth or beauty, even granting that nobility and beauty are severally greater Goods than skill upon the flute, and that their superiority to skill upon the flute is proportionally greater than the superiority of our supposed individual *to others* in flute-playing, still it is to him that we must give the finest flutes. For, *if we are to have regard to wealth and nobility in assigning the flutes,* superiority in these respects ought to contribute in some degree to the excellence of the performance; whereas they do not contribute at all. And further, the theory is one which would lead us to regard any Good whatever as comparable with any other Good. For if a certain amount of stature is preferable *to a certain amount of wealth or freedom,* it follows that stature generally may be weighed in the scales against wealth or freedom. Hence, if one person has a greater superiority in stature than another in virtue, and the distinction of stature generally is greater than that of virtue, all

things in the world will be comparable with each
other. For if a certain amount of stature is more
valuable than a certain amount of something else, it is
obvious that there is a certain amount of stature
which is equal to a certain amount of that something.
But as this *universal commensurability* is out of the
question, it is evidently reasonable in the realm of
politics not to regard any and every inequality as
constituting a title to the offices of State. For the
fact that some persons are slow and others swift is no
reason why they should enjoy a less or greater measure *of official power;* it is rather in the gymnastic
games that superiority of this kind receives its appropriate honour. The claim to office on the other hand
must be confined to those elements which enter into
the constitution of a State. Accordingly it is reasonable enough that noble or free-born or wealthy persons should lay claim to political honour. For a
State necessarily contains free persons and tax-payers
or a propertied class, as it can no more consist exclusively of paupers than of slaves. But if these elements
are indispensable, the same is obviously true of justice
and military virtue, both of which are essential to the
good administration of a State, although not, as were
the elements before mentioned, to its very existence.

CHAP.XIII.   If we look then to the mere existence of a State, it
would seem that all or at least some of the elements
named are rightful claimants *to political supremacy,*
whereas if we look to a good life, it would seem that
p. 126.   culture and virtue have the justest claims, as has been
already remarked. But as it is not right that persons
who are equal in one point only should have an equal

This then is one species of Kingship, viz. a life-generalship, and it may be either hereditary or elective. Besides it there is another species of Monarchy (2) The non-Greek. which includes such forms of Kingship as exist among certain non-Greek peoples. The power inherent in all these forms [1]closely resembles that of a Tyranny, but at the same time they are constitutional and hereditary. For as non-Greeks are naturally more slavish in character than Greeks and Asiatics than Europeans, they submit without a murmur to their despotic government. While then these forms of Kingship are tyrannical owing to the slavishness of the subjects, they are secure as being hereditary and constitutional. And for the same reason, *i.e. because they are hereditary and constitutional*, the body-guard *of these kings* is a kingly and not a tyrannical one. *The difference is* that, while kings are guarded by the citizens in arms, tyrants are guarded by a mercenary force; for the former rule constitutionally and over willing subjects, but the latter over unwilling subjects; and consequently the body-guard in the one case is derived from the citizens and in the other is maintained as a means of oppressing them. We have now considered two forms of Monarchy. There is a third (3) The Aesymneteia. which existed in ancient Greece, that of the Aesymnetes as they are called. This may be broadly designated as an elective Tyranny, differing from the

texts of Homer. It may be remarked that they are not found in *Nicom. Eth.* III. p. 1116 A_{34}, where Aristotle makes use of the same quotation and wrongly puts it into the mouth of Hector.

[1] Reading παραπλησίαν τυραννίσιν, εἰσὶ δὲ καὶ κατὰ νόμον.

non-Greek form of Monarchy, not in not being constitutional but solely in not being hereditary. The authority was exercised sometimes for life, sometimes for certain definite periods or until the performance of certain definite actions, as when Pittacus was elected by the Mitylenaeans to oppose the exiles headed by Antimenides and the poet Alcaeus. That they elected Pittacus tyrant is shown by Alcaeus in one of his drinking-songs, where he upbraids his countrymen [1] "for that Pittacus the low-born they had ordained to be tyrant of the craven ill-starred city, loud lauding, thronging round him." These *two last* forms of Kingship [2] in virtue of their despotic character are and always were tyrannical ; but their elective character and the voluntary obedience of the subjects make them kingly. A fourth species of kingly Monarchy is formed by the voluntary and hereditary constitutional Kingships which existed in the heroic times. *Their origin was as follows.* The founders of the Monarchy, having proved themselves benefactors of the people in arts or war or by having united a number of villages in a State or acquired new territory, received the voluntary submission of their subjects and handed down the kingdom as an inheritance to their successors. Their authority was supreme in military command and in sacrifices, except such as were reserved to the priesthood ; they also adjudged legal cases. This last they did sometimes under oath and sometimes

(4) The
heroic.

---

[1] This quotation appears, although with some variety of reading, as the 37th Fragment of Alcaeus in Bergk's *Poetae Lyrici Graeci*.

[2] Reading διὰ μὲν τὸ δεσποτικαὶ εἶναι τυραννικαί.

controlled in his authority by written formulae ; even
in Egypt a doctor is allowed to alter *the prescribed
course of treatment* [1] after three days, although, if he
does so sooner, it is at his peril. For the same
reason then it is obvious that a polity which rests
upon written formulae or laws is not the best. At
the same time *it must be admitted that* no officer of
State can dispense with the general principle *which
is embodied in a law,* and that that which is wholly
exempt from the emotional element is superior to
that in which it is innate. Now a law is unemotional,
whereas emotion is necessarily inherent in any
human soul. But perhaps it will be urged that in
compensation for this defect a person will be a better
judge of individual cases. It is clear then that an
officer of State should himself possess legislative
powers, and that there should ˙ be a code of laws,
but that their authority should not extend to cases
where they are wide of the mark, whereas in all
others they should be supreme.

But in cases where it is impossible for the law
to decide at all or to decide aright, ought authority
to reside in an individual of supreme merit or in
the whole body of citizens? For the existing practice is that the whole body meets to try cases and
to deliberate or decide upon matters of State,
although these decisions all refer to individual . cases.
It is true that, if we take any individual and compare
him *with the person of supreme merit,* he will probably be inferior. But the State consists of numerous

The author-
ity of an
individual
or of the
masses.

---

[1] μετὰ τὴν τριήμερον seems to be the better reading.

members *and is therefore superior to any indi-vidual,* as a picnic-repast is more sumptuous than a simple dinner given by a single person. It is for this reason that the masses are often actually better judges than any individual. [1]Also a large number is less liable to be corrupted. The masses are like a larger quantity of water ; they are not so easily corruptible as the few. If an individual is overcome by anger or any other similar passion, it necessarily follows that his judgment is corrupt ; but in the other case it is hardly possible that a whole people should simultaneously lose their temper and their judgment. When we speak of "the masses," it must be understood that we mean the free citizens, and that they never act without the sanction of the law, except in cases where it is necessarily inadequate.

The author-ity of an individual or of several persons.
Admitting however that this condition cannot easily be realized in a large number of persons, yet if we suppose the existence of several persons who are both good men and good citizens, we may inquire whether an individual in a position of rule or the several persons, all of whom are supposed to be good, will be the less liable to corruption. Surely the answer is plain—The several persons. But *it will be urged that* the larger number will [2]split into parties, which is impossible in the case of an indi-vidual. This objection however may perhaps be met by the reply that these persons are *ex hypothesi* virtuous in soul as much as the individual supposed

---

[1] Reading ἔτι μᾶλλον ἀδιάφθορον τὸ πολύ, καθάπερ ὕδωρ τὸ πλεῖον, οὕτω καὶ κ.τ.λ.

[2] Reading στασιάσουσιν.

and will therefore be free from party spirit. If then
the rule of a certain number of persons, all of whom
are good men, is to be called Aristocracy and the
rule of an individual Kingship, it would follow that
Aristocracy is in States preferable to Kingship,
whether the authority of the king is or is not supported by a military force, provided that it is possible
to find a number of persons equally virtuous. In The reason
fact it seems probable that the reason why kingly Kingship.
government was the rule in early times is that it was
rare to find persons of extremely eminent virtue,
especially as the States of those times were small.
And further, kingly power was then conferred upon
individuals as the reward of services rendered to the
State. But it is the function of good men to render
such services, *and if they were rewarded with kingly
power, the number of good men must have been very
small.* In process of time however there came to be Chrono-
a number of persons equally virtuous, and then they succession
no longer submitted to kingly rule, but sought to ments.
establish a sort of *commune* or constitutional government. And afterwards as men degenerated and
treated politics as a source of pecuniary gain, the
creation of Oligarchies was a natural result of such
a condition, as they had introduced the worship of
wealth. From Oligarchies they passed in the first
instance to Tyrannies and from Tyrannies again to
Democracy. For the Oligarchs, as in their miserable
avarice they perpetually narrowed the range of the
privileged class, so augmented the strength of the
populace that they rose in revolt and founded
Democracies. And now that States have grown to

still larger dimensions it is perhaps no longer easy
to establish any other form of polity than Democracy.

Hereditary Kingship. Supposing however it is determined that kingly
government is the best for States, *we may ask*, What
is to be the case with the children? Is the family
of the king to reign as well as himself? But in this
case, if the sons are no better than they often have
been, the interests of the State are prejudiced. [1]Is
it suggested that the king, although he has the
power, will not hand on the succession to his
children? This we cannot well believe; it is a hard
condition requiring superhuman virtue.

The military force of the king. There is a difficulty also as to the military power
of the king. Is the king designate to have such a
force attached to his person as will enable him to
enforce obedience upon unwilling subjects? or, if
not, how can he administer his office? Even on the
supposition that his authority is wholly constitutional
and that he never acts arbitrarily against the law,
he must still possess military power enough to guard
the laws. It is perhaps not difficult to fix the limit
in the case of such a constitutional king. He must
have a force at his disposal; but while it is large
enough to be stronger than any individual or knot
of individuals, it must be weaker than the collective
body of the citizens. It must be such a force as
the body-guard which the ancients usually assigned,
whenever they appointed an Aesymnete, as he was
called, or tyrant of the State, or which someone

---

[1] It is better to omit the mark of interrogation after τοῖς
τέκνοις. ἀλλ᾽ οὐ παραδώσει κ.τ.λ. introduces a supposed reply to
the question raised about hereditary Kingship.

advised the Syracusans to give Dionysius when he
asked for a body of guards.

The case of the king who acts in all things according to his arbitrary pleasure presents itself next
and claims consideration. For the so-called constitutional king does not, as we said, form a distinct
species of polity, as a perpetual generalship may exist in any polity, e.g. in a Democracy or Aristocracy,
and it is not uncommon to invest an individual with
the supreme control of the executive. There is an
office of this kind at Epidamnus among other places
and, [1]although with somewhat less extensive authority, at Opus. But to come to the case of universal Kingship, as it is called, or the form of Kingship in which the king exercises arbitrary authority
over all, it is by some considered absolutely unnatural that an individual should be master of all
the citizens where the State is composed of persons,
all of whom are alike. It is argued that, where
persons are naturally alike, there must naturally be
the same justice and the same desert for all; and
upon this principle, as it is hurtful to the physical
health that persons who are unequal should have
equal food or clothing, the same is true of public
honours. [2]Similarly it is hurtful that equals should
have unequal shares. Accordingly, *where the citizens
are alike*, it is just that they should have as large a
share of subjection as of rule. It follows that the
alternation *of rule and subjection* is likewise just.
But this alternation at once implies law; for such

CHAP. XVI.
Absolute or
universal
Kingship.

p. 148.

Objections
to it.

----

[1] Reading κατά τι μέρος ἐλάττων.
[2] Omitting τοίνυν.

a system is itself a law. The rule of law then (*it is
concluded*) is preferable to the rule of an individual
citizen. According to the same theory, even on the
supposition that it is advisable to have certain definite officers of State, they are to be constituted
merely guardians and ministers of the laws. It is
admitted that there must be certain officers of State ;
but that the officer should be a single individual is
declared to be unjust, as all the citizens are alike.
Against the supremacy of law however it may be
urged that an [1]individual would be able to decide
all such cases as apparently cannot be determined
by the law. The answer is that the law expressly
educates the officers of State and then sets them to
decide and administer all matters beyond its province
according to their most just judgment. And not only
so, but the law empowers them to introduce amend-
ments wherever experience suggests an improvement
of the existing ordinances. To invest the law then
with authority is, it seems, to invest God and intelligence only ; to invest a man is to introduce a
beast, as desire is something bestial and [2]even the
best of men in authority are liable to be corrupted
by anger. We may conclude then that the law is
intelligence without passion *and is therefore preferable to any individual.* There is a fallacy in the
illustration drawn from the arts, that it is a mistake
to let oneself be doctored according to formulae, and
we had better consult scientific physicians. For

---

[1] Reading ὁ δ' ἄνθρωπος in place of οὐδ' ἄνθρωπος.

[2] Reading καὶ ὁ θυμὸς ἄρχοντας καὶ τοὺς ἀρίστους ἄνδρας δια-
φθείρει.

physicians are never led by personal friendship to
offend against reason ; on the contrary it is only
when they have restored their patients to health that
they get their fee ; whereas officers of State have a
habit of acting in many matters out of spite or
favouritism. The truth is that when the patient sus-
pects his physician of taking bribes from his personal
enemies to poison him, he would then prefer to be
treated according to written formulae. Nay, physicians
in their illnesses call in other physicians, and gymnastic trainers in their own exercises other trainers, as
being unable to form true judgments in such cases,
because the judgment is one concerning themselves,
and they are prejudiced *in passing it.* It is evident
therefore that to seek justice is to seek something
free from bias, *or in other words to have recourse
to law,* as there is no bias in law. *It is to be
remembered* too *that* there are laws—the laws of
custom—more important and affecting subjects of
higher importance than those expressed in written
formulae, so that, even [1]if a personal ruler is more
to be trusted than the laws of written formulae,
he is not more trustworthy than the laws of custom.

Again, it may be said that an individual cannot
well attend to a large number of subjects. It will
be necessary therefore to have several officers appointed by him ; and, if so, what difference does it
make whether this system exists in the first instance
or the officers are appointed, as we suppose, by the
individual ? Further, as we remarked before, if a p. 150.

---

[1] Reading ὥστ᾽ εἰ τῶν κατὰ γράμματα κ.τ.λ.

virtuous man as being better than his fellows has a
claim to rule, then two good men are better than one;
witness the [1] *Homeric* saying :

> " if two together go,
> One thinks before the other ;" ·

and [2] Agamemnon's prayer,

> " Would I had ten such councillors as Nestor."

But there are even at the present time some matters
which it is within the competence of the officers of
the State, e.g. of a jury, to decide, matters which
cannot be determined by the law; for in cases which
it can determine no one denies that the rule and
decision of the law would be best. And in fact,
whereas there are some things which can and others
which cannot be embraced by the laws, it is the
latter which give rise to debate and examination
as to whether the rule of the best law or of the
best man is preferable. For it is a thing impossible
to legislate upon the ordinary matters of deliberation. Accordingly *the opponents of kingly government* do not dispute the necessity of having a person
to decide such cases ; they merely contend that
there should be a number of persons instead of
only one. For granted that each several officer, if
he has been educated by the law, decides well, yet
it would perhaps seem strange if a man were [3] better qualified to decide with only two eyes and ears
and to act with only two feet or hands than a number of people with many, especially as it is a fact

---

[1] *Iliad* x. 224.   [2] *Iliad* ii. 372.
[3] Reading εἰ βέλτιον ἔχοι.

BOOK IV.

[1]IN any attempt at an adequate investigation of the CHAP. I.
best polity it is necessary to begin by determining the
nature of the most desirable life. If we do not know
this, we cannot know the best polity, as it is natural
that persons who live under the best polity possible
to them in their circumstances should, unless for
some unforeseen circumstance, enjoy the best condition of life. And hence it must first be settled what
is the nature of that life which is, we may say, universally the most desirable, and secondly whether this life
is the same for the Commonwealth and the individual
or different.

Assuming then that the best life is the subject of The nature
of the best
sufficient discussion in many of our non-scientific dis- life.
courses, we have now merely to avail ourselves of the

---

[1] The imperfect sentence Ἀνάγκη δὴ τὸν μέλλοντα περὶ αὐτῆς
ποιήσασθαι τὴν προσήκουσαν σκέψιν which occurs in the MSS at the
end of Book III. is evidently only another form of the opening
words of Book IV. in Bekker's text, Περὶ πολιτείας ἀρίστης τὸν
μέλλοντα ποιήσασθαι τὴν προσήκουσαν ζήτησιν ἀνάγκη. I agree
with Congreve that it is probably the true reading and should be
placed at the beginning of Book IV. It was repeated with some
slight alterations by a copyist, when the original order of the
books had been disturbed.

W. A. 11

results there obtained. For undoubtedly, if we take one division of Goods, it will not be denied that, as there are three classes, viz. external Goods, Goods of the body and Goods of the soul, the happy man must possess all three. Nobody would predicate happiness of a man who had not a particle of valour, temperance, justice or prudence, who was terrified by the midges flying past him, who if he felt any desire of meat or drink abstained from no wickedness however extreme, who for a farthing would ruin his dearest friends, and who, to complete the picture, was intellectually as foolish and full of error as a child or a lunatic. [1]Yet while all would admit this in theory, there is a difference of opinion as to the degree *of these Goods necessary to perfect happiness* and as to their relative superiority. Thus people think it is enough to possess a degree however small of virtue; but of wealth, money, power, reputation and the like they seek an ever larger and larger share. We will tell them however that upon this point it is easy to satisfy themselves of the truth by the actual facts of life, if they observe that it is not the virtues which are gained and guarded by external Goods but these external Goods by virtues, and that happiness of life, whether men find it in·enjoyment or virtue or both, is rather the prerogative of those whose character and intellect are cultivated to a high degree, although they are moderate in the acquisition of external Goods, than of those who, while they possess a larger share than use requires of external Goods, are deficient in the Goods of character and intelligence. At the same

[1] Omitting ὥσπερ.

time it is equally easy to perceive this truth, if we take a theoretical view. ¹External Goods like instruments have a limit, viz. their utility, and it follows that the excess of them is either hurtful or in no way beneficial to their possessor ;· whereas, ²if we take any Good of the soul, the greater the amount of it, the greater is its utility, if utility no less than nobleness is to be attributed to Goods of the soul as well as of the body. Again, it is evident as a universal rule that, if we compare two things together, we shall lay it down that the best condition of the one is superior to the best condition of the other ³in a degree corresponding to the difference between the things of which these are themselves conditions, and consequently, as the soul is both absolutely and relatively to us a thing more honourable than either property or the body, it follows that the best condition of the soul is proportionately superior to the best condition of either of these. Further it is for the sake of the soul that the body and property are naturally desirable and should be desired by all sensible. persons, not the soul for the sake of these. We may regard it then as admitted that the degree of happiness which falls to the lot of any individual corresponds to his degree of virtue, prudence and virtuous or prudent action ; and herein we may appeal to the

¹ Reading τὰ μὲν γὰρ ἐκτὸς ἔχει πέρας ὥσπερ ὄργανόν τι (πέρας δὲ τὸ χρήσιμόν ἐστιν) ὧν τὴν ὑπερβολὴν κ τ.λ.

² It is possible to retain εἶναι in the text, if a colon instead of a full stop is placed after τοῖς ἔχουσιν.

³ Omitting the comma after ὑπεροχήν, so as to shew that the words ἥνπερ εἴληχε διάστασιν are equivalent to τῇ διαστάσει ἥνπερ εἴληχε and grammatically follow ἀκολουθεῖν.

11—2

witness of God who, while He is happy and perfectly blessed, is so owing not to any external Good but to Himself alone and His own intrinsic qualities. This is in fact the reason why good fortune is necessarily distinct from happiness ; for Goods external to the soul are the gifts of chance or fortune, whereas nobody is just or temperate from fortune or in virtue of his fortune.

The best life the same for the State as for the individual.

Our next point, although it does not require any fresh arguments, is that the same is true of the State, and that the best State is one which is happy and doing well. [1]But it is impossible to do well [2]without doing what is well ; nor can any work either of an individual or of a State be well done, if it is dissociated from virtue and prudence. But the valour, justice, prudence and temperance of a State are in effect and form identical with those, by participation in which an individual is described as brave, just, prudent or temperate.

We must be content however with these remarks by way of prelude to our argument ; it is equally impossible to avoid touching upon the subject and to pursue all the arguments proper to it, as it would require a separate discussion. For the present it may be taken as established that the best life, whether for each individual separately or for States collectively, is one which possesses virtue furnished with external advantages to such a degree as to be capable of

---

[1] The play or argument which turns upon the double meaning of καλῶς πράττειν, "to act well" and "to fare well," is not easy to reproduce exactly in English.

[2] Reading τοῖς μὴ τὰ καλὰ πράττουσιν.

actions according to virtue. The objections to this ⊦
doctrine we must neglect in the present inquiry and
submit to a full examination hereafter, if there are
any persons not convinced by our remarks.

We have still to discuss the question whether the
happiness of any individual and of the State is to be
considered as identical or different. Nor is this point
an obscure one; it would be universally admitted that
the happiness is the same. For those who believe
that a good life in the case of an individual depends
upon wealth agree in considering that the State also as
a whole is happy, if it is wealthy; those who hold a life
of tyranny in most honour *for individuals* will all
say that the State which has the largest number of
subjects is the happiest; and one who recognizes in
virtue the source of an individual's happiness will
assert that the more virtuous State also is the
happier.

However, there are these two points requiring
consideration, (1) which is the more desirable life, his
who lives as a member of the body politic and takes
part in affairs of State, or his who lives the life of
an alien holding aloof from the political association?
(2) what polity or what kind of political organization
is to be regarded as best, whether participation in the
affairs of State is desirable for all, or *for all* with some
few exceptions, i.e. for the large majority? But as it
is the second question rather than what is desirable
for individuals, which is the object of political reflexion and speculation, and as it is a political
inquiry which we have now undertaken, the question
as to the life of individuals is of minor importance,

whereas the second is the object of our present inquiry.

It is plain then that the best polity is necessarily the system under which anybody can do best and live happily. But even on the side of those who admit that the virtuous life is most to be desired, the question is raised whether it is a political and practical life which is desirable, or rather one of isolation from all external affairs, i.e. a speculative life, which is regarded by some as the only life worthy of a philosopher. These are practically the two lives which are chosen, as experience shows, by the persons most ambitious in the pursuit of virtue, whether in former days or at the present time, viz. the political life and the philosophical. Nor is it of slight importance on which side the truth lies, as the life of [1]any sensible individual or polity as a whole will necessarily be ordered in reference to the better goal. Now it is held by certain thinkers that the rule over others, if despotic in its character, implies [2]injustice in the most extreme degree, while, if constitutional, although it does not involve injustice, it presents an obstacle to the personal felicity of the ruler. There are others who entertain what we may call the diametrically opposite view that the practical or political life is alone worthy of a man on the ground that, whatever virtue we take, virtuous actions are far less possible to private persons than to persons who lead a public or political life.

[3]*Similarly,* while some contend *that a State*

Comparison of political and philosophical life.

The life of the State.

---

[1] Reading τόν γε εὖ φρονοῦντα.   [2] Omitting τινός.

[3] There is apparently a lacuna after πολιτευομένοις, and it has been necessary to insert some words in the translation in order to

task requiring divine power such as holds this our
Universe together[1]. Hence it follows that the noblest
State is one in which the proposed definition, *viz. good
order*, is combined with magnitude; for number and
magnitude are usual conditions of nobleness. But
there is a fixed measure of magnitude for a State as
for all other things, animals, vegetables or instruments, any of which, if extremely small or extrava-
gantly large, will not retain its proper efficacy but
will either be wholly divested of its natural character
or will be in bad condition. Thus a vessel, if it is a
span long or a quarter of a mile long, will not be a
vessel at all; while, if it reaches a certain size
*although not so small as a span or so large as a
quarter of a mile*, its smallness in the one case and
its inordinate magnitude in the other will make it
almost worthless for sailing in. Similarly a State,
if its members are extremely few, will not be independent, as a State must be; and if they are extremely
numerous, although it will be independent as regards
the necessaries of life in the sense in which a non-
Greek people is independent, yet it will not be a
State, as a polity cannot easily exist in it. For who
is to be general of this overwhelming multitude or
its public crier, if he has not the voice of a Stentor?
We may conclude then that, as a State is in the
nature of things first realized when the population
composing it is numerically the lowest which is
independent and capable of a good life, so one that

---

[1] The words ἐπεὶ τό γε καλὸν ἐν πλήθει καὶ μεγέθει εἴωθε γίνεσθαι
are inappropriate in their present position and should be transposed so as to follow ταύτην εἶναι καλλίστην ἀναγκαῖον.

is numerically larger than this may still be ¹a State, although this increase cannot continue indefinitely. Nor is it difficult, if we take a practical view, to ascertain the limit of excess. The actions of a State imply rulers on the one hand and subjects on the other, and the function of a ruler is to issue commands and pronounce judgments. If then they are to determine questions of justice and distribute offices of State according to desert, it is necessary that the citizens should know each other's character; for where this is not the case the distribution of offices and the judicial decisions will be wrong. For it is not just to form off-hand opinions upon these two points, as is plainly the case in over-populated States. Further in such States it is easy for foreigners and resident aliens to usurp the franchise, as the vastness of the population affords them a ready means of concealment. We see clearly then the best limit of population; it is that the number of citizens should be the largest possible in order to ensure independence of life, but not so large that it cannot be comprehended in a single view.

Such then may be our decision as to the magnitude of a State, and the case as to the country is very similar. If its character is in question, it is evident that every one will admire the country which is most independent. But in order to be so it must yield produce of every kind, as independence consists in possessing everything and having no wants. In extent and magnitude the country which will be admired is one which is so large that the

Chap. V. Nature of the country.

¹ Omitting μεί̓ζω.

the same kind. But when there are two things one
of which is a means and the other an end, between
these there is nothing common except in so far as
the one *viz. the means* produces and the other *viz.
the end* receives the product. This is the case e.g.
with any instrument or with the craftsmen on the
one hand and the work produced on the other ; there
is no factor common to a house and its builder, on
the contrary the builder's art is a means to the house
as an end. Similarly although property is indispensable to States, it is no part of a State ; and there are
many animate things, *it may be observed,* which fall
under the head of property.

But a State is an association of similar persons
for the attainment of the best life possible. And
as happiness is the *summum bonum* and happiness
consists in a perfect activity and practice of virtue,
and as it is a fact that there are some people who are
capable of this happiness and others who are capable
of it only in a slight degree or not capable of it at
all, it is evident that we have here an explanation of
the origin of different kinds of State and of varieties
of polity. For as there are various ways and means
by which people aspire to gain happiness, the lives
they lead and the polities they form are necessarily
different.

But we have to consider [1]what is the number of The elements in-
the things which are necessary to the existence of a dispensable
to a State's
State and will therefore certainly be found in it, as existence.
the parts of a State in our sense of the word will be

[1] Reading πόσα ταυτί ἐστιν ὧν ἄνευ πόλις οὐκ ἂν εἴη (καὶ γὰρ ἃ
λέγομεν εἶναι μέρη πόλεως ἐν τούτοις ἂν εἴη) διὸ ἀναγκαῖον ὑπάρχειν.

included among them. Let us take then the sum of the functions *of a State* as a test which will serve to elucidate the matter. The first requisite of a State then is food ; next arts, as there are various instruments, *which are made by the arts*, necessary to human existence ; thirdly arms, for the members of the political association require arms at home [1] to enforce their authority against recalcitrant persons as well as to defeat the attempts of enemies to inflict injury upon the State from without ; next a tolerable supply of money for purposes both domestic and military ; [2] fifthly the due worship of the Gods or ritual, as it is termed ; and sixthly, but most necessary of all, the means of deciding questions of policy and of justice between man and man. Such are the functions generally indispensable to a State. For a State according to our definition does not consist of any chance population but of one that is able to lead an independent life ; and if any of these functions is wanting, the association in question cannot be absolutely independent. It follows that all these processes must enter into the composition of a State. There must be in a State then a number of husbandmen who [3] supply the food, artisans, an army, a propertied class, a priesthood and judges of questions of justice and policy.

CHAP. IX.

The distribution of functions among the citizens.

Having now determined the functions of the citizens, we have still to consider the question whether all the citizens are to share them all—for it is pos-

---

[1] Reading ἔχειν ὅπλα πρὸς τὴν ἀρχήν.

[2] Omitting καὶ πρῶτον.

[3] Reading παρασκευάζουσι.

p. 103.

sible that the same persons should be all at one and
the same time husbandmen, artisans and deliberative
and judicial functionaries—or we are to assume the
existence of a separate class of citizens for each of
the functions specified, or again some necessarily
belong to a special class, while others are necessarily
open to all the citizens. The case is not ¹the same
in all polities. For, as we said, all the citizens may
have a share in all the functions, or on the other hand
only particular citizens in particular functions. This
is in fact the point of distinction among polities, as
in Democracies all the functions are open to all,
whereas in Oligarchies the contrary is the case. But
as we are engaged in a consideration of the best
polity, and this is the polity under which our State
will attain the *maximum* of happiness, and happiness,
as has been already remarked, cannot exist apart   p. 183.
from virtue, it is evident from these considerations
that in a State, in which the polity is perfect and the
citizens are just men in an absolute sense and not
merely in reference to the assumed principle *of the
polity*, the citizens ought not to lead a mechanical
or commercial life; for such a life is ignoble and
opposed to virtue. Nor again must the persons
who are to be our citizens be husbandmen, as
leisure *which is impossible in an agricultural life*
is equally essential to the culture of virtue and
to political action. But as besides these there exists in the State a military class and a class whose
function it is to deliberate on questions of policy
and to decide questions of justice, and these are

¹ Reading ταὐτό.

evidently in the strictest sense parts of the State,
the question arises, [1]Are these functions too to be distinguished or both to be assigned to the same persons ? And here again it is obvious that in one sense
they must be assigned to the same and in another
to different persons—to different persons in so far
as the two functions are severally suited to a different
prime of life, and the one requires prudence while
the other requires physical strength, but to the same
in so far as it is an impossibility that persons who
possess the power of compulsion and prevention
should put up with a permanent state of subjection ;
for the classes which have arms in their hands have
in their hands also the continuance or dissolution
of the polity. It remains then that in our polity [2]both
these functions should be assigned to the same persons,
not simultaneously however but [3]according to the
plan of Nature by which physical strength resides in
the younger and wisdom in the elder generation.
This method of distribution then among the two
is expedient and [4]just, as the division is one which
preserves the principle of desert. And further the
landed estates should be in the hands of these classes,
as affluence is a necessary qualification of our citizens, and these and these alone possess the citizenship. For neither the mechanics nor any other
[5]members of the State who do not cultivate virtue
are entitled to political rights, as in fact is evident

Landed
property.

---

[1] Omitting ἑτέροις.   [2] Reading ἀμφότερα.
[3] Reading ἀλλ', ὥσπερ πέφυκεν, ἡ μὲν δύναμις κ.τ.λ.
[4] Reading συμφέρει καὶ δίκαιόν ἐστιν.
[5] Reading μέρος.

from our fundamental principle ; for happiness, as
we said, can exist only in union with virtue and, p. 183.
when we speak of a State as happy, it is right that
we should regard not a single particular part of it
but the citizens collectively. And as the husbandmen are necessarily slaves or [1]members of a non-
Greek subject population, it is clear that landed property must belong exclusively to the military and the
deliberative or judicial classes. There still remains in
our list the priestly class whose position in the State is
also clear. No husbandman or mechanic may be appointed a priest, as it is proper that none but citizens
should pay honour to the Gods. And as the citizen
population is divided into two classes, the soldiers
and the deliberative body, and it is proper that
those who are past the age for these duties should
render to the Gods their worship and find their due
relaxation in their service, [2]they are the persons to
whom the priestly offices may properly be assigned.

We have now enumerated the things necessary to the composition of a State and its various
parts. Husbandmen, artisans, and hired labourers
generally are, it is true, indispensable to States, but
the only parts of the State *in the strict sense* are the
soldiery and the deliberative class. And further
there is in each case a separation ; but the separation
between the mere elements of a State and its parts
is perpetual, while the separation *between the military
and deliberative classes, both of which are parts of
the State,* is partial or temporary.

[1] Omitting ἢ before περιοίκους.
[2] Reading τούτοις ἂν εἴη τὰς ἱερωσύνας ἀποδοτέον.

CHAP. X.
Caste.

It may be said to be a discovery not made for the first time to-day or yesterday by political philosophers that there is a propriety in the division of the citizens into castes and in the separation of the military class from the agricultural. This organization prevails to the present day in Egypt where it was instituted, as is said, by Sesostris and in Crete where it was instituted by Minos. The system of common meals appears also to be of high antiquity, having been established in Crete at the era of the reign of Minos, and in Italy at a period considerably more remote. According to the local antiquaries there was a certain King of Œnotria called Italus, from whom the name of the Œnotrians was changed to Italians and the whole peninsula of Europe which lies between the Scylletic and the Lametic gulfs, [1]a distance of half a day's journey, received the name of Italy. This Italus, as the story goes, converted the Œnotrians, who until then had been a nomad people, into agriculturists, and, besides other laws that he gave them, was the first to establish the system of common meals. Hence the common meals as well as some of his laws are preserved to the present time among certain of his successors. The district bordering upon Tyrrhenia was occupied by the Opicans who still bear their old surname of Ausonians ; while that which extends in the direction of Iapygia and the Ionian sea, viz. [2]the country commonly known as the Siris, was the land of the Chonians, who were also of Œnotrian descent. It is from these parts that

The origin of common meals.

[1] Reading ἀπέχει δέ.
[2] Reading τὴν καλουμένην Σῖριν.

upon its having a supply of good water, [1]this last point is also one which deserves attention as of capital importance. For the things of which we make most and most frequent use for our bodies have the greatest influence upon our state of health, and the effect of water and air is of this nature. Accordingly in any sensible State, if the springs are not all equally good or there is not an abundance of good springs, a distinction should be made between the water which is used for drinking and the water which is used for other purposes.

Coming to the question of strongholds, we find that what is advantageous to one polity is not advantageous to another. Thus a citadel is suitable to an Oligarchy or a Monarchy, level ground to a Democracy, neither of these but on the contrary a number of strongholds to an Aristocracy. *Situations suitable to different polities.*

Although the arrangement of private houses is considered to be more agreeable and better suited to general purposes, if it is regular [2]according to the modern plan called after Hippodamus, yet for security in time of war a contrary arrangement such as existed in ancient times is more serviceable, as it is one in which it is difficult for an army of foreigners to escape or for an assailing force to make out its way. We conclude then that the city should combine the two arrangements—nor is this impossible, if we adopt a plan of construction like the planting of vines in quincunxes as they are sometimes termed among farmers— and that it should be laid out in regular sections *Plan of the city.*

---

[1] Reading δεῖ καὶ τούτου τὴν ἐπιμέλειαν ἔχειν.

[2] Omitting καὶ.

not as a whole but only partially and in certain places. It will then be equally well adapted for security and beauty of effect.

Walls.   Upon the question of walls, [1] the idea that they ought not to exist in States which affect a character for valour is a view that is utterly out of date, especially in the face of the fact that the States which prided themselves upon having no walls are proved by experience to be in the wrong. It is true that, when we have to deal with none but enemies similar to ourselves in character and only slightly superior in numbers, there is something discreditable in the endeavour to protect ourselves by the strength of our walls. But as it is often a fact and always a possibility that the superior force of the assailants should be too great [2] for the unaided personal valour of a small number of citizens, the only way to protect ourselves and be safe against injury and dishonour is to look upon the strongest defence in the way of walls as in the highest degree a resource of military skill, especially in these days when the missiles and engines of blockade have been brought to so high a pitch of perfection. The demand that we should not surround our cities with a ring of walls is much like the demand that we should choose for our country one that is easily exposed to invasion and should raze all the high ground *that protects it ;* or again that we should leave our private houses without walls for fear the inhabitants should turn cowards, *if they*

[1] Probably Aristotle has in mind the teaching of Plato in the *Laws*, Bk. VI. pp. 777—779.

[2] Reading τῆς ἀνθρωπίνης τῆς ἐν τοῖς ὀλίγοις.

excluded from power, are all the *unenfranchised*
inhabitants of the land ready for revolt, and it is an
impossibility that the members of the governing class
should be so numerous as to be stronger than the
two together.   On the other hand that the rulers
should be superior to the subjects is indisputable.
The means of arriving at this result and of giving all
the citizens a share in rule and subjection are matters
for the consideration of the legislator.   Or rather the
point is one which has been already discussed.   Nature has herself supplied the [1]distinction we need, in
that those who are in actual race the same she has
made some junior and others senior, and to the
former a position of subjection and to the latter one
of rule is appropriate.   Nobody feels indignant or
fancies himself superior to his place, if the ground of
his subjection is simply his youth, especially when he
is sure to enjoy this privilege *of rule* in his turn, as
soon as he has reached the proper age.   Our conclusion then is that the rulers and subjects are in one
sense the same and in another different.   And from
this it follows that their education too must be in one
sense the same and in another different.   *The point
of identity and of difference is the fact* that nobody,
as it is said, can be a good ruler without having first
been a subject.   Rule, however, according to the
remark we made at the outset of our treatise, may be
for the benefit either of the ruler or of the subject.
The former kind we call the rule of a slavemaster
over his slaves, the latter the rule which is exercised
over free persons.   But in the case of a certain class

p. 119,

---

[1] Reading διαίρεσιν.

of commands the distinction *between obedience which is free and obedience which is servile* lies not so much in the actual tasks enjoined as in their object. Accordingly there are many tasks regarded as menial which it is honourable even to free persons to perform in their youth, as the honour or dishonour of such actions depends not so much upon the actions in themselves as upon the end or object for which they are performed. And as the virtue of a citizen, while

p 110.

he actually holds a position of rule, is according to our definition identical with the virtue of the best man, and the same person is to become a subject first and a ruler afterwards, the endeavour of the legislator should be to make men good, to study what are the occupations which produce goodness and what is the end *and object* of the best life.

The parts of the soul.

The human soul is divided into two parts, one of which contains reason in itself, and the other, although not containing in itself reason, is at the same time capable of obeying it. Also it is to these parts that the virtues belong which entitle a man to be called good. Nor can it be doubtful to anyone who adopts our division of the soul in which of the two the end *of human existence* is to be regarded as properly residing. For it is a constant rule equally conspicuous in the realms of Art and Nature that the lower is for the sake of the higher, and in the case of the soul the rational part is the higher. The reason according to our usual method of division is divided into two parts, viz. practical reason and speculative reason. It follows evidently that the rational part of the soul must be similarly divided. We shall recognize a corresponding

division in the actions *of its parts ;* those of the part
which is naturally the higher deserve the preference
at the hands of anyone who is capable of all the
actions of the soul or of these two kinds of action ;
for in the case of any individual the highest of which
he is capable is most deserving of his preference.
Again, all life is divided into business and leisure, war
and peace ; and within the sphere of action there are
some things which are *at best* ind` ,ensable or salu-
tary and others which are moral *per se.* And here
too the same rule of preference must prevail as in
regard to the parts of the soul and their actions ; the
end or object of war should always be peace, of
business leisure, of things indispensable and salutary
things moral *per se.* It is right then that a States- The objects
man should in his legislation pay regard to all these tion.
points whether in respect of the parts of the soul or
of their actions, but especially to the higher points or
the ends. The same is true of the various kinds of
life and the different objects of action. It is right
that the citizens should possess a capacity for business
or war but still more for the enjoyment of peace and
leisure ; right that they should be capable of such
actions as are indispensable and salutary but still
more of such as are moral *per se.* It is with
a view to these objects then that they should be
educated while they are still children and at all
other ages until they pass beyond the need of
education.

But if we look at those of Greeks who are supposed to enjoy the best polities at the present time
and at the legislators who have established these

polities, it is clear that they had not ¹the highest end
in view in framing their political systems nor the sum
of all the virtues in their laws and education ; on the
contrary they took a lower line and turned aside in
search of such as are supposed to be profitable and
to afford a better chance of self-aggrandisement.
And following their example some later writers have
expressed the same sentiments, eulogizing the Lacedaemonian polity and admiring the object of their
lawgiver in that all his legislative measures were *exclusively* directed to conquest and war. This is a
view which not only can be easily refuted on logical
grounds but has been ²utterly refuted by history.
The truth is that, as most men ³covet a wide extent of
despotic authority as being the means to a rich abuud-
ance of external blessings, so ⁴Thimbron and all other
writers upon the Lacedaemonian polity make no
secret of the admiration they feel for the legislator,
because the Lacedaemonians being disciplined to face
dangers were enabled to rule an extensive empire.
Yet *on this hypothesis* it is evident that, as the Lacedaemonians have now lost their empire, they are no
longer happy, and their lawgiver must no longer be
called a good one. And besides this there is something ridiculous in the idea that, while remaining
true to his laws and absolutely unimpeded in the
exercise of them, nevertheless they have failed to

¹ Reading τὸ βέλτιστον τέλος.
² Omitting νῦν.
³ Reading ζηλοῦσι.
⁴ Θίμβρων is the form of the name which has the best MSS authority.

preserve a noble life. As a fact however *those who form this sort of estimate* are wrong in their conception of the rule upon which the legislator should set a conspicuous value. For *they prefer despotic rule, whereas* such rule as is exercised over free persons is ✗ nobler and implies a higher degree of virtue. And further it is no reason for esteeming the State happy or eulogizing the legislator [1] that he disciplined the citizens to endurance in order that they might enjoy ✗ external dominion; for such a principle as this is full of mischief. For it is evident that on *the same principle* any citizen who has the power should try to succeed in making himself ruler of his own State; yet this is a charge which the Lacedaemonians bring against their king Pausanias notwithstanding the high honours he enjoyed. No such [2]law or ✗ theory is statesmanlike, expedient or true. For the same principles of morality are best both for individuals and States, [3]and it is these which the legislator should implant in the souls of men. The object of War. military training should be not to enslave persons who do not deserve slavery, but firstly to secure ourselves against becoming the slaves of others, secondly to seek imperial power not with a view to a universal despotic authority, but for the benefit of the subjects whom we rule, and thirdly to exercise despotic power over those who are deserving to be slaves. That the legislator should rather make it his object so to order

[1] Reading καρτερεῖν ἤσκησεν ἐπὶ τὸ τῶν πέλας ἄρχειν.

[2] Reading νόμων καὶ λόγων.

[3] Reading καὶ κοινῇ, καὶ τὸν νομοθέτην ἐμποιεῖν δεῖ ταῦτα ταῖς ψυχαῖς.

his legislation upon military and other matters as to
promote leisure and peace is a theory borne out by
the facts of History. For such States as *aspire to
military success*, although they are saved in time of
war, generally collapse as soon as they have obtained
imperial power. [1] They lose their temper like steel
in time of peace. For this however the legislator
is to blame in that he did not educate them in the
capacity for enjoying leisure.

CHAP. XV.
The virtues
of the
citizens.

As it appears that the end is the same for men
both collectively *as members of a State* and individually, and the definition of the best man and the
best polity is necessarily the same, it is evident that
the virtues which are suited to leisure must be found

pp. 205 sqq.

in the best State. For war, as we have remarked
several times, has its end in peace, and business its
end in leisure. But the virtues which are useful to
leisure and to rational enjoyment are not only such
as find their sphere of action in leisure but such also
as find it in business ; for *it is the latter which produce the necessaries of life, and* the possibility of
leisure presupposes the possession of various necessaries. [2] Hence valour and endurance are virtues
suitable to our citizens, as it is proverbial that "slaves
know no leisure," and a people incapable of facing
dangers valorously are the slaves of every assailant.
And if valour and endurance are thus necessary to
business, intellectual culture is necessary to leisure,
and temperance and justice at both times but more
especially in time of peace or leisure ; for war necessi-

---

[1] Reading ἀνιᾶσιν.
[2] Omitting σώφρονα.

tates the practice of justice and temperance, whereas
the enjoyment of the gifts of fortune and a life of
peace and leisure have a tendency to produce an
insolent disposition. We conclude then that a high
degree of justice and temperance is necessary to
persons who are reputed to be most prosperous and
who enjoy all the Goods for which men are accounted
happy, e.g. to those, if such there be, who dwell, as
poets say, in the islands of the Blessed; for they
above all will need culture, temperance and justice
in proportion as their life is one of leisure amidst a
rich abundance of such Goods.

It is evident then that our State, if it is to be
happy and virtuous, must participate in these virtues.
For if it is disgraceful to be incapable of making
a right use of our Goods *at any time*, still more disgraceful is it to be incapable of so doing in seasons of
leisure, to display a good character in time of business or war and a slavish character in time of peace
and leisure. And from this it follows that we ought
not to practice virtue after the manner of the Lacedaemonians, who differ from the rest of the world not
in refusing to recognize the same things as the highest Goods but in imagining that they are best attained
by one particular virtue only [1]and also that these
Goods and the enjoyment of them are higher than
the enjoyment of the virtues.

[2]*It is evident from these considerations that it is*

---

[1] Reading ἀρετῆς, ἔτι δὲ μείζω τε ἀγαθὰ ταῦτα καὶ τὴν ἀπόλαυσιν
τὴν τούτων ἢ τὴν τῶν ἀρετῶν.

[2] If the reading given above, which is supported by p. 50, ll.
6—10, is correct, and indeed whatever view is taken of the pas-

*our duty to cultivate the virtue which has its sphere
in leisure* and to do so for its own sake. It is the
means and manner of attaining this virtue which now
remain to be considered.

p 201.   We have already decided that nature, habit and
reason are all indispensable to this end. *The first
point, viz.* the proper natural character of the citizens,
The order of has been already determined ; and it only remains to
education.
consider whether their education is to begin with the
reason or the habits. For it is necessary that there
should be the most perfect harmony between reason and
habits, as it is equally possible that the reason should
have quite missed the best principle of life and that the
citizens should have been led astray by force of habit.

One thing at least is perfectly evident at the
outset here as elsewhere, viz. that the process of
production starts from a beginning and that the
end to which a certain beginning leads is itself the
¹beginning of another end. Now reason or intellect is the end *or complete development* of our
nature ; consequently it is in reference to them that
we should order our process of production or in
other words the training of the habits. Further as
soul and body are two, so also in the soul itself we
find two parts, viz. the irrational and the rational, with
two distinct habits, the one appetite and the other

sage, it cannot well be doubted that there is a lacuna after
ἀρετῶν. The context suggests some remark about ἡ ἐν τῇ σχολῇ
ἀρετή. The reading adopted in the translation is purely conjectural, but gives, I hope, something like the true sense : <ὅτι μὲν
οὖν τὴν ἐν τῇ σχολῇ ἀρετὴν δεῖ ἀσκεῖν> καὶ ὅτι δι' αὐτήν, φανε-
ρὸν κ.τ.λ.

¹ Reading ἀρχῆς ἀρχὴ ἄλλου τέλους.

intellect. Also as the body in process of production
is prior to the soul, so is the irrational part of the
soul prior to the rational—a fact not difficult to perceive, as spirit, will and desire also exist in children
from the moment of their birth, while ratiocination
or intellect is in the course of Nature not developed
in them until they grow older. And hence in the
first place the care of the body must precede that
of the soul, that of the appetite must be second, but
always that of the appetite for the sake of the intellect
and that of the body for the sake of the soul.

Seeing then that it is from the first the legislator's Chap. XVI.
business to provide for the best possible physical The physical condi-
condition of the persons he has to educate, he must tion of the
citizens.
at the outset devote his attention to the question
of marriage. He must consider the right times for Marriage.
persons to contract the matrimonial alliance and the
proper sort of persons to contract it. And in legislating about this association, *viz. marriage,* he should
have in view not only the persons themselves who are
to marry but their time of life, so that they may
arrive simultaneously at corresponding periods in
respect of age, and there may not be a discrepancy
between their powers, whether it is that the husband
is still able to beget children and the wife is not or
vice versa, as this is a state of things which is a
source of mutual bickerings and dissensions. Secondly
the legislator ought to have regard to the time at
which the children *will be grown up and* will be
ready to take their parents' places. They should
not be too much younger than their parents nor too
nearly of the same age. In the former case the

14—2

seniors lose the benefit of such services as their children might render them *in old age,* and the children of the support they might derive from their parents *in youth;* and the latter is one full of difficulty, as the children feeling themselves to be nearly of an age with their parents entertain less reverence towards them, and the proximity of years is a cause of dispute in domestic matters. Another point *deserving the legislator's attention* is the one with which our present digression began, viz. that the bodily condition of the children shall be such as he desires. Practically all these results may be secured by a single precaution. As it is a general rule that seventy among men and fifty among women is the extreme limit of age at which they are capable of begetting children, the beginning of marriage should be fixed at such a time that the parents may reach these ages simultaneously. Marriage at a youthful age has a prejudicial influence upon the procreation of children. It is a law of the whole animal world that the offspring of youthful parents are imperfectly developed, are apt to procreate females and are small in body, and we must conclude the same to be the case among human beings. We infer it from the fact that in all States, in which the practice of youthful marriage is in vogue, the citizens are imperfectly developed and small in stature. Another *objection to such marriages* is that young women are greater sufferers in their travail and die oftener; in fact it is sometimes said that this was the explanation of the [1]oracular response

---

[1] The oracle was μὴ τέμνε νέαν ἄλοκα, according to a gloss upon the present passage.

which was given to the Troezenians, referring not to
the ingathering of the fruits of the earth but to the
great mortality among their women in consequence of
the practice of marriage at an early age. Again, it
is expedient in the interest of continence that the
women should not be given in marriage until they
are older, as experience shews there is a greater
danger of unchastity, if they are young at the time
of cohabitation. Further it seems that the bodies
of males are apt to be stunted in their growth, if they
marry before the body has finished growing ; for the
body too has its fixed limit of time after which it
ceases to grow. It is convenient then to marry the
women at about the age of eighteen and the men
at about thirty-seven[1]; they will thus be at the height
of their physical vigour at the time of marriage and
will come simultaneously and at the right season
to the period of life when they cease to beget children. Finally as regards the time when the children
will succeed to their parents' places, the children, if
they are born as we may expect immediately after
the marriage, will be entering upon their prime at
the time when the parents are already well stricken
in years and are drawing near to the age of seventy.

So much as to the age for entering upon the matrimonial state. In regard to the seasons of the year [2]it
is well to follow the wise system generally retained
at the present time, by which it is fixed that this
union should take place in winter. [3]The parents them-

---

[1] Omitting $\mathring{\eta}$ μικρόν.

[2] Reading χρόνοις δεῖ χρῆσθαι οἷς οἱ πολλοί.

[3] Reading δεῖ δέ.

selves too in view of the procreation of children should pay attention to the rules of physicians and natural philosophers, the former of whom are competent authorities upon the occasions suitable to their physical condition and the latter upon the various kinds of winds, northerly winds being in their judgment preferable to southerly.

What is the physical condition of the parents which will be most beneficial to the children they beget is a question we shall have to discuss more particularly when we come to treat of the supervision of children. For the present a mere sketch of the subject must suffice. For a vigorous habit of body in one who is to lead a political life, for health and for the procreation of *healthy* children, what is wanted is not the bodily condition of an athlete nor on the other hand a valetudinarian and invalid condition, but one that lies between the two. The right condition then, although it is one of discipline, is disciplined not by violent exercises nor for one purpose only like an athlete's, but for all the actions of a liberal life. Also this condition should be [1]the same for women as for men.

Again, the women should take care of their bodily health during pregnancy, not leading a life of indolence nor yet adopting a scanty diet. This care of their bodies may be easily secured by the legislator, if he ordains that they should daily take a certain walk to render due service to the Gods whose function it is to preside over childbirth. But their mind unlike their bodies should at such a time be comparatively indo-

---

[1] Reading ταὐτὸ.

lent *and free from anxiety*, as we see that the
children are affected by the state of the mother during
pregnancy just as plants by the condition of the soil.

As to the question of exposing or rearing the [The exposure of children.]
children [1]born, there should be a law against rearing
any cripple. [2]On the other hand the exposure of
children simply on the ground of their number is
prevented by the established customs of the State, as
there is to be a limit set to the number of children
the citizens may beget. If however a larger number
are born to some parents in marriage, abortion should
be procured before they acquire sensation or life ; for
the morality or immorality of such action depends
upon whether the child has or has not yet obtained
sensation and life.

Further as we have determined the time of life at
which a man and a woman [3]are to enter respectively
upon matrimony, it is right to settle also the limit of
time during which they are to beget children for the
service of the State. For the children of parents who
are above, as also of those who are below the proper
age are imperfectly developed in body and mind,
while those of aged parents are feeble. Hence *the
limit* must depend upon the intellectual prime *of the
parents*, and this is generally, as it has been stated
[4]by certain poets who divide human life into periods

---

[1] Reading γενομένων.

[2] Reading διὰ δὲ πλῆθος τέκνων ἡ τάξις τῶν ἐθῶν κωλύει μηδὲν
ἀποτίθεσθαι τῶν γενομένων· ὡρίσθαι γὰρ δεῖ κ.τ.λ.

[3] Reading δεῖ.

[4] See e.g. the well-known lines which appear as the 25th
Fragment of Solon in Bergk's *Poetae Lyrici Graeci.*

of seven years, about the age of fifty. If this is true,
it follows that as soon as a person is four or five years
above this age he should be discharged from the duty
of begetting children who are to see the light of day,
and such persons should in future enjoy such sexual
intercourse only as is good for health or some other
similar object.

And lastly as to the connexion of a man with a
woman who is not his wife or of a woman with a man
who is not her husband, while such intercourse
in whatever form or under whatever circumstances
must be considered absolutely discreditable to one
who bears the title of husband or wife, so especially
any one who is detected in such action during the
time reserved for the procreation of children should
be punished with such civil degradation as is suitable
to the magnitude of his crime.

CHAP.
XVII.
Early edu-
cation.
(1) Infancy.

The children being now supposed to be born, the
character of their diet, [1]we must consider, has an important influence on their physical powers. Whether
we examine the case of the other animals or of nations
which set themselves to encourage such a condition
of body as is useful in war, it is evident that a diet
containing plenty of milk is best suited to the bodily
health of children; it should consist of as little wine
as possible for fear of the diseases which a wine-diet
produces. Also it is expedient that [2]children at this
early age should indulge in all such movements as
are possible to them. As a means of preventing their
limbs which are so supple from getting twisted, it is

---

[1] Reading οἴεσθαι δεῖ.
[2] Reading τηλικούτους.

the practice among some nations even at the present
day to employ certain mechanical instruments which
keep the bodies of young children straight. It is well
too from a very early age to inure the children to
cold; such a practice is highly useful not only as a
source of health but also as a preparation for military
duties. It is accordingly the custom among many
non-Greek peoples either to plunge their newborn
babes into a cold river or, as the Celts do, to cover
them with scanty clothing. For wherever it is possible to habituate children to anything, it is best to
begin the process of habituation [1]early in life and
continue it gradually; and the bodily condition of
children from its warmth is naturally adapted to such
a training in the endurance of cold. [2]Nor is it right
to prohibit, [3]as do some persons in their Laws, the
spasmodic stretchings and screamings of the children;
they are helpful to growth, as being virtually a sort
of gymnastic exercises for their bodies. For just as
labourers get strength by holding their breath, so do
infants by these spasmodic cries.

Such then or similar to these are the precautions
to be taken in the first months of a child's life. In
the subsequent period up to the age of five, when as
yet it is not well to make them apply themselves to

(2) From
infancy to
the age of
five.

---

[1] Reading ἀρχομένων.

[2] The natural sequence of the subjects discussed is somewhat
confused in the mss text which Bekker retains. But I have not
ventured to do more in the way of transposition than to insert
after τὴν τῶν ψυχρῶν ἄσκησιν the two sentences τὰς δὲ διατάσεις
τῶν παίδων......καὶ τοῖς παιδίοις διατεινομένοις, p. 128, ll. 4—9.

[3] Plato Laws, VII. p. 791 E sqq.

study of any kind or compulsory bodily exercises for fear of injuring their growth, they should be allowed just so much movement as not to fall into a sluggish habit of body, and this should be secured among various forms of action by the amusement they take. But their amusements themselves should not be of an illiberal sort nor yet too laborious or effeminate. Further it should be the duty of the officers who are called overseers of the youth to determine the character of the tales and legends which the children at this tender age are to hear. For all this early education should be preparatory to their subsequent pursuits, and accordingly their amusements should for the most part be imitations of their serious occupations in the future. The overseers of the youth too, while superintending their general manner of life, should take especial precautions against their associating more than is necessary with slaves ; *and there is a certain danger of their so doing,* as children at this age and up to the age of seven are necessarily brought up at home.

There is then, as we see, a strong probability that they may [1]derive a taint of ungentlemanliness even at this tender age from the objects which meet their ears and eyes. And hence, as light talking about foul things is closely followed by doing them, it is the duty of the legislator to banish foul language [2]as much as any other foulness from his State, [3]from

---

[1] Reading ἀπολαύειν ἀπὸ τῶν ἀκουσμάτων καὶ τῶν ὁραμάτων ἀνελευθερίαν.

[2] Reading ὥσπερ τι ἄλλο.

[3] The construction becomes clearer, if the words ἐκ τοῦ ·γὰρ

among the young especially, who should not be
allowed either to say or hear anything of the kind,
[1]while anyone who is convicted of using such language
or doing any such action as is prohibited should be
punished with [2]reprimands and stripes, if he is a
free man but not yet of an age to take his seat at
the public tables, and, if older, should be visited with
civil degradation involving the loss of a free man's
rights because he has conducted himself in a manner
worthy of a slave. And as we banish all foul language
from our State, so undoubtedly should we also banish
from the observation of the citizens all indecent pictures or tales. It should be the business then of the
officers of State to see that there is no image or
picture representing indecent scenes, except in the
temples of those Gods to whose worship scurrilous
jesting is by law declared to be appropriate; [3]and
besides it is only [4]persons of a suitable age who are
permitted by law to render honour to these Gods on
their own behalf and on behalf of their children[5].
Nor again should the younger generation be [6]allowed
to be present at the performance of satirical plays or
comedies until they have attained the age at which

εὐχερῶς λέγειν......τὸ ποιεῖν σύνεγγυς are regarded as a parenthesis
and the full stop after σύνεγγυς is changed to a colon.
    [1] Placing a comma only, instead of a full stop, after μηδὲν
τοιοῦτον.
    [2] Reading ἐπιτιμήσεσι.
    [3] Reading πρὸς δὲ τούτοις.
    [4] Reading τοὺς τὴν ἡλικίαν ἔχοντας τὴν ἱκνουμένην.
    [5] Omitting καὶ γυναικῶν.
    [6] Reading θετέον. .

they will be admitted to a seat at the common tables and to a share in convivial meetings and will in all cases be secured by their education against the injury resulting from such performances.

We have alluded to these matters now only in passing. It will be proper hereafter to dwell upon them more at length and set them at rest by a thorough examination of the question whether in the first place the young citizens are or are not *to be admitted to such performances,* and *secondly, if so,* on what conditions they are to be admitted. For the present however, *as I say,* we have alluded to it only so far as is necessary to our purpose. For it was perhaps a wise judgment of the famous tragic actor Theodorus, when he never allowed any actor however insignificant to come upon the stage before himself on the ground that the audience surrender themselves to anyone or anything that they hear first. The same is the case in all our dealings with men and things; the first favourable impressions are always the strongest. Hence we should keep our youth from all acquaintance with evil, especially such as involves vice or [1]coarseness.

(3) From five years to seven. After the age of five the two following years up to seven they should spend in observation of the lessons which they will be required in the future to learn themselves.

The division of human life. There are two periods into which their education *in the proper sense of the word* should be divided : the one from the age of seven to puberty, the other

---

[1] Reading δυσγένειαν.

from puberty to twenty-one. For the division of human life into periods of seven years is upon the whole not a bad one; but it is best to follow strictly the division of Nature herself, as it is the purpose of all art and culture to supply the deficiencies of Nature.

BOOK V.

[1]WE have to consider then in the first place whether it is desirable to establish a definite system in the education of children, secondly whether it is expedient that the superintendence of them should be the concern of the State or, as is now the case in most States, of private individuals, and thirdly, *if there is to be a system,* [2]what should be its character.

That the education of the young is a matter which has a paramount claim upon the attention of the legislator will not be disputed. The neglect of it in existing States is prejudicial to their polities. For the [3]educational system must always be relative to the particular polity, as it is the character proper to each polity which is its habitual preservative, as it is in fact the original cause of its creation, e.g. a democratic character of a Democracy, an oligar-

---

[1] The last sentence of Book IV. in Bekker's text is so closely connected with the subject of Book V. and forms so natural an introduction to the chapters on education, that I have had no scruple about transferring it with Spengel and Susemihl to the beginning of the present Book.

[2] Reading ποίαν τινὰ δεῖ εἶναι ταύτην.

[3] Reading παιδεύεσθαι in place of πολιτεύεσθαι.

chical of an Oligarchy and so on, and, the higher
this character *of the citizens,* the higher is the polity
it produces. And further there is no faculty or art
in which a certain process of education or habituation
is not essential as preparatory to its exercise; and
it follows as an evident consequence that the same is
true of the practices of virtue.

Again, as the end proposed to the State as a
whole is one, it is clear that the education of all the
citizens must be one and the same and the superintendence of it a public affair rather than in private
hands, as it now is, when each individual superintends
his own children privately and with such private
instruction as he thinks good. The training in
public business should itself be public. And further
it is not right to suppose that any citizen is his own
master but rather that all belong to the State; for
each individual is a member of the State, and the
superintendence of any part is naturally relative to
that of the whole. This is one point in which the
Lacedaemonians deserve praise; they devote a great
deal of attention to the educational needs of their
children, and their attention takes the form of action
on the part of the State.

The propriety of legislating upon education and
of treating it [1]as an affair of the State is now evident.
But we must not leave out of sight the nature of the
education and the proper manner of imparting it. For
at present there is a [2]practical dissension upon this
point; people do not agree upon the subjects which

The educational system. CHAP. II.

----

[1] Reading κοινῇ.
[2] Reading διὰ τῶν ἔργων.

The subjects of education.

the young should learn, whether they take virtue *in the abstract* or the best life as the end to be sought, and it is uncertain whether education should properly be directed rather to the cultivation of the intellect or the moral discipline of the soul. The question is complicated too, if we look to the actual education of our own day; [1]nobody knows whether the young should be trained in such studies as are merely useful as means of livelihood or in such as tend to the promotion of virtue or in the higher studies, all of which have received a certain number of suffrages. Nor again, *if virtue be accepted as the end*, is there any agreement as to the means of attaining it; for at the very outset there is a difference of opinion respecting the nature of the virtue that is held in honour and consequently, as might be expected, a disagreement as to the method of training young people in it.

That such useful studies as are absolutely indispensable ought to be taught is plain enough; not all useful studies however, for in face of the distinction which exists between liberal and illiberal occupations it is evident that our youth should not be allowed to engage in any but such as being practically useful will at the same time not reduce one who engages in them to the level of a mere mechanic.

Mechanical studies.

It may be observed that any occupation or art or study deserves to be regarded as mechanical, if it renders the body or soul or intellect of free persons unfit for the exercise and practice of virtue.

---

[1] Reading καὶ δῆλον οὐδενὶ.

Accordingly we describe as mechanical not only those
arts which degrade the condition of the body but also
all mercenary employments, as depriving the intellect ✗
of all leisure or dignity. And even if we confine
ourselves to the liberal sciences, there are some in
which, although the study of them up to a certain
point involves no departure from liberal culture,
yet [1]an excessive assiduity and endeavour after perfect mastery are subject to the drawbacks just mentioned. It is the object of any action or study which
is all-important. There may be nothing illiberal in
them if undertaken for one's own sake or the sake of
one's friends or the attainment of virtue; whereas
the very same action, if done to satisfy others, would ✗
in many cases bear a menial or slavish aspect.

The studies established at the present day are,
as has been already remarked, of an ambiguous
character. We may say that there are four usual CHAP. III.
subjects of education, viz. Reading and Writing, Gym- The usual subjects of
nastic, Music, and fourthly, although this is not uni- education.
versally admitted, the Art of Design. Reading and ✗
Writing, and the Art of Design are taught for their ✗
serviceableness in the purposes of life and their
various utility, Gymnastic as tending to the promotion of valour; but the purpose of Music is in- ✗
volved in great uncertainty. Although it is generally
studied at the present day solely for the pleasure it
affords, yet in the first instance it was made a branch
of education because the endeavour of Nature herself, as we have frequently remarked, is that men pp.205 sqq.

---

[1] Reading τὸ δὲ προσεδρεύειν λίαν πρὸς ἀκρίβειαν.

may be able not only to engage in business rightly but also to spend their leisure nobly ; and *the guidance of Nature deserves to be followed, as* Nature, if we may repeat what we have already said on the subject, is the first principle of all things. For if *the right conduct of business and the noble employment of leisure* are both requisite, and at the same time leisure is preferable to business [1]*and is the end of human existence,* we are bound to investigate the right manner of employing leisure. It should evidently not be spent in mere amusement ; else it would follow that amusement is the end and object of our life. But if this supposition is impossible, if amusements are to be our resource in times of business rather than of leisure—*as may well be the case,* since it is persons who exert themselves that need such recreation as is the object of all amusement, and business necessarily involves exertion and effort—it follows that in introducing amusements [2]one must carefully observe the seasons proper to their use and consider that they are applied as a sort of medicine. For the motion of the soul thereby produced is a relaxation and from its pleasurable effects a recreation ; whereas the enjoyment of leisure is admitted to contain in itself not only pleasure but happiness and a life of pure bliss. Such a life is the prerogative not of persons engaged in business but of those who enjoy leisure. For the man of business seeks by his business to attain some end and therefore *ex hypothesi* is not in possession of it

The employment of leisure.

---

[1] Reading ἀσχολίας καὶ τέλος, ζητητέον.
[2] Reading καιροφυλακοῦντα and προσάγοντα.

already; whereas happiness, which is universally allowed to be associated with pleasure and not with pain, is itself an end, *and is therefore to be found only in leisure. But this general agreement extends no further.* There is no consensus of opinion as to the definition of this pleasure; each individual is guided by his own personality and habit of mind, and it is the perfect man whose pleasure is perfect and derived from the noblest sources.

It is evident then *from our consideration of business and leisure* that there are certain things in which instruction and education are necessary [1] with a view to leisure, and that these branches of education and study are ends in themselves, while such as have business for their object are pursued only as being indispensable and as leading to some ulterior object. Accordingly Music was introduced into the educational system by our forefathers not as indispensable— it has no such characteristic—nor as practically useful in the sense in which Reading and Writing are useful for pecuniary transactions, domestic economy, scientific study and a variety of political actions, or as the Art of Design is in the general opinion useful as a means of forming a better judgment of works of art, nor again as useful like Gymnastic in promoting health and vigour. Neither of these two results do we find to be produced by Music. It remains therefore that Music is useful for the rational enjoyment of leisure; and this is evidently the purpose to which it was in fact applied by our forefathers, as it is ranked by them as an element of the rational enjoyment

The object of Music.

[1] Omitting ἐν τῇ διαγωγῇ.

15—2

which is considered to be appropriate to free persons.
It is thus that Homer described *the bard* as one

¹ "Meet to be bidden to the festive board;"

and similarly after the mention of certain other classes
of persons he adds

² "Who bid the bard, to gladden all men's hearts."

So too in another place Odysseus says there is no
enjoyment so good as when men make merry

³ "And i' the hall the feasters list the bard
Seated in rank."

Utilitarian education. We see clearly then that there is a certain education which our sons should receive not as being
practically useful nor as indispensable but as liberal
and noble. Whether it comprises a single branch or
several, and, *if the latter*, what is their character and
how they should be taught are questions which we
shall have to discuss hereafter. At present however

¹ It may be suggested on metrical grounds that the true
reading of the line is

.ἀλλ' οἷόν γε μέν ἐστι καλεῖν ἐπὶ δαῖτα θαλείην.

But it does not occur in the existing text of Homer, although
the same sentiment is found in *Odyssey* XVII. 381—6, the passage
from which the next quotation seems to be taken.

² Aristotle cites from memory and not quite accurately, if the
reference is as is probable to *Odyssey* XVII. 381—6 and the words
οἱ καλέουσιν ἀοιδόν are part of the quotation. The actual lines are

τίς γὰρ δὴ ξεῖνον καλεῖ ἄλλοθεν αὐτὸς ἐπελθὼν
ἄλλον γ', εἰ μὴ τῶν οἳ δημιοεργοὶ ἔασιν,
μάντιν ἢ ἰητῆρα κακῶν ἢ τέκτονα δούρων,
ἢ καὶ θέσπιν ἀοιδόν, ὅ κεν τέρπῃσιν ἀείδων;
οὗτοι γὰρ κλητοί γε βροτῶν ἐπ' ἀπείρονα γαῖαν.

³ *Odyssey* IX. 7.

we have advanced so far as to see that antiquity itself supplies us, in the shape of the established studies, with a certain testimony *to the importance of a right use of our leisure;* for Music makes this point clear. And further even among such subjects as are practically useful we see there are some, e.g. Reading and Writing, in which our children must be educated not only for their utility but because they are a means to the acquisition of various other kinds of learning. Similarly they must be taught the Art of Design, not only that they may avoid serious mistakes in their private purchases and may not be cheated in the purchase and sale of household goods, [1]but rather because it renders them scientific observers of physical beauty. The universal pursuit of utility on the other hand is far from becoming to magnanimous and free spirits.

As it is evident that the education of the habits must precede that of the reason and the education of the body must precede that of the intellect, it clearly follows that we must surrender our children *in the first instance* to Gymnastic and the Art of the Trainer, as the latter imparts a certain character to their physical condition and the former to the feats they can perform. The order of education.

At the present day the States, which enjoy the highest repute for care in the education of children, generally produce in them an athletic condition whereby they mar their bodily presence and development; while the Lacedaemonians, although they Chap. IV. Gymnastic.

---

[1] Reading ἀλλὰ μᾶλλον.

avoided this mistake, render them brutal by the ex-
ertions required of them in the belief that this is the
best means to produce a valorous disposition. Yet,
as we have several times remarked, valour is neither
the only ¹virtue nor the virtue principally to be kept
in view in the superintendence of children ; and, even
if it were, the Lacedaemonians are not successful in
devising the means to attain it. For neither in the
animal world generally nor among uncivilized nations
do we find valour associated with the most savage
characters, but rather with such as are gentle, like
the ²lion's. There are many uncivilized nations who
think very little of slaying and eating their fellow-
creatures, e.g. the Achaeans and Heniochans on the
shores of the Black Sea and other nations of the
mainland *in those parts,* some of whom are as savage as
these and others more so ; yet although their existence
is one of piracy, they are absolutely destitute of valour.
Nay if we look at the case of the Lacedaemonians
themselves, it is well known that, although they maintained their superiority to all other peoples so long as
they alone were assiduous in the cheerful endurance
of laborious exercises, they are now surpassed by
others ³in the contests both of the wrestling-school
and of actual war. The fact is that their preeminence
was due not to their disciplining their youth in this
severe manner but solely to their giving them a course
of training, while the other nations *with whom they*

¹ Reading οὔτε πρὸς μίαν ἀρετὴν οὔτε κ.τ.λ.
² Aristotle's view of the lion's character is expressed more
fully περὶ τὰ ζῷα ἱστοριῶν I. p. 629 B 8 sqq.
³ Reading καὶ τοῖς γυμνικοῖς ἀγῶσι καὶ τοῖς πολεμικοῖς.

had to contend did not. [1]But it is right that we
should base our judgment not upon their achievements in the past but at the present day; for at
present they have competitors in their educational
system, whereas in past times they had none. We
may conclude then that it is not the brutal element *in
men* but the element of nobleness which should hold
the first place—for the power of encountering noble
perils must belong not to a wolf or to any other
brute but only to a brave man—[2]and that to give up
our children overmuch to bodily exercises and leave
them uninstructed in the true essentials, *i.e. in the
rudiments of education,* is in effect to degrade them
to the level of mechanics by rendering them useless
in a statesman's hands for any purpose except one
and, as our argument shews, not so useful as other
people even for this.

The duty then of employing Gymnastic and the
method of its employment are admitted. Up to the
age of puberty gymnastic exercises of a comparatively
light kind should be applied with a prohibition of
hard diet and compulsory exercises, so that there may
be no impediment to the growth. The fact that these
[3]may have the effect of injuring growth may be clearly

*The period
of gym-
nastic
exercises.*

---

[1] There is here again some confusion in the order of sentences, and it is desirable to insert after μὴ πρὸς ἀσκοῦντας ἀσκεῖν
the single sentence δεῖ δὲ οὐκ ἐκ τῶν προτέρων ἔργων......πρότερον
δ' οὐκ εἶχον, ll. 23—25, which is evidently out of place in its present context.

[2] Changing the full stop after ἀνὴρ ἀγαθός to a colon, so as
to shew that the sentence is still continued.

[3] Reading δύνανται.

inferred from the circumstance that in the list of
Olympian victors it would not be possible to find
more than two or three who have been successful in
manhood as well as in boyhood; for the effect of
their training in youth is that they lose their physical
vigour in consequence of the enforced gymnastic
exercises they perform. When our youths have devoted
three years from the age of puberty to other studies,
it is then proper that the succeeding period of life
should be occupied with hard exercises and severities
of diet. For the intellect and the body should not be
subject to severe exertion simultaneously, as the two
kinds of exertion naturally produce contrary effects,
that of the body being an impediment to the intellect
and that of the intellect to the body.

CHAP. V.
Music.
p. 225.

Coming to the subject of Music, although we have
already in the course of our treatise entered into a
discussion of some of the points in dispute concerning
it, it is right to resume and continue the discussion
now, in order that it may serve as a sort of keynote to
the theory which may be put forward by a systematic
writer on the subject. It is not easy to define the

The object
for which it
is studied.

faculty of Music or the object for which it should be
studied. Should the object of Music be amusement
and relaxation as it is of sleep or conviviality, which
are not in themselves virtuous but pleasant and, as
Euripides says, are at the same time "[1]dull care's
lullaby"? It is, in this view that Music is ranked *with
sleep and conviviality*, all the three are treated alike,

---

[1] ἄμα μέριμναν παύει is the reading which has the best MSS
authority. In *Bacchae* 378—381, the passage from which the
quotation is taken, the MSS. give ἀποπαῦσαι τε μερίμνας.

and dancing is included in the same category. [1]Is it
on the other hand to be considered that Music has a
certain moral tendency because, as Gymnastic produces a certain condition of the body, so it is within
the power of Music to produce a certain condition of
the character by training the young in the faculty of
enjoying themselves in a right manner? Or again
does Music contribute more or less to rational enjoyment and intellectual culture? for this must be
regarded as a third supposition.

That mere amusement should not be our object in
the education of the young is plain enough; for
learning does not mean amusing ourselves, as it
necessarily involves a painful effort. Nor again is
rational enjoyment a proper occupation for children
or persons of a youthful age, as *rational enjoyment
is the end or perfect state of human existence, and
*[2]perfection is not suited to one who is imperfect *like
a child.* It may perhaps however be supposed that
the serious pursuits of children are intended as means
of amusement for them when they have grown to the
perfect state of manhood. But on this hypothesis we
may ask why they should themselves be taught
Music instead of following the example of the Persian

---

[1] The construction of the original Greek will be perspicuous,
if the colon after μέθης, l. 15, and the full stops after τὴν ὄρχησιν ἐν
τούτοις, l. 19, and χαίρειν ὀρθῶς, l. 23, are changed to commas, and
ll. 15—19 ταῦτα γὰρ καθ᾽ αὑτὰ μὲν...τὴν ὄρχησιν ἐν τούτοις enclosed
in brackets as a parenthesis.

[2] It is difficult to express at all without a periphrasis, and
even then to express satisfactorily the force of the play upon
words in the Greek οὐθενὶ γὰρ (or, as the better reading is, οὐδὲ γὰρ)
ἀτελεῖ προσήκει τέλος.

and Median kings and enjoying the pleasure it
affords [1]by means of the performances of others, *i.c.
of professional musicians,* [2]without receiving instruction in it themselves. For the execution of
persons who have adopted Music as their special occupation or art will necessarily be superior to theirs
who have studied it only so far as to acquire an
ordinary musical education. We may add that, on
the principle that they are personally to undertake
the labour of musical performances, they ought also
to be educated in cookery; which is absurd. The
same difficulty is involved in the supposition that
Music is capable of improving the moral character.
Why—*it may be asked*—should our young citizens be
personally taught musical performances instead of
enjoying themselves in a right manner and acquiring
a correct musical judgment by listening to the performances of others, as is the case with the Lacedaemonians who are not taught Music and yet are able,
as they say, to form correct judgments of good or
bad pieces? The same remark may be made, if *we
assume that* Music is to be used as a means to
happiness and the rational enjoyment of a liberal
life. Why should the young be personally taught it
instead of enjoying it in the performances of others?
We may consider *in this connexion* our conception of
the Gods. Zeus is never represented by the poets as
himself singing or playing upon the cithern. On the
contrary we regard professional musicians as on a
level with mere mechanics and musical execution as

---

[1] Reading δι' ἄλλων αὐτὸ ποιούντων.
[2] Reading καὶ ἄνευ τῆς μαθήσεως.

unworthy of a man, unless in some moment of conviviality or amusement.

These however are perhaps matters for future investigation. The first question which meets us now is whether Music is or is not to be made a branch of education, and, *if it is,* which of the three disputed effects it may produce, viz. moral discipline, amusement or rational enjoyment. It may reasonably be ranked under all three heads and be regarded as capable of all these different effects. For the object of amusement is relaxation, and relaxation is necessarily pleasant, being as it were a process of healing the pain of labour. Again, it is admitted that there should be an element of pleasure as well as of nobleness in rational enjoyment; for happiness, *which is attained only in rational enjoyment,* consists of both. It is a truism however to say that nothing is pleasanter than Music whether instrumental or accompanied by the voice.

[1] " Song, mortals' sweetest pleasure "

[2]says Musaeus himself, and accordingly Music in virtue of its power to make glad the heart of man is naturally introduced into social gatherings and festivities. From this fact alone we might infer the propriety of giving the younger citizens an education in Music, as all pleasures of a harmless kind are suitable not only to the end *or perfect state of human life* but also as means of relaxation. And as it is

---

[1] The words βροτοῖς ἥδιστον ἀείδειν should be printed as a quotation.

[2] Reading φησὶ γὰρ.

seldom the fortune of men to find themselves in the
perfect state, whereas they frequently take relaxation
and indulge in amusements not merely for the profit
they afford but for the pleasure as well, it will be
useful to them to find relaxation from time to time
in the pleasures of Music. The world has come however to treat its amusements as the end or perfect
state. The reason is probably that there is a certain
pleasure in the end as well as in amusement, although
it is not a pleasure of a commonplace kind, and that
in the endeavour after this *true pleasure* men mistake for it the commonplace one, because there is in
this last a certain resemblance to that which is the
end of all human actions. For it is the characteristic
of the end that it is not desirable for the sake of any
future object ; and similarly the pleasures of amusement have their cause not in the future but in the
past, i.e. in the labour or pain *we have undergone.*
This then may reasonably be supposed to be the
reason why men seek to obtain happiness by the
pleasures of amusement. But they take up Music not
on this account only but also because it is conceived
to be useful for purposes of recreation. At the same
time it is a question worthy of consideration whether,
if we grant this to be an incidental quality of Music,
it is not in its nature more honourable than merely
to supply the need of recreation, whether it is not
the right principle not merely to enjoy the universal
pleasure it affords, of which all the world is sensible,—
for the pleasure of Music is a natural one, and hence
the use of it is attractive to persons of all ages and
characters—but to consider whether it has also any

tendency to form the moral character and influence
the soul. Nor will there be any room for doubt
about the matter, if *it can be shewn that* Music produces in us certain conditions of character. But
this effect of Music is proved by various instances and
especially by the musical compositions of Olympus ;
for it is admitted that they make our souls enthusiastic, and enthusiasm is an emotional condition of the
character of the soul. And further, when we listen to
imitations, we all acquire a sympathy *with the feelings
imitated,* even apart from the actual rhythms and
melodies. And as Music is in fact a pleasant thing,
and virtue consists in enjoying right pleasures and
entertaining right feelings of liking or dislike, it is
evident that there is nothing in which it is so important that men should be instructed and trained
as in forming right judgments and feeling pleasure
in honourable characters and noble actions. But it
is in rhythms and melodies that we have the most
realistic imitations of anger and mildness as well
as of courage, temperance and all their opposites
and of moral qualities generally. This we see from
actual experience, as it is in listening to such imitations that we suffer a change within our soul. But to
acquire the habit of feeling pain or pleasure upon
the occurrence of resemblances is closely allied to
having the same feelings in presence of the real
originals. For instance, if a person feels pleasure in
the contemplation of somebody's picture for no
reason except the beauty of the form itself, it necessarily follows that the contemplation of the man
himself whose picture he contemplates will be plea-

sant to him ; ¹and this is a sensation enjoyed by all
alike. The fact is however that there is no imitation
of moral qualities in the objects of sense generally,·
e.g. in the objects of touch and taste, except indeed
in the objects of sight and here only in a slight
degree. For figures possess this imitative power,
although only to a small extent; and indeed they are
not actual imitations of moral qualities, but the
figures and colours which are produced are rather
symbols of moral qualities, and their influence works
²through the body upon the emotions. Nevertheless
as there is a considerable importance attaching to
the contemplation of pictures, it is proper that the
young should contemplate not the works of Pausou
but those of Polygnotus or any other painter or
sculptor who has an ethical character. Melodies on
the other hand contain in themselves representations·
of moral qualities. This is a fact beyond dispute, as
there is an initial distinction between the natures of
different harmonies, so that we are variously affected
by the sound of them and do not experience the
same mood when we listen to all, but in listening to
some, e.g. the mixed Lydian as it is called, experience
a mood of comparative melancholy and restraint ; in
listening to others, e.g. the lax harmonies, a more
tender mental mood ; and again an intermediate and
sedate mood in listening especially to a third—for
such is, as it seems, the effect of the Dorian har-

¹ It is probable that the clause καὶ πάντες τῆς τοιαύτης αἰσθή-
σεως κοινωνοῦσιν, ll. 18—19, should be transposed, as it is in the
translation, so as to follow ἡδεῖαν εἶναι, l. 15.

² Reading ἀπὸ τοῦ σώματος.

mony alone—while we are excited to enthusiasm
by the Phrygian. This is well set forth by writers
who have treated this branch of education from
a philosophical point of view; for they appeal to
the evidence of experience in support of their
theories. [1]And the same is true of rhythms: some
have a more sedate, others again an exciting character, and among these last the means of excitement are in some cases more vulgar and in others
more refined. [2]In fact there seems to be a sort of
relationship between *the soul on the one hand and*
harmonies and rhythms on the other; and hence
there are many [3]philosophers who hold either that
the soul is itself a harmony or else that it contains
a harmony.

It is evident then from these considerations that
Music possesses the power of affecting in a certain
way the character of the soul; and, if so, it is clear

---

[1] Reading τὸν αὐτὸν δὲ τρόπον.

[2] The sentence καί τις ἔοικε συγγένεια...οἳ δ' ἔχειν ἁρμονίαν, ll.
14—17, should probably follow ἐλευθεριωτέρας, l. 8. But it is not
necessary to insert the words πρὸς τὴν ψυχὴν as Bekker has done,
although they serve to bring out the true meaning of the
passage.

[3] Compare the discussion in περὶ ψυχῆς, i. ch. 4. The passage
which Aristotle had chiefly in mind was doubtless Plato *Phaedo*,
pp. 86 sqq. But it is worth while to refer to the Fragment of
Parmenides beginning

ὡς γὰρ ἕκαστος ἔχει κρᾶσιν μελέων πολυκάμπτων
τὼς νόος ἀνθρώποισι παρέστηκεν κ.τ.λ.,

which will be found in Ritter and Preller, *Historia Philoso-*
phiae, § 102, to Lucretius III. 100 sqq., and to Cicero *Tusc. Disp.*
I. 20, 21.

that we ought to make use of it and educate the younger generation in it. For instruction in Music is appropriate to the natural disposition of the young, as from their tender years they do not willingly put up with anything that is not sweetened, and there is a natural sweetness in Music.

CHAP. VI.
Are the young to practise Music themselves?
p. 233.

We have now to discuss the question, which has been already raised, whether their instruction should or should not take the form of personally singing and performing upon musical instruments. Nor can it be doubted that personal acquaintance with the practice of anything is far the best way of acquiring certain qualifications; for it is in fact difficult, if not impossible, to become a good critic without any such practical experience. And besides this children require some occupation. We cannot but approve as a capital invention the *so-called* rattle of Archytas, which is given to children to keep them employed and to prevent their breaking furniture, as young people are unable to keep quiet. As this rattle then is suitable to babes, so the education they receive serves as a rattle *or amusement* to children of a more advanced age.

Such considerations as have been adduced shew clearly the propriety of educating the young in Music to the point of actual acquaintance with the practice. It is not difficult however to determine what is or is not becoming to different periods of life and to meet the objection of those who maintain that the practice of Music is worthy only of mechanics. In the first place, as the acquisition of a right judgment is the sole object with which they are to take part in musical performances, it follows that they should perform only during their youth and, when they have grown older, should be released from all performance and yet be enabled by the instruction they have received in youth to form a judgment of noble pieces of music and enjoy pleasures of a right kind. Nor is it difficult to meet the objection sometimes brought against Music as reducing its students to the level of mere mechanics, if we consider what are the limits to be set to actual performances in the case of persons whose education is directed to political virtue, what kind of melodies and rhythms they should practise, and thirdly—for this too is probably a point of some importance—what is the nature of the instruments to be used in their instruction. It is here that the answer to the objection lies, as it is quite possible that some species of Music may produce the ill effects above described.

It is evident then that their musical education ought not to prove an impediment to their subsequent actions or render their body mechanical and unfit for the exercise of war and politics, i.e. [1]for instruction in them at the present time and for its practical application in the future. And *the result we desire* will be attained in their education, if they do not spend their time and labour upon perform- The nature of the ances which are suitable only with a view to the Music. contests of professional musicians or upon performances of an extraordinary and exceptional kind, such as have lately been introduced into these con-

---

[1] Reading πρὸς μὲν τὰς μαθήσεις ἤδη, πρὸς δὲ τὰς χρήσεις ὕστερον.

tests and from them into the educational curriculum, [1]and if they carry their musical studies only so far as to acquire a capacity for enjoying noble melodies and rhythms and not merely that general effect of Music which is enjoyed by some of the lower animals, as well as by a number of slaves and children, no less than by men.

Musical in-
struments.

We see from this too the sort of instruments to be used. It is not proper to introduce into education the flute or any other instrument which requires professional skill, like a cithern or other instrument of the kind, but only such as will make them apt recipients either of musical education or of education generally. And further the flute is an instrument of a strongly exciting rather than of an ethical character and should consequently be employed only upon occasions when the object of the audience is the purging of the emotions rather than the improvement of the mind. We may add, as an incidental objection to the use of the flute in education, that flute-playing prevents the use of the voice. It was with justice then that our forefathers banished the flute from the education of the young and of persons of free birth, although they had originally employed it. For [2]as the increase of wealth afforded them better opportunities of leisure and quickened the moral aspirations of their souls, the result was, even before the Persian wars and still more after them in the full flush of their achievements, that they

[1] Placing a comma, instead of a full stop, after παιδείαν and omitting καὶ before τὰ τοιαῦτα.

[2] Reading γινόμενοι.

essayed every kind of education, drawing no line any-
where but making experiments in all directions. Thus
the use of the flute among other things was introduced into the educational curriculum. For there
was a master of a chorus at Lacedaemon who himself
accompanied his chorus upon the flute, and at Athens
the use of the flute became so popular that the
majority of free persons may be said to have had
some knowledge of it, as we see from the tablet set
up by Thrasippus on the occasion when he acted as
master of the chorus for Ecphantides. At a later
date however the flute was rejected upon actual trial,
when it was possible to form a better opinion of what
was or was not conducive to the practice of virtue.
The same was the case with not a few antique instruments, e.g. [1]dulcimers, psalteries and others which
serve merely to tickle the ears of the audience, sept-
angles, triangles, sackbuts and all such as require
manual dexterity. The old legend about the flute
has much truth in it. It is said that Athene discovered [2]the flute and afterwards flung it away. It
is not a bad idea that the goddess did so in consequence of the disgust she felt at the disfigurement
of her countenance *by flute-playing ;* but at the same
time the reason is more likely to have been that

---

[1] I do not think it is possible to find English equivalents for
the names of instruments given in the text. They seem to have
been all stringed instruments, some of native Greek invention
like the βάρβιτος, and others, like the σαμβύκη, borrowed from
foreign nations. The names τρίγωνα and ἑπτάγωνα are evidently
descriptive of shape.

[2] τοὺς αὐλούς. The Plural, as it was usual for the Greek performer to play two flutes.

education in flute-playing has no intellectual value, as it is to Athene that we ascribe science and art.

Professional musicians.   Professional education then, whether in respect of the instruments or of the execution, we reject, meaning by "professional" such as is suitable to public contests. For in it the object of the performer is not the promotion of his own virtue but the pleasure of his audience, and this a vulgar sort of pleasure. Accordingly we regard such execution as unworthy of free men and as being rather a species of hired labour. It is a fact too that *the professionals* sink to the level of mechanics, as the object which they have in view in the choice of their end is a debased one. For the low character of the audience usually necessitates a *corresponding* variety in the Music; and hence a *deteriorating* effect is produced not only upon the character of the musicians, whose study is directed solely to the pleasure of the audience, but upon their bodies too by the *ungraceful* movements which they make *in playing*.

CHAP. VII.   There still remains the question of harmonies and
Harmonies and rhythms.   rhythms. [1]We have to consider *firstly* whether it is proper to make use of all the different harmonies and rhythms indiscriminately or to draw a distinction between them, secondly whether we are to adopt the same distinction [2]or some other in the case of persons who are serious students of Music for educational purposes, and thirdly, as Music consists of melody and rhythms and we ought not to be ignorant of the educational value of either, whether the preference

[1] Omitting καὶ πρὸς παιδείαν.
[2] Reading θήσομεν ἤ τινα ἕτερον, τρίτον δὲ κ τ.λ.

should be given to melodious or to rhythmical Music.
Believing then that the subject is fully and excel-
lently treated by some musicians and on the philosophical side by such philosophers as have a practical
acquaintance with musical education, we will leave
anyone who chooses to refer to these authorities for a
detailed discussion of particular points and will at
present determine them from a legislative point of
view, contenting ourselves with a mere outline of the
subject.

We accept the classification of melodies adopted Classifica-
tion of
by some philosophical writers, who distinguish them melodies.
as ethical, practical and enthusiastic, and hold that
different harmonies are in their nature appropriate to
the several different [1]melodies. Further we maintain
that Music should not be employed for a single benefit
only but for several, i.e. as a means of education, as a
purgative of the emotions—what we mean when we
speak of purging the emotions, although here stated
only in general terms, will be explained more clearly
hereafter in our [2]treatise on Poetry—and thirdly [3]for
the relaxation or recreation of the tense condition
of the soul. It is evident then that, although it is
right to make use of all the different harmonies,
they ought not all to be used in the same manner,
but the harmonies of the most strictly ethical
character for educational purposes, and the practical and enthusiastic harmonies when we listen to
the performances of others. It is to be observed that

---

[1] Reading μέλος.

[2] The passage referred to is *Poet.* ch. 6.

[3] Omitting πρὸς διαγωγήν.

an emotion, which is strongly incident to one soul, is
existent in all, although they differ in their degree of
it, whether it be compassion or fear or even enthusiasm; for there are some people who are exceedingly liable to the emotion of enthusiasm. [1]And
in the case of the sacred melodies we observe that
such persons, after listening to melodies which raise
the soul to ecstasy, relapse into their normal condition, as if they had experienced a medical or
purgative treatment. The same is of course the
case with compassionate and fearful persons and
emotional persons generally, and with others in proportion as each participates in such emotions : they
all experience a sort of purging and a pleasurable
feeling of relief. Similarly melodies of a [2]practical
sort produce in men a feeling of innocent joy. Hence
it is with harmonies and melodies of this sort that
persons who practise [3]music professionally should be
set to contend. But as there are two sorts of audience, one free and cultivated, the other vulgar,
consisting of mechanics, hired labourers and the like,
the second class no less than the first requires appropriate musical contests and exhibitions for its
relaxation. And as their souls are distorted from
their natural condition, so are there *correspondingly*
corrupt forms of harmony and melodies of a strained
and artificially coloured character. A feeling of
pleasure is excited in every class of persons by what-

The pur-
ging of the
emotions.

---

[1] The ἱερὰ μέλη are apparently the same as the Ὀλύμπου
μέλη p. 137, l. 28.

[2] Reading τὰ μέλη τὰ πρακτικὰ.

[3] θεατρικὴν is not found in the best mss.

ever has an affinity to their own nature, and accordingly performers, who compete for the prize before a vulgar audience, must be allowed to employ this species of Music. As a means of education, on the other hand, the ethical melodies and the corresponding harmonies should be employed. The Dorian harmony, as we remarked before, has an ethical character; nor may we refuse to accept any other that is recommended to us by those who are versed in philosophical studies and in musical education. But Socrates in the [1] *Republic* is wrong in making an exception in favour of the Phrygian harmony, which he allows as well as the Dorian, especially when he has rejected the flute as an instrument. For the Phrygian harmony corresponds in its effects to the flute among instruments, both being of a strongly exciting and emotional nature. We may find an evidence of this fact in poetry. For all revelry and such excitement is expressed by the flute better than by any other instrument; while, if we look to harmonies, it receives its appropriate expression in the Phrygian melodies. Thus it is generally allowed that the dithyramb is a composition which requires a Phrygian melody; and of this there are various proofs adduced by those who are competent authorities upon the subject, especially the circumstance that Philoxenus failed in the attempt to set his dithyrambic poem "The Mysians" to a Dorian harmony and was driven by the nature of the case to fall back upon the appropriate Phrygian. The Dorian harmony on the contrary is recognized on all hands as preeminently

p. 239.

[1] *Republic,* III. p. 399 A.

staid and characterized by a spirit of valour. And further as it is the mean between two extremes that we always admire and regard as the proper object of our pursuit, and as the Dorian harmony stands midway between the others, it is evident that Dorian melodies are particularly suited to the education of the young. There are always two objects to be kept in view, viz. possibility and propriety; for it is such things *and such only* as are within his capacity and appropriate to his character that each individual should choose to undertake. But the conditions of possibility and propriety are determined by the ages of the persons in question. For instance, people who are old and feeble cannot easily sing the strained harmonies ; it is rather the lax ones that Nature suggests at this time of life. Accordingly there is justice in the reproach brought against Socrates by some musical authorities that [1]he rejected the lax harmonies in his educational system, regarding them as intoxicating, not in reference to the effects of intoxication *at the time*—for it rather produces a disposition to revelry—but of intoxication when the actual fit has passed away. Hence it is in view of their later or more advanced years that they should essay harmonies and melodies of this kind. And further if there is any harmony appropriate to the age of childhood in virtue of its capacity for combining propriety with culture, as seems to be particularly the property of the Lydian harmony[2]...... It

---

[1] The passage referred to is Plato *Republic*, III. p. 398 E.

[2] It can hardly be doubted that the true apodosis of the sentence has fallen out of the text. How much more has been

is evident that these are the three canons to be laid Canons of down *respecting the use of Music* in education, viz. education. that it should be of an intermediate character, that it should be within the capacity of the learner and that it should be appropriate to his age.

lost before δῆλον ὅτι τούτους ὅρους κ.τ.λ. cannot now be determined; but the whole discussion of Music as an educational agent is imperfect.

BOOK VI.

IN all the roll of arts and sciences, which are not
restricted to a single branch of a subject but are
complete treatments of some one subject as a whole,
it is the province of one and the same art or science
to consider all the questions appropriate to a given
subject, e g. *if we take the case of Gymnastic, to consider firstly* the sort of discipline which is beneficial
to particular physical constitutions ; secondly the
nature of the best discipline, as it is certain that the
best discipline is such as is appropriate to the person
who enjoys the finest constitution and is endowed
with the richest natural advantages ; and thirdly the
discipline which is uniformly beneficial to the great
majority of people taken collectively ; [1] for this is
equally a function of Gymnastic. And further if a
person is content with aspiring to something short of
his proper physical condition or scientific expertness
in athletic exercises, it is none the less the business
of the trainer or gymnastic master [2] to produce even
this inferior measure of capacity. Similarly we find

---

[1] Reading καὶ γὰρ τοῦτο τῆς γυμναστικῆς ἔργον ἐστίν.
[2] Omitting τε.

this to be the case in Medicine or Shipbuilding or Tailoring or any other art. It is evidently therefore the business of the selfsame science to consider the nature of the best polity or in other words the character of polity which would best satisfy our ideal, if there, were no impediment in external circumstances, and *secondly* the nature of the polity appropriate to particular classes of persons. For as the best polity is probably out of the reach of large numbers of people, it is right that the ¹good legislator and the true statesman should keep his eyes open not only to the absolutely best polity but also to the polity which is best under the actual conditions. We may add thirdly an assumed polity; for it is right that in the case of any given polity he should be competent to consider the means of calling it into existence and, when it has come into existence, the method of endowing it with the longest life. I am referring to the case where the conditions of a particular State are such that the polity under which it exists is not the best *nor indeed can ever be the best, as* it is unprovided with the very essentials *of the best polity,* nor again is the best which is possible in the circumstances, but some polity of an inferior kind. And besides all this it is right that he should understand the polity which is most appropriate to the mass of states, *especially* as the great majority of political writers, even if successful in their treatment of the other points, utterly miss the mark of practical utility. For it is

¹ Reading τὸν ἀγαθὸν νομοθέτην.

not only the *absolutely* best polity which is the proper
subject of consideration, but also that which is possible *in any given case* and similarly that which is comparatively easy of attainment and has a closer affinity
to the polities of all existing States. But our modern
writers either aspire to the highest polity, for which a
number of external advantages are indispensable, or,
if they describe a form more generally attainable, put
out of sight all existing forms *except the favoured one*
and pronounce a panegyric upon the Lacedaemonian
or some other polity. What we want however is to
introduce some system which the world will easily be
induced and enabled to [1]accept as an innovation upon
the existing forms ; for it is quite as troublesome a
task to amend a polity as to establish it in the first
instance, just as the task of correcting one's knowledge is quite as troublesome as that of acquiring it
at first.

The qualifi-
cations of a
statesman.
It is proper then that in addition to the points
specified *by these political writers* the true statesman
should be capable of coming to the rescue of existing
polities, as has been already said. Nor can he possibly do this, if he is unacquainted with all the various
kinds of polity. [2]*I say this*, because in our own day it
is the opinion of some writers that there is only one
kind of Democracy or Oligarchy. This however is not
the true state of the case. The eyes of the statesman
therefore should be open to all the shades of difference between the various polities and to the number

---

[1] Reading καινοτομεῖν.
[2] Reading νῦν γὰρ μίαν δημοκρατίαν κ.τ.λ.

of possible combinations; [1]and by the light of the same practical science he should discern the best laws and the laws appropriate to each form of polity, as it is the laws enacted which should be, and in fact are universally relative to the polities rather than the polities to the laws. For whereas a polity is the general system of any State in regard to the distribution of the executive offices, the supreme political authority and the end which [2]the citizens propose to themselves in their association, laws, as distinct from the institutions which express the character of the polity, are merely the conditions according to which the officers of state are to hold office and to exercise surveillance over lawbreakers. And from this we see clearly the necessity, even from a legislative point of view, of a familiarity with the differences between polities and the number *of the varieties* of each *in a general classification of polities;* for the same laws cannot be beneficial to all Oligarchies or Democracies alike, as there are several species of Democracy and Oligarchy rather than a single species only.

As at the beginning of our treatise we divided [3]polities into the normal polities, which are three in number, viz. Kingship, Aristocracy and Polity, and the perversions of these which are also three, viz. Tyranny the perversion of Kingship, Oligarchy of Aristocracy and Democracy of Polity; as Aristocracy and Kingship have been already discussed—for the consideration of the best polity is nothing else than a

CHAP. II
The ar-
rangement
of the
Politics.
pp. 119, 120.

---

[1] The construction becomes clearer, if the full stop after ποσαχῶς is changed to a colon.

[2] Reading ἑκάστοις.   [3] Omitting περί.

discussion of the polities which bear these names, as in theory each of them is constituted on the basis of virtue furnished with external means—and as further the points of difference between Aristocracy and Kingship and the occasions when a polity is to be regarded as regal have been determined, it remains to describe the form which is called by the general name of all polities, *viz. the Polity,* and the remaining forms, Oligarchy, Democracy and Tyranny.

The comparative badness of the perverted polities. It is evident, if we consider these perversions, which is the worst and which is the next worst. For the perversion of the primary or most divine form must be the worst; and as Kingship must either be a mere name and not a reality or must have its justification in the vast superiority of the reigning king, it follows that Tyranny is the form which is worst and farthest removed from a constitutional government, Oligarchy the next worst—for Aristocracy, *it must be remembered,* is widely different from Oligarchy— and Democracy the least bad. [1]An earlier writer has already expressed himself in this sense, although not from the same point of view as ours. For *he recognized a good and a bad form of each of these polities and* held that of all the polities when they are good, i.e. of good Oligarchy and the like, Democracy is the worst, but that when they are bad it is the best. We maintain on the contrary that these polities are wholly vitiated, and it is not right to speak of one Oligarchy as being better than another but only as being less bad.

---

[1] The reference is to Plato *Politicus,* pp. 302 sqq.

This discussion however we may dismiss for the present. We have now first to determine the different species of the various polities, assuming that there are several kinds of Democracy and Oligarchy, and next the polity that is most generally attainable and most desirable with the exception of the best polity and any other that is aristocratical and constituted on noble principles—I mean the polity which is suited to the great majority of States. We have then to determine among the remaining forms of polity what special form is desirable for particular people, as it is probable that in some cases Democracy is necessary rather than Oligarchy, and in others Oligarchy rather than Democracy, and next to consider the right means to be employed by one who wishes to establish these polities, i.e. the several species of Democracy and again of Oligarchy. And finally, after briefly noticing as best we may all these points, we must try to enumerate the agencies destructive and preservative of polities both generally and individually and the causes which tend especially to produce them.

The existence of a number of polities is due to the fact that in any State there are a number of parts. For in the first place all States, as we see, are composed of households; then again the population so formed necessarily consists partly of the rich, partly of the poor and partly of the middle class, and further the rich and poor may both be subdivided into soldiers and civilians. Again, one people, as we see, is agricultural, another commercial and a third mechanical. And among the upper classes themselves there are again distinctions in

CHAP. III.
The causes of a variety of polities.

respect of their wealth and the magnitude of their
property, as e. g. in regard to keeping a stud of
horses ; for it is only persons of large property who
can easily afford to keep horses. It was thus that
in older times in any State, whose military strength
resided in its cavalry, there was always an oligarchical
government. Cavalry, it may be observed, was used
in wars with border States as e. g. by the Eretrians,
the Chalcidians, the Magnetians on the Maeander
and many other Asiatic peoples. To the differences
of wealth may be added differences in race or virtue
or in anything else of the same kind which has been
described as a part of a State in our discussion of
pp 182 sqq. Aristocracy, where we defined the number of parts
necessary to the existence of a State, as political
rights are sometimes enjoyed by all these parts and
at other times by only a smaller or larger number
of them. It is evident then that there must be a
number of polities differing specifically from one
another, as there is a specific difference between
these their parts. For a polity is simply the system
of the offices of State, and this is distributed by
all the citizens among themselves either in virtue of
the superior power of the privileged class or of some
qualification common to both alike—I mean e. g. in
virtue of the power of the poor *in numbers* or of the
rich *in wealth* or of some power which they possess
in common. It follows as a necessary consequence
that there is a number of different polities equal to
the number of systems dependent upon the superiori-
The two ties or differences of the members of a State. But it
principal
polities. seems that there are principally two polities, that as

in the case of winds some are described as northerly, others as southerly and all the rest as perversions or variations of these, so the polities may be reduced to two viz. Democracy and Oligarchy. For Aristocracy is reckoned as a species of Oligarchy, being regarded as in a certain sense an Oligarchy, and the so-called Polity is reckoned as a Democracy, as among winds the West wind is called a species of North wind and the East wind a species of South wind. It is much the same with harmonies according to some authorities, who reckon only two species, the Dorian and Phrygian, and describe all the other combinations as either Dorian or Phrygian. [1]This then is the usually accepted view of polities. But it is not so true or good as our classification, according to which there are only two polities or even only a single polity constituted on noble principles, and all the rest are perversions of the best polity, corresponding to the variations of the well-tempered harmony *in Music*, the more intense and despotic polities being oligarchical and the lax and mild polities democratical.

The true classification of polities.

But it is not right to follow the fashion of some contemporary writers in defining Democracy without any qualification as a polity in which the masses are supreme. For it is equally the case in an Oligarchy and in any other polity whatever that the supreme power is in the hands of the greater part. Nor again may we define Oligarchy without any qualification as a polity in which the Few are supreme. For sup-

CHAP. IV.
The definition of Democracy and Oligarchy.

---

[1] Reading μάλιστα μὲν οὖν εἰώθασιν.

pose that the gross population of a State amounted
to thirteen hundred, of whom one thousand were
rich, and that the thousand rich persons did not
allow any share of rule to the three hundred poor,
although they were personally free and similar to the
thousand in every respect except riches; nobody
would maintain that the polity of this State was
democratical. Similarly suppose the case of a small
number of poor persons who are yet stronger than
a larger number of the rich; here again nobody
would describe such a polity as an Oligarchy, if the
mass of the population being rich were excluded, *as
they are ex hypothesi*, from the honours of State.
It is more correct then to say that the polity is a
Democracy when the supreme power is in the hands
of the free citizens, and an Oligarchy when it is in the
hands of the rich, [1]and that it is only an accidental
circumstance that the former constitute [2]a majority
and the latter a minority of the population, as there
are many free persons in the world and only a few
persons of property. For *on the assumption that it
is the supremacy of the Few which makes an Oligarchy* it would follow that, if the distribution of the
offices of State among the citizens were regulated by
stature, as [3]according to some authorities is the case
in Æthiopia, or by personal beauty, the polity would
be an Oligarchy; for the number of beautiful or tall
persons is small. *This however is evidently out of*

----

[1] There should be a comma, instead of a full stop, after
πλούσιοι.

[2] Reading πλείους.

[3] See Herodotus III. ch. 20. Cp. p. 118, l. 25.

the question. But at the same time even wealth and personal freedom taken alone are not sufficient as the determining characteristics of Democracy and Oligarchy. On the contrary, as both these polities include a variety of members, it is proper to draw a further distinction and to lay down on the one hand that the polity is not a Democracy, if a minority of simply free citizens rule a majority[1] as e.g. at Apollonia upon the Ionian sea and at Thera, in both which States the civic honours were engrossed by the families which claimed a preeminent nobility as having been the original founders of the colonies, although they were numerically few and their subjects were many, and on the other hand that it is not an [2]Oligarchy, if the rich rule solely in virtue of their numerical superiority, as was formerly the case at Colophon, where the majority of the citizens had acquired a large property before the era of the Lydian war. The truth is that a Democracy exists when the authority is in the hands of the free and poor who are in a majority, and an Oligarchy when it is in the hands of the propertied or noble class who are in a minority.

Thus the fact that there are more polities than one and the reason of the fact have been stated. We have now to show that there are more than the two we have mentioned, *viz. Democracy and Oligarchy,* and to describe the nature and the cause of each, starting from the consideration which has been already adduced. We all allow that every State con-

p. 255.

---

[1] Omitting καὶ μὴ ἐλευθέρων.
[2] Reading ὀλιγαρχία.

17—2

The parts of a State. tains not one part only, but several. Accordingly we must proceed in the same way as if it were our purpose to ascertain the different species of animal. We should begin in that case by specifying the organs indispensable to any animal; I mean certain of the organs of sense, the organs which receive and digest food, viz. the mouth and stomach, and also the members by means of which each animal moves. Supposing that this is an exhaustive list of the different organs, and that of each organ there are different kinds, I mean, supposing that there are several kinds of mouth, stomach and organs of sensation as well as of the members which are organs of movement, we see that the number of possible combinations of these organs will necessarily produce several kinds of animals, *although the number of different species will not be unlimited,* as the same animal cannot have several different kinds of mouth or ears. Hence if we take all the possible combinations of these organs, they will produce different species of animals, and there will be as many different species of animals as there are combinations of the organs necessary to their existence. It is the same with the polities in question; for States like animals are composed not of a single part, but of several, as has been more than once remarked. One of these parts is the class which is concerned with the supply of food, viz. the husbandmen as they are called. A second is the so-called mechanical class, viz. the class [1]which is occupied with such arts as are indispensable to the administration of a State, whether they are absolutely necessary

---

[1] Reading ἔστι δὲ τοῦτο τὸ περὶ τὰς τέχνας.

to its existence or conducive to luxury and refinement of life. A third is the commercial class, by which I mean the class that devotes itself to the sale and purchase of goods and to business both wholesale and retail. There is fourthly the class of hired labourers; fifthly, the military class which is quite as indispensable as the foregoing, if the citizens are not to be the slaves of any assailants. *And this power of self-defence is absolutely requisite;* for it is an impossibility, we may say, that a State which is naturally the slave of others should deserve to be called a State at all, as independence is a characteristic of a State, and slaves are destitute of independence. Hence this subject has been treated inadequately although ingeniously in the [1]*Republic* of Plato. Socrates there says that a State is composed of four absolutely indispensable elements which he specifies as a weaver, a husbandman, a cobbler and a builder; but at a later point, as if he felt the insufficiency of these four for independence, he adds to the number a smith, people to take charge of the necessary live stock, and still further a merchant and a retail trader; and all these elements collectively form the complement of the State in its primary-form, as if it were [2]only the necessaries of life which are the objects of the constitution of any State, and refinement or nobleness were not more indispensable to a State than cobblers or husbandmen. The military class he does not assign to the State until the increase of its territory and its

Criticism of the view of Socrates.

---

[1] *Republic* II. p. 369 B sqq.

[2] Reading τῶν ἀναγκαίων γε and below ἀλλ' οὐ τοῦ καλοῦ μᾶλλον δεομένην σκυτέων τε καὶ γεωργῶν.

contiguity to that of a neighbouring people have
landed the citizens in war. But it may fairly be
objected that among his four associates or whatever
the number may be, there must be somebody to pronounce and adjudge justice. And on the same principle as we should regard the soul as being more
properly a member of an animal than the body, so it
is right to regard the corresponding classes in the
State, viz. the military class, the class which is invested with the administration of legal justice, and
thirdly, the deliberative body—for deliberation is a
task which demands political intelligence—as being
members of a State in a higher sense than the classes
which merely serve to supply the necessary wants of
life. Nor does it make any difference to our argument whether these functions are appropriated to
particular classes or are united in the same hands,
as is often the case; for it happens not infrequently
that the soldiers are at the same time the husbandmen. Thus as the classes which constitute the soul of
the State, as well as those which constitute its body
are to be regarded as members of the State, it is evident that the military class is necessarily a member[1].

.   .   .   .   The seventh class consists of those

---

[1] It would appear that some words have fallen out of the text
after μόριον τῆς πόλεως. For after mentioning five parts or elements
of a State (p. 151, ll. 7—18) Aristotle is led into a digression
upon the necessity of a military class and a criticism of the views
put forward by Socrates in the *Republic* (p. 151, l. 19 – p. 152, l. 10);
then he resumes his enumeration of the parts of a State with the
words ἕβδομον δὲ τὸ ταῖς οὐσίαις λειτουργοῦν. A comparison of
the present passage with Bk. IV. ch. 8 suggests the insertion of
ἕκτον δὲ οἱ ἱερεῖς.

whose properties enable them to bear the public burdens, or in other words of the rich. The eighth comprises the executive magistrates who serve the State in the different public offices, as officers are indispensable to a State. It is necessary therefore that there should be a class of persons who are capable of holding office and who render this service to the State either continuously or by a system of alternation. There remain the classes which we incidentally defined just now, viz. the body ¹which is to deliberate, and the body which is to adjudicate upon questions of justice between litigants. And as all the functions we have named ought to be discharged and nobly and justly discharged in a State, it is indispensable that there should be also a class of public men endowed with virtue.

It may be observed, that all the faculties we have described may with one exception be often united in the same hands. Thus the same persons may constitute the military, agricultural, and artisan classes, and also the deliberative and judicial bodies. All classes too affect to possess the requisite virtue and consider themselves competent to fill nearly all the public offices. But it is impossible that the same persons should be poor and rich. And hence it is supposed that these two classes, viz. the rich and the poor, are in a preeminent sense parts of a State. And further, as the one class is almost always numerically small, while the other is numerically large, it appears that these are the really antagonistic mem-

---

¹ Reading τὸ βουλευσόμενον καὶ κρινοῦν.

bers of a State. The result is that the character of
all existing polities is determined by the predominance of one or other of these classes, and it is the
common opinion that there are two polities and two
only, viz. Democracy and Oligarchy.

pp. 255 sqq.   We have already stated that there are several
The cause of polities and have indicated the causes. We have
varieties of
Democracy now to show that there are several kinds of De-
and
Oligarchy. mocracy and Oligarchy. But the remarks we have
already made serve to elucidate this point. For
there are various classes among the commons as well
as among the so-called upper orders. One class of
commons is composed of husbandmen, another of
artisans, a third of merchants who are occupied with
the purchase and sale of goods, a fourth of seafar-
ing people, whether engaged in war, business, transport service or fishing, for each of these classes is
numerous in different places, as e.g. fishermen at
Tarentum and Byzantium, marines at Athens, traders
in Ægina or Chios, and persons engaged in transport
service in Tenedos. To these we may add manual
labourers and all who possess so little property
as to be incapable of leisure, as well as all who are
free but not descended from citizens on both sides,
and any other similar class of population. Among
the upper classes on the other hand, the differences
consist in wealth, nobility, virtue, culture, and other
recognized characteristics not less distinctive than
these.

Democracy according to the primary conception
of it is the polity which is preeminently based upon
equality. According to the law of Democracy as so

conceived equality implies that the poor should not
be in any sense ¹rulers rather than the rich, that neither the one party nor the other should be supreme
but that both should stand upon the same footing.
For if we grant that freedom and equality are, as
some suppose, especially found in a Democracy, they
will best be realized where all the citizens have the
largest share of political rights upon equal terms.
But as the commons form a numerical majority and
the will of the majority is supreme, it follows that
the polity in which these conditions are realized
must be a Democracy. ²One, species of Democracy The various
then is that in which eligibility to the offices of State species of
is dependent upon a property qualification, but the
qualification is a low one and, as anyone who acquires the amount of property enjoys the privilege of
eligibility, so anyone who loses it ceases to be eligible.
There is a second species of Democracy in which all
the citizens who are not liable to any objection *on
the score of birth* are eligible to office but the law is
supreme. A third is that in which everybody is eligible to the offices of State, provided only that he is a
citizen, *i. e. is actually in the enjoyment of the rights
of citizenship,* but the law is supreme. There is yet The
another species which is similar to the last in all extreme
respects except that the people rather than the law is
here supreme. This is the case when it is popular
decrees which are the supreme or final authorities,
and not the law. It is the demagogues who are
to blame for this state of things. For in States

---

¹ Reading ἄρχειν.　　² Omitting τοῦτο, ἄλλο δὲ.

which enjoy a democratical polity regulated by law
no demagogue ever makes his appearance, and it is
the best citizens who enjoy the posts of honour. But
it is where the laws are not supreme that demagogues appear. For the commons in such a State
are converted into a monarch, i. e. into an individual
composed of many other individuals; for the supreme
power is vested in the many, not indeed as individuals but collectively. What is the nature of the "mul-
"titude of lords," which in the language of [1]Homer is
"no blessing," whether it is this or a number of rulers
exercising individual authority, is a question involved
in obscurity. But in any case the commons whom we
are supposing aspire in virtue of their monarchical
character to exercise monarchical power, as being
exempted from the control of the law; they become
despotic and consequently pay high honour to sycophants, and in fact a Democracy of this description is
analogous to Tyranny among monarchical forms of
government. Thus in both there is the same character, in both an exercise of despotic rule over the
better classes; the popular decrees in the one case
answer to the edicts *of the tyrant* in the other, and the
demagogues and sycophants are the same and correspond. Nor is there any class so influential as the sycophants and demagogues in their respective spheres, the
former in the court of tyrants and the latter in the
kind of Democracy which I have described. It is the
demagogues who are responsible for the supremacy
of the popular decrees rather than of the laws, as they

[1] *Iliad* ii. 204.

always refer everything to the commons. *And they
do so*, because the consequence is an increase of their
own power, if the commons control all affairs, and
they themselves control the judgment of the commons, as it is their guidance that the commons
always follow. Another *circumstance which leads to
the last form of Democracy* is that all who have any
complaint against the officers of State argue that the
judicial power ought to be vested in the commons;
and as the commons gladly entertain the [1]indictment,
the result is that the authority of all the offices of
State is seriously impaired. It would seem a just
criticism to assert that this kind of Democracy is not
a constitutional government at all, as constitutional
government is impossible without the supremacy of
laws. For it is right that the law should be supreme
universally and the officers of State only in particular
cases, [2]if the government is to be regarded as constitutional. And as Democracy is, *as we have seen*, a
form of polity, it is evident that the constitution, in
which all business is administered by popular decrees, is not even a Democracy in the strict sense of
the term, as it is impossible that any popular decree
should be capable of universal application.

The various species of Democracy may be thus
determined.

Among the species of Oligarchy the first is [3]one in
which a property qualification is the condition of eligibility to the offices of State, but it is only so high that

---

[1] Read πρόσκλησιν.

[2] Reading καὶ ταύτην πολιτείαν κρίνειν.

[3] Reading ἐν μὲν τὸ ἀπὸ τιμημάτων κ.τ.λ.

the poor who are excluded from office may form a majority of the population, and everyone who acquires the amount of property enjoys full political privileges. Another species is when eligibility to office is dependent on a high property qualification and the officers themselves elect to the vacancies. In this case, if the election takes place from among the whole body of qualified citizens, the system may be regarded as tending towards an Aristocracy, but if it is confined to particular classes, as *essentially* oligarchical. A third species of Oligarchy is one in which a son succeeds to his father's office, *i.e. is based upon the principle of heredity;* a fourth one in which the same hereditary principle exists, and the supreme authority rests with the Executive and not with the law. This last species of Oligarchy is the counterpart of Tyranny among monarchical forms of government and of the extreme form of Democracy, as we defined it, among Democracies and is commonly described as a Dynasty.

There are thus all these various species of Oligarchy and Democracy. But it would not be right to ignore the fact that it happens in a considerable number of States that, while the polity as expressed in the laws is not democratical, the [1]habit and tendency of the citizens produce a democratical spirit in the administration, and so conversely in other cases that, while the polity as expressed in the laws is comparatively democratical, it is from the tendency and habits of the citizens more oligarchical in its

---

[1] Reading ἔθος.

administration. And this is especially the case after political revolutions, as men do not pass easily from one political régime to another but are content in the first instance with petty encroachments upon the privileges of their rivals, so that the laws which existed before the revolution continue in force, although the revolutionary party has got the upper hand.

That this is an exhaustive classification of the different species of Democracy and Oligarchy is sufficiently proved by the nature of facts we have alleged. For it is inevitable that political privileges should be enjoyed either by all the classes of the commons as we have specified them or by some of them only.

Chap. VI. Recapitulation of the species of Democracy and Oligarchy.

This being the case, whenever it is the agricultural class or in other words the class possessed of a moderate property which enjoys the supreme authority in the polity, the administration is based upon an observance of law. For as an agricultural population is obliged to work for its living and is incapable of a mere life of leisure, they bow their necks to the law and content themselves with holding only such meetings of the Assembly as are indispensable. But political privileges in this polity are open to any inhabitant of the State upon his acquiring the legally determined property qualification[1]. The reason of these conditions is that the absolute exclusion of any individual from political privileges is a mark of Oligarchy; while on the other hand the possibility of leisure is out of the question, if there is not an adequate pecuniary income. This then is one species

---

[1] Omitting διὸ πᾶσι τοῖς κτωμένοις ἔξεστι μετέχειν.

of Democracy, and such are the circumstances which give rise to it. There is a second species based upon the next principle of eligibility. For political privileges may be open theoretically to any inhabitant against whom no objection can be brought on the score of his descent, although they are not practically exercised by anyone, unless he is able to enjoy a life of leisure. The result is that in this second form of Democracy the laws are supreme owing to the want´ of pecuniary means among the citizens. The third species is one in which political privileges are open to all the inhabitants, provided only that they are of free birth, although they are prevented from actually exercising them by the reason alleged in the last case, *viz. want of means*, so that in this polity too the law is necessarily supreme. The fourth species of Democracy is the one which was chronologically developed last in States. For it results from the great increase in the size of States as compared with their original dimensions and from the accession of large pecuniary resources that not only do all the inhabitants theoretically enjoy political privileges in consequence of the predominant influence of the masses, but they actually exercise them in the conduct of political business, as even the poor are enabled by the pay they receive to enjoy the leisure *necessary to political life*. And indeed it is a population of this kind which has the largest amount of leisure; for they are not impeded in any way by the management of their private affairs as is the case with the rich, who are thus frequently prevented from attending the Assembly or the Courts of Law. The cousequence is that it is the mass of the poor rather than the laws that become the supreme authority in the polity.

So much for the number and character of the species of Democracy as determined by the force of the circumstances we have described.

We come now to those of Oligarchy. When there is a considerable number of people possessing an amount of property which is comparatively small or at the most not very large, this is the first species of Oligarchy, one in which anybody who acquires the amount of property is entitled to the exercise of political privileges and in which, as there is a large number of members of the governing class, it is a necessary consequence that the supremacy resides not in human beings but in the law. For the more widely the citizens are removed from monarchical government, and the more nearly it is the case that the amount of property which they possess is not so large as to enable them to enjoy leisure [1]without attending to business or so small that they require to be supported at the expense of the State, the more certainly will they approve the supremacy of the law in their case rather than their own supremacy. If on the other hand the propertied class is smaller than in the last case, and the requisite amount of property larger, the second species of Oligarchy is realized. For the increase of their resources leads them to aspire to a proportionate increase of their power; and the result is that they

---

[1] Reading ἀμελοῦντες.

exercise the right of coopting the members of the
governing body from the ¹masses and, as they have
not yet attained sufficient strength to dispense with
the authority of law, they accommodate the law to
the general principle of the polity. If again they
intensify the form of polity by still further diminishing the number of the governing body and augmenting the requisite amount of property, they arrive at
the third stage of Oligarchy, in which not only are
the offices of State in the hands of the privileged
class, but the tenure of office is regulated by a law
which prescribes that at the death of the parents the
children shall succeed to their places. But when the
accumulation of vast properties and the presence of a
numerous *clientèle* leads to an exaggerated intensification *of the oligarchical principle,* a dynastic government of the kind thus constituted approaches closely
to a Monarchy, and the supreme authority is vested
in human beings rather than in the law. This is
the fourth species of Oligarchy, the counterpart of
the latest development of Democracy.

CHAP. VII.   Apart from Democracy and Oligarchy there are
still two forms of polity or constitutional government,
one of which is generally recognized and has been
mentioned in this book as one species of the four
acknowledged polities, viz., Monarchy, Oligarchy,
Democracy, and fourthly the so-called Aristocracy.
But there is a fifth which is called by the general
name of all polities, viz., a Polity, although from the
infrequency of its actual realization writers who en-

---

¹ Reading ἐκ τῶν πολλῶν.

deavour to enumerate the species of polities pass it·
over and confine themselves, like Plato in the books of
his *Republic*, to the usual four.

Properly speaking we should confine the name of Aristocracy·
Aristocracy to the form of polity described in the early
part of our treatise. For the only polity which in jus- The strict
definition of
tice deserves the name of Aristocracy is that in which the term.
the citizens are the best persons in an absolute sense,
according to the standard of virtue and not in reference·
to any arbitrary definition of goodness. For it is here
and here only that the good man and the good citizen
are absolutely the same; whereas in every other polity
the goodness of the good is relative to their own polity.
However there is a class of polities which present cer- Its popular
use.
tain points of difference as compared with oligarchical
polities on the one hand[1] and with the so-called Polity
on the other, as in them the elections to office are not
determined by wealth only but also by virtue. This
form of polity differs both from Polity in the strict
sense and from Oligarchy, and is called aristocratical.
It arises from the fact that even in States which do
not treat the promotion of virtue as a matter of public
interest there are still certain persons whose name
stands high and who are generally regarded as the
better classes. Any polity then in which regard is
paid to wealth, virtue and numbers, as at Carthage, is
aristocratical; so too is any polity in which regard is
paid to two of these only, viz., to virtue and numbers as in the Lacedaemonian polity[2], and there is
a fusion of the two elements, numbers and virtue.

---

[1] Omitting καὶ καλοῦνται ἀριστοκρατίαι.
[2] There should be a comma after οἷον ἡ Λακεδαιμονίων.

There are thus two species of Aristocracy besides the
primary or best polity; and we may reckon as a third
species all the forms of the so-called Polity which
have rather an inclination to Oligarchy.

CHAP. VIII.   It remains for us to speak of the form specially
called Polity and of Tyranny. We have adopted this
order, although neither the Polity nor anyone of the
forms of Aristocracy just described is properly a perversion, because in strict truth they all fall short of
the absolutely normal polity and consequently are
placed in the same catalogue with the perversions, and
the perversions properly so-called are perversions of
p. 120.   these, *i.e. perversions in the second degree*, as we said
at the outset. And it is reasonable to discuss Tyranny
last as being of all polities the least worthy to be called
a polity or constitutional government, and it is only
with polities that our treatise is concerned.

Polity.   Having then stated the justification of our arrangement, we have now to speak of the Polity. Its essential character will be clearer after our determination
of the features of Oligarchy and Democracy; for a
Polity may be described in general terms as a fusion
The   of Oligarchy and Democracy. It is the fashion how-
distinction
between   ever to assign the name of Polity to such forms only
Polity and
Aristocracy.   of the fusion as incline to Democracy, and of Aristocracy rather to such as incline to Oligarchy, inasmuch as culture and nobility, *which are the characteristics of an Aristocracy*, are more usually the con-
comitants of wealth. Another reason *for regarding
as aristocratical the forms of fusion which have a tendency to Oligarchy* is the assumption that the rich are
in possession of the advantages for which crimes are

usually committed, *and are therefore likely to lead
virtuous lives;* hence they are designated the gentle
or upper classes. And thus as it is the purport of
Aristocracy to assign the superiority to the best citizens, it is held that the citizens in Oligarchies are
also likely to be the gentle classes. But it may be
said to be an impossibility [1]that a State should be
well-ordered, if it is governed not by the best but by
the lower classes, and similarly that a State should be
under the government of the best, if it is not well-
ordered. Good order however does not consist in the
mere enactment of good laws, if they are not obeyed.
Hence we must distinguish two kinds of good order,
one consisting in the obedience of the citizens to the
existing laws, and the other in the wise enactment of
the laws by which they abide; for it is possible to
obey bad laws as well as good ones. But this wise
enactment of the laws may take two forms; they may
be either the best laws possible to the citizens in
question or the best absolutely. It seems that Aristocracy consists principally in the distribution of the
honours of State according to virtue. (For the principle of Aristocracy is virtue, of Oligarchy wealth and
of Democracy freedom; but the definition that the
will of the majority is supreme is true of all, as it is
the case in Oligarchy and Aristocracy no less than in
Democracy that the will of the greater part of those
who enjoy full political privileges is supreme[2].) In the

---

[1] Reading τὸ εὐνομεῖσθαι τὴν μὴ ἀριστοκρατουμένην πόλιν ἀλλὰ
πονηροκρατουμένην.

[2] The brackets mark the parenthetical nature of the sentence,
which is not necessary to the progress of the argument.

great majority of States then it is the species which is
really a Polity that is called an ¹Aristocracy; *it is
really a Polity*, because the fusion of rich and poor
aims merely at *the representation of* wealth and freedom, *but it is generally called an Aristocracy*, because
the rich are in fact popularly regarded as occupying
the position of the gentle classes. But as there are
three things, viz. freedom, wealth and virtue, which
claim to be the standard of equality in a polity—for
the fourth or nobility, as it is called, is a necessary
concomitant of the last two, being nothing else than
²ancestral virtue and wealth—it is evident that, while
the fusion of the two elements, the rich and the poor,
ought to be called a Polity, that of the three deserves
the name of Aristocracy more than any other polity,
except the genuine or primary form.

It has been stated then that there are other
species of polity besides Monarchy, Democracy and
Oligarchy. It is clear too what is the character of
these several species, what are the points of difference
between the forms of Aristocracy and between Aristocracy on the one hand and the various forms of Polity
on the other, and how nearly they are related to one
another.

CHAP. IX.
The consti-
tution of a
Polity.
As a sequel to these remarks we have now to
describe the manner of creating the so-called Polity
as distinct from Democracy and Oligarchy and the
method of setting it up as a constitution. This will
be made clear at once by a simple statement of the
characteristics of Democracy and Oligarchy; for we

¹ Reading καλεῖται ἀριστοκρατία.
² Reading ἀρετὴ καὶ πλοῦτος ἀρχαῖος.

have only to ascertain the points of distinction between them and then to take the corresponding half, so to say, of each and put the two together.

But there are three principles of this combination or fusion. The first consists in the adoption of both the institutions [1] of the two parties, *viz. the Oligarchs and Democrats.* Take for instance the question of attendance in the Courts of Law. It is customary in Oligarchies to inflict a fine upon the rich for non-attendance but not to give the poor any fee *for attendance,* and in Democracies on the other hand to pay the poor but not to inflict a fine upon the rich. The combined or intermediate system is a union of both and is therefore appropriate to a Polity, as consisting in a fusion of the two principles. This then is one method of combination. Another consists in taking a mean between the systems of the two parties. Thus if we take the privilege of attendance in the public Assembly, in the one case there is no property qualification required or it is a very small one, and in the other it is large; the combined system is not to adopt either of these qualifications but to strike a mean between the two. A third method is to adopt parts of both systems, i.e. part of the oligarchical and part of the democratical law. For instance, if the appointment of the offices of State by lot is, as is generally supposed, democratical, while the appointment by suffrage is oligarchical, if it is democratical not to require a property qualification and oligarchical to require it, then the aristocratical

---

[1] Reading ἃ ἑκάτεροι νομοθετοῦσιν.

or political system is to take part from each of the
two polities, viz. to take from Oligarchy the system of
election by suffrage and from Democracy the absence
of a property qualification.

The cri-
terion of a
Polity.

And as this is the method of fusing the two
polities, Democracy and Oligarchy, so the criterion of
a good fusion is the possibility of calling the same
polity a Democracy and an Oligarchy; for it is evident
that the cause of this uncertainty in language is the
success of the fusion. It is in fact a general characteristic of the mean that the two extremes are dis-
cernible in it. This is just the case with the Lacedaemonian polity. There are many people who
endeavour to describe it as a Democracy because of
the many democratical elements in its constitution.
We may instance first the education of the children.
The children of the rich are brought up in the same
way as those of the poor and receive an education
which would not be beyond the children of poor
parents. And the same is true of the years succeeding childhood, and again afterwards when they
reach man's estate ; there is no distinction between
rich and poor. So too they all fare alike in the common meals, and the rich wear a dress which any poor
man would be able to procure. Another *democratical
feature* is that of the two chief offices of State to the
one the commons elect and to the other they are
themselves eligible ; for they elect the Senate and
are themselves eligible to the Ephoralty. Others
again call the Lacedaemonian polity an Oligarchy
because of its numerous oligarchical elements, e. g.
the appointment of all the officers of State by suffrage

instead of by lot, the concentration in a few hands
of the powers of life and death and exile, and many
other similar features. Where the fusion is successful
it is proper that the polity should appear to be both
an Oligarchy and a Democracy and to be neither, and
further that it should owe its preservation to internal rather than to external causes, and to internal
causes [1]not merely in the sense that the party which
is anxious for its preservation should form a majority,
as this may be the case even in a bad polity, but that
there should be no element of the State whatever
which is anxious for a change of polity.

The proper manner of establishing a Polity as
well as the so-called Aristocracies has now been
stated.

It remains for us, as we said, to speak of Tyranny, CHAP. X.
not that there is much to be said on the subject, but Tyranny
Its various
in order to give it its proper place in our treatise, as species.
we regard it as one among the various kinds of
polity. We entered into a discussion of the forms [p. 144 sqq.
of Kingship in the early part of our treatise, when
we were investigating Kingship in the strict sense
of the term, the advantage or disadvantage of it to
States, the nature and antecedents of the king and
the manner of instituting kingly government. There
are two species of Tyranny which we distinguished in
our investigation of Kingship ; for their character in
a certain sense approximates to Kingship and over-
laps it, inasmuch as both these forms of rule are
regulated by law. I refer to the absolute monarchs

---

[1] Omitting ἔξωθεν.

elected among some non-Greek peoples and to the
corresponding monarchs who were formerly created
among the ancient Greeks and were known as Æsym-
netes. No doubt there are certain points of difference between these two forms; but they both
approximate to Kingship in their constitutional character and the voluntary obedience of the subjects,
while they resemble a Tyranny in the despotic ¹and
wholly arbitrary nature of the rule. There is a third
species of Tyranny which may be regarded as Tyranny in the strictest sense, being the counterpart of
the absolute Kingship. A Tyranny of this kind is
necessarily realized in the form of Monarchy which
is an irresponsible ²exercise of rule over subjects, all
of whom are the equals or superiors of the·ruler,
for the personal advantage of the ruler and not of
the subjects. And hence the obedience is in this
case involuntary; for no free person submits willingly
to such rule.

Such then for the reasons alleged are the character
and number of the species of Tyranny.

CHAP. XI.   But ³what is the best polity and the best life for
The best
average   the great majority of States and persons, as tested
polity.   by the standard not of a virtue which is beyond the
attainment of ordinary human beings, nor of such an
education as requires natural advantages and the
external resources which Fortune alone can give, nor
again of the ideally constructed polity, but of such a
life as the majority of people are capable of realizing

¹ Reading δεσποτικῶς ἄρχειν καὶ κατὰ τὴν αὐτῶν γνώμην.
² Reading ἀρχή.
³ Putting a mark of interrogation after μετασχεῖν.

in a political association and such a polity as the
majority of States are capable of enjoying? For as
the so-called Aristocracies of which we recently
spoke lie in some respects beyond the reach of ordinary States and in others approximate to the Polity
in the limited sense of the term, we may speak of the
two forms, *viz. Aristocracy and Polity,* as one and
the same.

In the determination of all these questions we
may start from the same principles. If it has been
correctly stated in the [1]*Ethics* that the happy life is a
life which is unimpeded in the exercise of virtue, and
that virtue is a mean between two extremes, it follows
that the mean life, [2]viz. the attainment of the mean
condition possible to the citizens of any State, is the
best. And further the same canons of virtue and vice
necessarily hold good for a State and for its polity, as
the polity is, so to say, the life of a State.

In every State without exception there are three
parts, viz. the very rich, the very poor and thirdly the
intermediate class. As it is admitted then that the
moderate or intermediate condition is best, it is evident that the possession of Fortune's gifts in an intermediate degree is the best thing possible. For this is
the condition in which obedience to reason is easiest;
whereas one who is excessively beautiful, strong, noble
or wealthy, or on the contrary excessively poor or
weak or deeply degraded cannot easily live a life

The middle class

---

[1] The reference would seem to be to *Nicom. Eth.* VII. ch. 14,
p. 1153 B_9 sqq.; but perhaps it is rather the general doctrine of
the *Ethics* than any particular passage that Aristotle has in mind.

[2] There should be a comma after βέλτιστον.

conformable to reason. Such persons are apt in the
first case to be guilty of insolence and criminality on
a large scale, and in the second to become rogues and
petty criminals. But all crimes are the results either
of insolence or of roguery¹, both which are conditions
prejudicial to the interests of States. And further
persons, who are in the enjoyment of an extraordinary
amount of Fortune's gifts, strength, wealth, friends
and so on, have neither the disposition nor the knowledge necessary for submission to authority—a fault
which they derive from their home-training in early
years, as they are educated amidst such indulgence
that they do not get the habit of submitting ²even
to their masters—while persons who suffer from too
great deficiency of these blessings are reduced to a
state of mental degradation. Thus while the latter
do not understand how to rule, but only how to be
ruled like slaves, the former do not understand how to
submit ³to any rule, but only to exercise the rule of
slave-masters. The result is a State composed exclusively of slaves and slave-masters instead of free men,
with sentiments of envy on the one side and of contempt on the other. But such sentiments are the very
negation of friendship and political association; for
all association implies friendship, as is proved by the

---

¹ Omitting the words ἔτι δ' ἥκισθ' οὗτοι φυλαρχοῦσι καὶ βου-
λαρχοῦσι; for the "unwillingness to hold military and civil office"
is not a point that deserves mention here. If they are retained
in the text, ἀμφότερα will mean, not insolence and roguery, as
in the translation, but the disposition to commit crimes on the
one hand and the unwillingness to hold office on the other.

² Reading οὐδὲ τοῖς διδασκάλοις.

³ Reading οὐδεμίαν ἀρχήν.

fact that people do not choose even to walk on the same
road with their enemies. But in theory at least the
State is composed as far as possible of persons who
are equal and similar, and this is especially the condition of the middle class. And from this it follows
that, if we take the parts of which the State in our
conception is composed, it is a State of this kind, *viz.*
composed largely of the middle class, which enjoys
the best political constitution. Further it is this
middle class of citizens which runs the least risk of
destruction in a State. For as they do not like paupers lust after the goods of others, nor do others lust
after theirs, as paupers after the property of the rich,
they pass an existence void of peril, being neither the
objects nor the authors of conspiracies. Hence it was
a wise prayer of [1] Phocylides

> The middle class within the State
> Fares best, I ween;
> May I be neither low nor great
> But e'en between.

It is clear then that the best political association is
the one which is controlled by the middle class, and
that the only States capable of a good administration
are those in which the middle class is numerically
large and stronger, if not than both the other classes,
yet at least than either of them, as in that case the
addition of its weight turns the scale and prevents the
predominance of one extreme or the other. Accordingly it is an immense blessing to a State that the
active citizens should possess an intermediate and

---

[1] Fragment 12 in Bergk's *Poetae Lyrici Graeci.*

sufficient amount of property; for where there is a
class of extremely wealthy people on the one hand and
a class of absolute paupers on the other, the result
is either an extreme Democracy or an untempered
Oligarchy, or, as the outcome of the predominance
of either extreme, a Tyranny. For Tyranny results
from the most violent form of Democracy or from
Oligarchy, but is far less likely to result from a polity
in which the middle class is strong and the citizens all
stand much on the same level. The reason of this we
will state hereafter when we treat of the revolutions
of polities. It is evident however that the intermediate form of polity is best, as it is the only one which
is free from political disturbances. For it is where
the middle class is large that there is the least danger
of ¹disturbances and dissensions among the citizens.
And this too, viz. the largeness of the middle class, is
the reason why great States are comparatively little
liable to political disturbances; whereas in small
States it is easy to divide the whole population into
two camps, leaving no intermediate class, and all the
citizens in them are practically either poor or rich.
It is the middle class too which imparts to Democracies a more secure and permanent character than to
Oligarchies, as the middle class are more numerous
and enjoy a larger share of the honours of State in
Democracies than in Oligarchies; for if there is no
middle class, and the poor in virtue of their numbers
are preponderant, the consequence is failure and
speedy destruction of the State.

pp. 356, 360, 363.

¹ Reading στάσεις.

We may fairly regard it as an indication *of the same fact, viz. of the superiority of the middle class,* that the best legislators belong to the middle class of citizens, e.g. Solon, as is evident from his poems, Lycurgus—for he was not king—Charondas and most others.

We see too from these facts why it is that the great majority of polities are either democratical or oligarchical. The reason is that, as the middle class is generally small in them, whichever of the two other classes enjoys the superiority in any case, whether it be the propertied class or the commons, it is a party which transgresses the rule of the mean that imparts its own bias to the polity, and thereby produces either Democracy or Oligarchy. And there is the further fact that in consequence of the political disturbances and contentions between the commons on the one hand and the rich on the other whichever party happens to get the better of its opponents, instead of establishing a polity of a broad and equal kind, assumes political supremacy as a prize of the victory and sets up either a Democracy or an Oligarchy. We may add that the two States, which have attained an imperial position in Greece, having regard solely to their own respective polities always established either Democracies or Oligarchies in the different States, not out of any consideration for the interests of the States in question, but simply for their own interest. And the result of all these circumstances is that the intermediate polity is either never realized at all or only seldom and in a few States; for among all who have hitherto attained a commanding position there has

been only a single ¹individual who was prevailed upon
to restore this political system, *viz. a Polity*. And
indeed it has become a settled habit among the citizens of Greek States not even to desire the principle
of equality but to seek a position either of rule or of
patient submission to a dominant power.

The com-
parative
excellence
of different
polities.

p 264

The nature of the best polity and the reason why
it is the best are now clear. But taking the general
list of polities and remembering that according to
our ²former statement there are several varieties of
Democracy and Oligarchy, we shall not after our determination of the best polity find a difficulty in discern-
ing what kind of polity is to be placed first, second
and so on in due order according to their comparative
excellence and inferiority. For the nearer a polity is
to the best polity, the better of course it will be, and
the further it is removed from the mean, the worse it
will be, unless indeed it is tried with reference to an
arbitrary standard. And when I speak of an arbitrary
standard, I mean that there are many cases in which
one of two polities is preferable *in itself*, but the other
³may well be more advantageous to a certain State.

Chap.XII.

The polities
suitable to
particular
States.

The nature and character of the polities suited to
particular natures and characters is the next question
which we have to consider.

¹ It is impossible to determine who was the "individual" meant
by Aristotle among the ten or more different names suggested
by commentators. The language in which he describes the
Solonian polity (p. 56, ll. 8 sqq.) would lend itself to the view
that he is here referring to Solon. But ἀποδοῦναι is in favour of
Congreve's suggestion that it is the Lacedaemonian Pausanias
who was in his mind.

² Reading ἔφαμεν.   ³ Reading κωλύει.

It is necessary to begin by assuming a principle of general application, viz. that the part of the State which desires the continuance of the polity ought to be stronger than that which does not. But in every State there is a qualitative and a quantitative element. By the former I mean freedom, wealth, culture and nobility; by the latter mere numerical superiority. But it is possible that of the parts of which the State is composed the quality may belong to one and the quantity to another, e.g. that the ignoble classes may be numerically larger than the noble or the poor than the rich, but that their superiority in quantity may not be commensurate with their inferiority in quality. It is necessary therefore to institute a comparison between the two elements.

Where the numerical superiority of the poor bears the proportion we have indicated *to the qualitative superiority of the rich, i.e. is vastly superior to it*, it is natural that the polity established should be a Democracy, and that the species of Democracy should be determined by the character of the commons to whom the superiority belongs, i.e. that, if it is the agricultural population which is predominant, it should be the primary form of Democracy, if the mechanical and wage-earning population, the latest development of Democracy, and so for all the intermediate forms. Where on the other hand the superiority of the rich or upper classes in quality is greater than its inferiority in quantity, it is natural that the polity should be an Oligarchy, and as in the last case that the species of Oligarchy should be determined by the character of the oligarchical population in whom the superiority resides.

The importance of the middle class.

But the legislator in his political system ought always to secure the support of the middle class. For if the laws which he enacts are oligarchical, he should aim at *the satisfaction of* the middle class ; if democratical, he should engage their support in behalf of the laws. But it is only where the numbers of the middle class preponderate either over both the extremes or over only one of them that there is a possibility of a permanent polity. For there is no danger of a conspiracy among the rich and the poor against the middle class, as neither rich nor poor will consent to a condition of slavery[1], and if they try to find a polity which is more in the nature of a compromise, they will not discover any other than this, *viz. the polity which rests upon the middle class.* For the mutual distrustfulness *of the Oligarchs and Democrats* will prevent them from consenting to an alternation of rule. All the world over on the other hand there is nobody so thoroughly trusted as an arbitrator, and the middle class occupies a position of arbitration *between the rich and the poor.*

But the permanence of the polity will depend upon the excellence of the fusion. It is a common and serious mistake made even by those who desire to set up aristocratical polities not only to give an undue share of power to the rich but to endeavour to deceive the commons. For the spurious advantages are sure in time to produce a real evil, as the usurpations of the rich are more fatal to the polity than those of the commons.

---

[1] Omitting τοῖς ἑτέροις.

The artifices usually adopted in polities as pretexts CHAP.XIII.
to impose upon the commons are five in number, Political artifices:
having reference to the Public Assembly, the offices
of State, the Courts of Law, the possession of arms
and [1]gymnastic exercises.

In regard to the first the artifice is that, while at- (1) oligar- chical,
tendance in the Public Assembly is a privilege allowed
to all alike, the rich are liable to a fine either exclusively or to a fine of a much more serious amount for
non-attendance. In regard to the offices of State it is
that the poor enjoy the privilege of declining office,
which is not accorded to persons possessing a certain
property assessment. In regard to the Courts of Law
it is that, whereas the rich are subject to a fine for
non-attendance, the poor enjoy an immunity, or the
former are mulcted heavily and the latter only in a
small sum, as is the case in the laws of Charondas.
There are some States also in which the entire population is entitled after registration to attend the
Assembly and the Courts of Law, but if after registration they fail to attend, they are liable to a heavy fine,
the object being that the poorer citizens may be
deterred by fear of the fine from registering themselves and in consequence of not being registered
may be unable to attend the Courts of Law or the
Public Assembly. The same principle prevails in the
legislation respecting the possession of arms and
gymnastic exercises. It is a penal offence to be without arms in the case of the rich but not of the poor,
and similarly it is a penal offence in the rich but not

[1] Reading γυμνάσια.

in the poor to omit their gymnastic exercises ; and here again the object is that the former may be induced by fear of the fine to engage in such exercises and the latter having no such fear before their eyes may not engage in them.

(2) demo-
cratical,

And as ¹these artifices of legislation are oligarchical in their character, so there are counter-artifices in Democracies. Thus, *to take a single instance*, a fee is given to the poor for attendance in the Assembly and the Courts of Law, but no fine is inflicted upon the rich for non-attendance.

(3) suited to
a fusion of
Oligarchy
and Demo-
cracy.

It is evident therefore that anyone who is anxious to produce a just fusion should combine the characteristics of the two polities, *Democracy and Oligarchy*, i.e. he should fee the poor and fine the rich. This will be a means of securing the participation of all the citizens *in the business of the Assembly and the Courts of Law*, whereas in any other case the polity falls entirely into the hands of the one class or the other.

The limit of
citizenship
in a Polity.

The Polity should be exclusively in the hands of the class which possesses heavy arms ; but it is not possible to define absolutely the amount of the property assessment *requisite for the enjoyment of political privileges* and to say that it must reach a certain figure. We must rather consider what is the ²highest property assessment which in each particular case is consistent with the hypothesis that those who are admitted to the exercise of political privileges are more numerous than those who are not, and then determine it at this amount. For the poor are content

¹ Reading ὀλιγαρχικὰ τὰ σοφίσματα.
² Reading πόσον.

to keep the peace despite their exclusion from the
honours of State, if nobody insults them or despoils
them of any of their property. Not indeed that this
is an easy condition ; for it is not the case that the
members of the governing body are invariably persons
of a delicate sense of honour. And again it is the
custom of the poor on occasion of war to refuse to serve,
if in spite of their poverty they are not supplied with
the means of subsistence ; although, if the means are
given them, they consent to take the field. But there
are some States in which the Polity is in the hands
not only of all who are actually serving as heavy-
armed soldiers but of all who ever have so served
and are now past the military age ; while among the
Malians, although both these classes enjoyed political
privileges, it was only the persons actually serving in
the army who were eligible to the offices of State.

The first polity or constitutional government in Historical
Greece, which was formed after the era of the kings, succession
of polities.
included none but the military class. The original
polity of all was in the hands of the knights, as it
was the cavalry that at that time constituted military
strength and superiority. For heavy infantry is useless without organization and, as there was no such
thing as any experience or system in the organization
of infantry among the ancients, their strength resided
wholly in the cavalry. But as the different States
increased in size, and the heavy-armed soldiers acquired greater power, a larger number were admitted
to political privileges. This is the reason why the constitutions which we call Polities were called by our
forefathers Democracies, and the Polities of antiquity

19—2

were, as might be expected, oligarchical and regal
in their character; for as owing to the paucity of
inhabitants the middle class in them was not large,
their numerical and strategical insignificance inclined
them to acquiesce in a position of subjection.

We have now stated the reason why there are
varieties of polity and why there are more than the
actual names imply, there being more kinds than one
of Democracy and so on ; we have also described the
points of difference between them and the reason of
the difference, the nature of the best average polity
and the character of polity suited to particular kinds
of people.

CHAP. XIV. Let us proceed to discuss the points which naturally follow not only generally but in reference to
particular polities, taking them in order and starting
from the suitable basis of the subject.

The three
depart-
ments of a
Polity.
Every polity comprises three departments, and a
good legislator is bound to consider what is expedient
to particular polities in respect of each. For the good
order of the polity necessarily follows from the good
order of these departments, and the differences of
polities necessarily depend upon the differences in
these respects.   .

The first of the three points is [1]the nature of the
body which deliberates on affairs of State, secondly
the nature of the Executive, i.e. the offices to be created,
the extent of their jurisdiction and the right system
of election, and thirdly the nature of the Judicial
Body.

---

[1] Reading ἐν μὲν τί τὸ βουλευόμενον.

The Deliberative Body is supreme upon all ques- (1) The Deliberative
tions of war and peace, the formation and dissolution Body:
of alliances, the enactment of laws, sentences of death,
exile and confiscation ; to it belongs [1]the election of
the officers of State, and to it they are responsible at
the expiration of their term of office. It is necessary
that all these decisions [2]should be committed either
to the citizens collectively or to some of them, i. e. to
a single definite office or to several, or that different
decisions should be committed to different offices, or
that some of them should be committed to the citizens
collectively and others to some of the citizens only.

The exercise of deliberative powers by all the in a Democracy,
citizens upon all subjects is a characteristic of popular
government ; for this universal equality is in the spirit
of Democracy. But there are various modes of ordering this general deliberative power. The first is that
it should be exercised by all the citizens not collectively but by alternation, as e. g. in the polity of the
Milesian Telecles or in other polities in which it is the
various official boards which meet for deliberative
purposes, but all the citizens enter upon official positions according to a rotation of tribes or whatever
are the very smallest divisions of the State, until the
tenure of office has passed down the entire body.
The citizens only assemble collectively under this
system to enact laws, to settle constitutional questions
and to receive the reports of the officers of State.
Another mode is that the citizens collectively should
form the Deliberative Body but should not assemble

---

[1] Reading δημεύσεως καὶ περὶ ἀρχῶν αἱρέσεως.
[2] Reading ἀποδίδοσθαι.

except ¹to elect officers of State, to enact laws, to
determine questions of war and peace and to hold
the audit of the officers' accounts, while upon all other
matters the power of deliberation is vested in officers
appointed for the particular duties, these officers
being appointed from the whole body of citizens
by suffrage or by lot. A third mode is one by which
the citizens all meet for the election of officers of
State, for the audit of their accounts and for deliberation upon questions of war and of alliance, while all
other matters are administered by the officers of State,
who are appointed by suffrage so far as is possible *in
this advanced form of Democracy*, viz. in all cases
where special knowledge is required in the officers.
A fourth mode is one in which the citizens meet
collectively to deliberate upon all questions, and the
officers of State do not possess the power of decision
in any case but merely of preliminary examination—
a method of administration prevailing at the present
day in the latest development of Democracy, which is
in our view analogous to an Oligarchy of a dynastic or
a Monarchy of a tyrannical type.

In an Oli-
garchy,
          As the modes we have hitherto described are all
democratical, so the system in which deliberation upon
all matters is confined to certain citizens is oligarchical.
And in this case too there are several different forms.
When the election to the Deliberative Body is simply
dependent upon a comparatively low property assessment and the body is in consequence comparatively
numerous, when they do not interfere with any legally

---

¹ Omitting αἱρησομένους.

prohibited subject but are always obedient to the law,
and when participation in the deliberative procedure
is open to anyone upon his acquiring the requisite
property assessment, the constitution in question is
an Oligarchy, but an Oligarchy which in virtue of its
moderate character is a close approximation to a
Polity. When again the privilege of deliberation is
not open to all the citizens *who possess the requisite
property assessment* but is limited to an elected body,
but as in the last case their authority is conformable
to law, the system is *in the strict sense* oligarchical.
And when the body with whom the deliberative power
resides has the power of cooption, and *similarly* when
a son succeeds to his father's place in the Deliberative
Body, *i.e. when the hereditary principle is introduced*,
and the Deliberative Body is superior to the laws, the
system in question must be an [1]extreme form of
Oligarchy.

Where again there are certain matters which are in an Aristocracy,
in the control of certain persons, e.g. where questions
of war and peace and the audit of the officers' accounts
come before the citizens collectively, while everything
else is left to executive officers and the officers are
appointed by [2]suffrage, the polity is an Aristocracy.

If on the other hand the subjects of deliberation in a Polity.
come in some cases before persons appointed by suffrage
and in others before persons appointed by lot, whether
appointed by lot absolutely or from a body previously selected, or before persons appointed partly
by suffrage and partly by lot, these conditions are

---

[1] Reading ὀλιγαρχικωτάτην.
[2] Omitting ἢ κληρωτοί.

characteristic partly of an aristocratical form of polity and partly of a Polity in the strict sense.

The Deliberative Body is distinguished in the way we have described relatively to the several polities, and the [1]administration of each polity corresponds to the distinction we have stated.

Expedients appropriate to the extreme Democracy, But in the interest of the [2]Democracy of our own day which is supposed to have a pre-eminent title to the name—I mean the Democracy in which the commons are superior even to the laws—it is well, if we would improve the deliberation, to adopt the same expedient as is adopted in reference to the Courts of Law in Oligarchies, where a fine *for non-attendance* is imposed upon the class whose presence in the Courts is desired, as a means of securing their attendance (while the advocates of popular government give a fee to the poor *for their attendance*), and to apply it to the meetings of the Public Assembly. For the deliberation [3]is better conducted, if all the citizens collectively take part in it, the commons as well as the upper classes and the upper classes as well as the masses. It is advisable too that an [4]equal number of members of the Deliberative Body should be appointed by suffrage or by lot from each division of the citizens. And further, if the Democrats have a vast numerical preponderance over the capable statesmen, it is advisable either to give the fee for attendance not to the whole number but to a number corresponding to

---

[1] Reading διοικεῖται.
[2] Reading δημοκρατίᾳ τῇ νῦν.
[3] Reading βουλεύονται.
[4] Reading ἴσους.

the numerical strength of the upper classes or to
throw out by lot all who are in excess of the proper
number.

In an Oligarchy on the other hand it is advisable *and to Oli-garchy*
either to elect by anticipation certain representatives
of the people *as members of the Deliberative Body* or
to establish such an office as exists in certain polities
under the name of Preliminary Councillors or Guardians of the Laws and to allow the whole body of
citizens to take into their consideration such matters
only as have already received the preliminary decision
of these boards. This will be a means of giving the
commons a share in the deliberation and at the same
time of preventing them from abolishing any institution of the polity. It is advisable too that the
commons either should simply confirm the resolutions brought before them *by the Preliminary Councillors or the Guardians of the Laws* or *at least*
should not pass any resolution of a contrary nature
or, that while the privilege of giving advice is conferred upon all, the right of actual deliberation, *i. e. of
voting,* should be confined to the officers of State.
It is proper too to adopt just the opposite course to
the one usually adopted in polities, i. e. to make the
veto of the masses final but not their positive resolutions, and always to let a bill *which has been rejected
by the commons* be referred back to the executive
officers. For in existing polities the converse is the
practice ; it is a small body that has a supreme power
of veto but not of positive resolution, and there is
always a power of reference back to the masses.

Such then is the result of our discussions respect-

ing the Deliberative Body and therefore of course the
supreme authority in the polity.

CHAP. XV.   We come next to the distinction in respect of the
(2) The Exe-
cutive.   offices of State. For in this department of the polity
as in the last there is room for a good many variations.
The questions arise what is to be the number of the
offices of State, the extent of their jurisdiction and
the period of each—for in some States the officers
are appointed for six months, in others for a shorter
period, in others again for a year and in others for a
still longer time—and further whether the offices are
to be tenable for life or for a long period, or neither
of these is to be the case, but they are to be tenable
several times by the same person, or they are never in
any circumstances to be tenable by the same persons
twice. And coming to the appointment of the officers
of State, we have to inquire into the nature of the
persons eligible and of the electing body and into the
method of election. For it is right that upon all these
various points we should be able to distinguish all the
various possible arrangements and then to adapt the
different offices to the [1] polities to which they are suited.

Nature and
number of
the offices
of State.   But it is not an easy matter at the outset to determine the character of the positions which are properly
described as offices of State. For there are many
mere superintendents necessary to the political association and, *as these are certainly not officers of State,*
it is not correct to regard all functionaries appointed
either by suffrage or lot as officers. The priesthood
is an obvious case in point ; it should be regarded

---

[1] Reading πολιτείαις.   .   .   .   .

not as an office in the strict sense but as something distinct from and parallel to political offices. Then again there are masters of choruses and heralds *who are elected,* and we elect [1]ambassadors also ; *but none of these are officers of State.* Some offices of superintendence are political, whether the superintendence is over all the citizens in respect of a particular function, as e. g. the superintendence of a general in the field of battle, or departmental, like that of a censor of women or boys. Others again are economic—it is a common thing e. g. to elect inspectors of weights and measures —and others again simply menial, to which people, if they are wealthy, appoint slaves. Strictly speaking however we must define offices generally as all positions to which are assigned the functions of deliberation, decision and command on certain points and more especially the last, as to command is an especial characteristic of official power. But such a question as the exact meaning of the term office is in fact one of no practical significance ; for no controversy about the name has ever yet been raised or decided; although it has a distinct speculative import.

It is more to the point to raise a question in respect of all polities without exception and especially of small States as to the character and number of the offices indispensable to the existence of a State and the character of such offices as, although not indispensable, are yet serviceable to a high order of polity. For in large States it is equally possible and right to have a single office appointed to a single

---

[1] Reading πρεσβευτάς.

work, as on the one hand it results from the large
number of the citizens that there are many persons
ready to be admitted to the official board, so that [1]in
some cases the office is held a second time only after
a long interval and in others is never held more than
once, and on the other hand every work is better
done when the attention is exclusively devoted to
it instead of being distracted by a number of things.
In small States on the other hand it is necessary
to concentrate a number of offices in a few hands, as
the scantiness of the population makes it difficult for
a large number of people to be in office at the same
time. For *if this is the case,* who are to relieve the
first set of officers? But it sometimes happens that
small States require the same offices and laws as
great ones, with this difference that in the latter case
[2]they are required frequently and in the former only
at considerable intervals. Hence there is no reason
why several functions should not be assigned to the
same persons ; for they will not be any impediment
to one another, and in view of the scanty population
it is necessary to constitute the offices on the principle of [3]spit-candlesticks. If we are in a position
then to enumerate the offices necessary to any State
and the offices which are [4]appropriate, although not
wholly indispensable, the knowledge will facilitate

---

[1] Reading τὰς μὲν διαλείπειν and below τὰς δ᾽ ἅπαξ ἄρχειν.

[2] Reading αὐτῶν for τῶν αὐτῶν.

[3] i. e. articles which were spit and candlestick in one. See note
on Bk. I. ch. 2.

[4] It is better to interchange the positions of δεῖ and ἑρμόττει.

a conclusion as to the character of the offices which may properly be united in a single one.

Nor is it fitting to neglect the further question, what is the [1]character of the subjects which should be under the superintendence of many local officers and of the subjects over which a single office should be supreme universally, e.g. whether public propriety should in the market be under the control of a censor of the market and of different officers in different places or of the same office everywhere. There is the further question whether the division should depend upon the subject or the persons, I mean e.g. whether there should be a single minister of public propriety or different officers for children and women. And yet again, looking to the different polities we have to ask whether there is a special class of offices suited to each polity or not; in other words whether the same offices are supreme in Democracy, Oligarchy, Aristocracy and Monarchy, although the persons eligible to them are not equal and similar but [2]differ in the different polities, being the cultured classes in an Aristocracy, the wealthy in an Oligarchy and all free-born persons in a Democracy, or whether on the other hand there are [3]different kinds of office corresponding to the differences between the polities, and the same offices are in some cases similar and in others different in consequence of these differences, as it is appro-

---

[1] Reading ποίων δεῖ κατὰ τόπον ἀρχεῖα πολλὰ ἐπιμελεῖσθαι.

[2] Reading ἑτέρων.

[3] Reading κατὰ ταύτας τὰς διαφορὰς διαφοραὶ τῶν ἀρχῶν and below καὶ ὅπου διαφέρουσι διὰ ταύτας.

priate that the same offices should be influential in
one polity and insignificant in another. It must be
Offices peculiar to particular polities.   admitted however that there are certain offices peculiar
to particular polities, e.g. a Preliminary Council, which
unlike a Council is distinctly non-democratical. For
there must be some body to undertake the business
of preparing measures for the consideration of the
Public Assembly and thereby enabling the commons
to attend to business. But if the members of it are
numerically few, the institution is characteristic of
Oligarchy ; and as a Preliminary Council is necessarily small, it is therefore oligarchical. Where however both these offices, *viz. a Council and a Preliminary Council*, exist, the latter is established as
a controlling influence upon the former ; for while
the Council is an institution of Democracy, the Preliminary Council is an institution of Oligarchy. But
the authority of the Council is gradually undermined
in all Democracies in which the commons themselves
assemble for the transaction of business of every
kind. And this is usually the case when the members
of the Public Assembly are in receipt of large pay for
their attendance, as in that case they have sufficient
leisure to assemble frequently and themselves pronounce decisions upon all questions. On the other
hand a censorship of women or children or any
other office charged with similar superintendence is
characteristic of an Aristocracy, but not of a Democracy, as it is impossible *in a Democracy* to prevent the wives of the poor from going out of doors,
nor yet of an Oligarchy, as the wives of the actual
Oligarchs lead luxurious and unrestrained lives.

So much however at present for these questions.
We must now endeavour to enter upon a thorough
discussion of the various methods of appointing the
officers of State. The points of difference are comprised under three general heads, the combinations
of which will certainly give us all the possible modes
of procedure. The questions which arise are firstly,
who are the persons that appoint the officers of
State? secondly, who are eligible to office? and
thirdly, what is the mode of election? And further
under each of those heads there is a [1]certain number
of possible variations.

The power of appointment may be in the hands
either of all the citizens or of some, and the persons
eligible may be either all or some, the some being
determined e. g. either by property assessment or
birth or virtue or some other similar qualification,
as at Megara where they were the exiles who had
come home in a body and fought against the commons; and further the appointment may be made
either by suffrage or by lot. Again, there are combinations of these different modes ; I mean that some
of the officers may be appointed by some citizens
and others by all, to some offices all the citizens may
be eligible and to others only some, and in some
cases the appointment may be made by suffrage and
in others by lot. Further each of these different
possibilities admits of four variations. For either all
may appoint from all by suffrage or all from all by
lot, [2]or all from some by suffrage or all from some by

The various
modes of
appointing
officers of
State.

---

[1] Reading διαφοραί τινές εἰσιν.

[2] Inserting the words ἢ πάντες ἐκ τινῶν αἱρέσει ἢ πάντες ἐκ τινῶν

lot ; and ¹in appointing from all the appointment may
be made either by a system of rotation, i.e. according
to tribes, townships and clans, until it has passed
through the entire body of citizens, or in all cases
from the whole body, or again partly in one way
and partly in the other. Again, if it is some only of
the citizens who appoint, they may appoint either
from all by suffrage or from all by lot or from some
by suffrage or from some by lot or partly in one way
and partly in another, I mean ²partly by suffrage and
partly by lot. We thus arrive at twelve as the
number of possible modes, not including the two
combinations. ³And of these there are two systems
of appointment which are democratical, viz. that all
should appoint from all by suffrage or lot or by a
combination of the two, i.e. to some offices by lot and
to others by suffrage. On the other hand the system

κλήρῳ, without which the δώδεκα τρόποι cannot be satisfactorily
made out.
    ¹ Omitting ἢ before ἐξ ἁπάντων.
    ² Omitting ἐκ πάντων.
    ³ The text which I have adopted—it is mainly Spengel's—is as
follows : τούτων δ' αἱ μὲν δύο καταστάσεις δημοτικαί, τὸ πάντας ἐκ
πάντων αἱρέσει ἢ κλήρῳ ἢ ἀμφοῖν, τὰς μὲν κλήρῳ τὰς δ' αἱρέσει τῶν
ἀρχῶν. Τὸ δὲ μὴ πάντας ἅμα μὲν καθιστάναι, ἐξ ἁπάντων δ' ἢ κλήρῳ
ἢ αἱρέσει ἢ ἀμφοῖν, ἢ τὰς μὲν ἐκ πάντων τὰς δ' ἐκ τινῶν ἢ κλήρῳ ἢ
αἱρέσει ἢ ἀμφοῖν (τὸ δὲ ἀμφοῖν λέγω τὰς μὲν κλήρῳ τὰς δ' αἱρέσει)
πολιτικόν· καὶ τὸ τινὰς ἐκ πάντων τὰς μὲν αἱρέσει καθιστάναι τὰς δὲ
κλήρῳ. Τὸ δὲ τινὰς τὰς μὲν ἐκ πάντων τὰς δ' ἐκ τινῶν πολιτικὸν
ἀριστοκρατικῶς ἢ κλήρῳ ἢ αἱρέσει ἢ τὰς μὲν αἱρέσει τὰς δὲ κλήρῳ.
Τὸ δὲ τινὰς ἐκ τινῶν αἱρέσει ὀλιγαρχικόν, καὶ τὸ τινὰς ἐκ τινῶν κλήρῳ,
καὶ τὸ τινὰς ἐκ τινῶν ἀμφοῖν· ὀλιγαρχικώτερον δὲ το αἱρέσει ἢ τὸ
κλήρῳ ἢ ἀμφοῖν. Τὸ δὲ τινὰς ἐξ ἁπάντων τό τε ἐκ τινῶν πάντας
αἱρέσει ἀριστοκρατικόν.

in which the appointment is not vested in all the citizens collectively but all are eligible, and the appointment is made either by lot or suffrage or both, or in which the persons eligible are in some cases all the citizens and in others some of them and the appointment is made either by lot or suffrage or both, i.e. in some cases by lot and in others by suffrage, is characteristic of a Polity ; and the same is true of the system in which some appoint from all partly by suffrage and partly by lot. The system in which the appointment is made by some partly from all and partly from some either by lot or suffrage or partly by suffrage and partly by lot is suited to a Polity of an aristocratic type. The system in which some appoint from some by suffrage or some from some by lot or some from some by a combination of the two ways is oligarchical, although the appointment by suffrage is more strictly oligarchical than that by lot or by a combination of the two. Finally the appointment by some from all or by all from some by suffrage is suited to an Aristocracy.

Such is a complete catalogue of the modes of appointment to office and such their division according to the different polities. The institutions suitable to particular people, the methods of appointment and the nature of the [1]authority appertaining to the several offices of State will now be evident. And when I speak of the authority of an office, I mean e.g. the control it exercises over the revenues or the defences of the State ; for there are different kinds of authority, as we see if we compare the

[1] Omitting καὶ.

authority of a general and of a superintendent of commercial transactions in the market.

CHAP. XVI.
(3) The Courts of Law.
Their constitution.
p. 503.

The third point which still remains to be discussed is [1]the constitution of the Courts of Law. And here we must follow the same principle as before in ascertaining the modes of constituting them. The points of difference in respect of the Courts of Law fall under three general heads, viz. the persons eligible, the extent of their jurisdiction and the manner of their appointment. By the persons eligible I mean the question whether they are to be the whole population or only a class ; by the sphere of their jurisdiction, the various kinds of Courts ; by the method of appointment, the choice between lot or suffrage.

The different kinds of Court.

Let us begin by determining the different kinds of Court. They are eight in number, viz. a Court of scrutiny, a Court to try offences committed against the State, another to try all constitutional questions, a fourth to try cases that arise between officers of State and individuals respecting fines, fifthly the Court which deals with important cases of private contract, and besides these sixthly the Court of homicide, and seventhly the Court of aliens. The Court of homicide is of various kinds, whether the judges who hear the suits are the same or different, according as it deals with homicide of malice prepense, involuntary homicide, cases where the fact is admitted but the justice of it is in dispute, cases where persons [2]who have left the country *in consequence of an accidental homicide* are on their return tried upon a charge

---

[1] Reading εἰπεῖν περὶ δικαστηρίων.

[2] Reading τοῖς φεύγουσιν ἐπὶ καθόδῳ ἐπιφέρεται φόνου.

of murder, as is said to be the case at Athens in the
Court at Phreatto, although at the [1]present time
such cases are of rare occurrence even in large States.
The Court of aliens too has two divisions, one dealing
with cases between two aliens, the other with cases
between an alien and a citizen. And lastly there is
a Court for the trial of petty contracts to the amount
of a drachma or *at the most* five drachmae or a little
more ; for it is necessary that these cases like others
should be decided, although they are not suitable to
come before a number of judges.

These cases however, like cases of homicide and
cases in which aliens are concerned, we may dismiss.
We have now to discuss political cases, which must
be satisfactorily ordered, if we are to avoid dissensions and disturbances of the polity.

If all the citizens are capable of judicial office, The modes
the various cases we have distinguished must either of judicial
Procedure.
all come for decision before all the judges, who are
appointed by suffrage or lot or partly in one way
and partly in the other, or some of them must invariably come before certain judges appointed partly
by lot and partly by suffrage. These modes of organization then are four in number ; and there is an
equal number, if it is only a portion of the citizens
who are eligible to the judicial office. For with this
limited eligibility there may be a Court of universal
jurisdiction appointed by suffrage or by lot or partly
in one way and partly in the other ; or there may be
particular Courts with special jurisdiction composed
of members elected by lot or suffrage.

[1] Reading παρόντι.

Such then, as we have described them, are the possible modes of organization in the cases mentioned. There are also combinations of the same, e.g. cases where the persons eligible are sometimes all the citizens, sometimes some and sometimes again both, as when the members of the same Court are appointed partly from all and partly from some and either by lot or by suffrage or by a combination of the two.

All the possible modes of constituting the Courts of Law have now been stated. The systems first described, viz. the various conditions of universal eligibility and universal jurisdiction, are democratical. The next, viz. limited eligibility and universal jurisdiction, are oligarchical. The third, viz. the combination of universal and limited eligibility, are characteristic of an Aristocracy and a Polity.

BOOK VII.

THE number and nature of the different forms of the Deliberative or Supreme Body in the polity, of the system of the executive offices and the Courts of Law and the several forms of these institutions which are appropriate to the various polities have already been the subjects of discussion[1]. But as there are in fact several kinds of Democracy and similarly several kinds of the other polities, it is worth while to investigate any point which has not yet been considered in regard to them, and at the same time to determine the proper and convenient organization of each polity. We have also to consider the various ways in which the different methods of organizing the institutions in question may be combined; for it is the combinations of them that cause polities to overlap, producing Aristocracies which have an oligarchical bias on the one hand and Polities which have a democratical bias on the other. And when I

---

[1] The clause ἔτι δὲ περὶ φθορᾶς τε καὶ σωτηρίας τῶν πολιτειῶν ἐκ ποίων τε γίνεται καὶ διὰ τίνας αἰτίας, relating as it does to the subject of Bk. VIII., is necessarily omitted in Bekker's order of the Books.

speak of such combinations as deserve consideration but have not yet been considered, I mean e.g. the case where the system of the Deliberative Body and the election of the executive officers are constituted on oligarchical and the system of the Courts of Law on aristocratical principles, or where the Courts of Law and the Deliberative Body are constituted on oligarchical and the election of the executive officers on aristocratical principles, or again in some other way the institutions characteristic of a particular polity are not all found in combination.

p. 287.   The character of Democracy suited to a particular State or of Oligarchy to a particular population or the form of any other polity which is advantageous to particular people are subjects which have been already discussed. Still[1] it is not enough to elucidate the form in which any of the polities we have mentioned is [2]best for a particular State; we must proceed to examine briefly the proper method of establishing these or any others. We will begin with Democracy, as the consideration of Democracy will serve to display the characteristics of the polity antagonistic to it, i.e. of the polity sometimes called Oligarchy.

For the purpose of this investigation it is necessary to ascertain the characteristics which are democratical or regarded as consequent upon Democracy; for it is their combinations which give rise to the different species of Democracy and indeed to the exist-

---

[1] It is not necessary to insert ἐπεὶ, as Bekker has done, if the commas after ὅμως δὲ and κατασκευάζειν are omitted.

[2] Reading ἀρίστη.

ence of a plurality of Democracies differing from each other. For there are two reasons for a plurality of Democracies. The first is that which has been already alleged, viz. the variety in the character of the populations. For the population consists in one case of agriculturists, in another of mechanics or labourers, *and so on;* and if the first is added to the second and again the third to the first two, the difference in the Democracy is not merely one of superiority or inferiority but amounts to an actual change of kind. The second is the reason we are now considering, viz. that the various combinations of the characteristics consequent upon a Democracy and regarded as proper to this form of polity produce corresponding differences in the Democracy, as a smaller number of these characteristics will be consequent upon one form of Democracy, a larger number upon another, and all of them upon a third. The knowledge of these several characteristics is valuable as enabling us not only to establish any polity we may desire but also to effect the necessary reforms *in those which already exist.* For the founders of polities generally endeavour to combine all the characteristics proper to the principle of their polity and in so doing fall into an error[1]. But we may now proceed to describe the fundamental assumptions, the moral features and the objects of the different polities.

The primary principle of a democratical polity is

The reasons for a plurality of Democracies.

Chap. II.

---

[1] It is necessary in Bekker's order of the Books either to omit the clause καθάπερ ἐν τοῖς περὶ τὰς φθορὰς καὶ τὰς σωτηρίας τῶν πολιτειῶν εἴρηται πρότερον or, as Spengel proposes, to alter εἴρηται πρότερον to ἐροῦμεν ὕστερον.

personal liberty. Such is the language which is in
everybody's mouth, as if Democracy were the only
polity in which liberty is enjoyed ; for it is this, *viz.*
the enjoyment of liberty, which is said to be the end
and object of every Democracy. But one feature of
liberty is the alternation of rule and subjection. For
justice in the democratical view consists in equality
as determined not *proportionally or* by merit but
arithmetically, *i.e. by merely counting heads;* and
where this is the principle of justice, it necessarily
follows that the masses are supreme, and that, whatever is the will of the majority, this is [1]final, and in
this justice consists. For the theory being that all the
citizens should share alike, the result is that in a Democracy the poor exercise higher authority than the
rich ; for they constitute a majority of the population,
and the will of the majority is supreme. This then is
one token of liberty, which is represented by all
friends of popular government as a criterion of a
democratical polity. The other is that every citizen
lives according to his own pleasure. For this is said
to be a function of liberty, as the converse is a
function of one whose life is spent in a condition of
slavery. This is then a second criterion of Democracy ; and from this has been deduced the exemption of the citizens from authority, in the extreme
case from all authority whatever, but at all events
from anything more than such authority as they
themselves exercise in turn. And thus this second
criterion of liberty coincides with the liberty that
consists in equality.

        [1] Omitting καὶ before τέλος.

In view of these primary principles and of the The characteristics character of the authority which we have described, *viz.* of a popular govern- *alternate authority*, the following features are charac- ment. teristic of a popular government, viz. the eligibility of all the citizens to the offices of State and their appointment by all, the rule of all over each individual and of each individual in his turn over all, the use of the lot in the appointment either to all the offices of State or to all that do not require experience or special skill, the absence of a property qualification or the requirement of the lowest possible qualification for office, the regulation that the same person shall never hold any office twice or shall not hold it much oftener than once or shall do so only in a few cases with the exception of military offices, a system of short tenure of office either in all cases or in all cases where it is possible, the power of all or[1] of a body chosen from all to sit as judges in all or almost all or at least the greatest and most important cases, such as cases arising out of the audit of the officers' accounts, constitutional cases and cases of private contract, the supreme authority of the Public Assembly in all questions or[2] at least the most important, and of no individual office over any question or only over the smallest number possible. Of all offices of State the most democratic institution is a Council, except where all the citizens receive a large fee for attendance in the Assembly ; in which case they despoil the Council as well as all the other

---

[1] Reading πάντας ἢ ἐκ. πάντων.

[2] The words ἢ τῶν μεγίστων, which in Bekker's text follow ὀλιγίστων, should be placed after πάντων.

offices of their authority.' For the commons, being
well paid *and consequently having leisure to attend
the Assembly frequently*, draw all decisions without
p. 270.   exception into their own hands, as has been said in
the preceding part of this treatise. Another democratical feature is the payment of the members of all
the three powers in the State, viz. the Assembly, the
Courts of Law and the executive offices or, if this is
impossible, of the executive offices, the Courts of
Law[1] and the regular assemblies or, *if not of all
offices*, of those whose members require a common
table. And further as it is birth, wealth and culture
which are the characteristics of Oligarchy, it would
seem that those of Democracy are the opposites, viz.
low birth, poverty and intellectual degradation. And
in respect of the offices of State it is democratical
that none should be held for life, and that, if any
such office survives from an ancient revolution, its
power should be curtailed under the Democracy,
and the appointment to it should be by lot instead of
by suffrage.

Such being then the general features [2] of Democracy, Democracy or a democratic population in
the strict sense of the word as now conceived is an
outcome of the principle of justice which is admitted
to be democratical, i.e. of universal arithmetical
equality. For the condition of equality is one in
which the rule is not any more [3] in the hands of the
poor than of the rich, in which neither party enjoys

---

[1] Omitting καὶ τὴν βουλήν.
[2] Reading τῆς δημοκρατίας.
[3] Reading.τοὺς ἀπόρους ἢ τοὺς εὐπόρους.

an exclusive supremacy, but all stand upon a numerical equality. It is in these circumstances that equality and liberty would *in the judgment of Democrats* be realized in the [1]State.

The next point, viz. the manner in which the citizens are to enjoy equality, presents a certain difficulty. The question is whether it is right to consider the assessed properties of (*let us say*) five hundred citizens as distributed among, *or in other words balanced by, the properties of* a thousand others and to give the thousand only equal power with the five hundred—or perhaps instead of ordering the equality of property thus, it is right, while we adopt this method of distribution, to select an equal number of representatives of the five hundred and the thousand and to invest them with the supreme authority over the [2]election of the executive officers and the procedure of the Courts of Law—Is it then, *we may ask*, a polity so constituted or one in which the principle is simply that of counting heads, that is the justest according to the popular conception of justice? *I say the popular or democratical conception of justice,* for it is contended by the friends of popular government that the decision of the majority is just ; while the oligarchical party makes justice to consist in the decision of the wealthier, maintaining that the amount of property is the standard that should determine the decisions. But in either case there is a certain inequality and injustice. The theory that the decision of the Few is just will justify Tyranny, as if we suppose the

CHAP. III.

The nature of democratical and oligarchical equality.

----

[1] Reading πόλει.
[2] Reading ἀρχαιρεσιῶν.

case of an individual possessed of larger means than
all the other members of the wealthy class, the oligarchical principle of justice will entitle him to a
monopoly of rule, and the theory that the decision
of the mere numerical majority is just will [1]justify,
p. 127. as has been already said, the confiscation of the
property of the wealthy minority. The nature of
the equality to which both Oligarchs and Democrats
will yield assent is a question which must be considered by the light of their respective definitions of
justice. They agree in the view that the decision of
the majority of the citizens should be supreme. This
we may admit, although not without some limitation.
As there are two elements of which the State is composed, viz. rich and poor, we may determine that the
decision of the [2]majority of both, if they agree, and,
if they disagree, of the absolute majority, or in other
words of those whose collective property assessment
is higher, should be supreme. Suppose e.g. that there
are ten rich and twenty poor and that there are six rich
on one side and fifteen poor on the other ; there are
then four rich on the side of the fifteen poor and five
poor on the side of the six rich. Reckoning the poor
and rich together on both sides, we determine that
the decision of the side which has the larger property
assessment is supreme. But supposing that the sides
chance to come out equal, we must look upon this as
a difficulty which is liable to occur in any system of
voting and actually does occur when e.g. the Public
Assembly or the Court of Law is evenly divided.

[1] Reading οὐκ ἀδικήσουσι.
[2] Omitting ἤ.

The only thing to be done then is to appeal to the lot or to adopt some other similar expedient. But where the question is the principle of equality or justice, difficult as it is—and it is most difficult— to discover the truth, still it is an easier task to arrive at it than to win the practical compliance of those who have it in their power to aggrandize themselves. For appeals to [1]justice and equality have ever been the resource of the weaker and are systematically disregarded by the strong.

While there are four forms of Democracy, it is the first in order which is the best, as was remarked in the earlier part of our treatise, not to say that it is the most ancient of all. When I speak of the first or primary Democracy, I refer to the natural classification of populations. As the agricultural population is best, it is only possible to realize [2]the best Democracy where the people live by agriculture or grazing. For the members of a population so composed, not possessing a large property, are occupied about their business, so that they cannot hold frequent meetings of the Assembly; while, as they [3]do possess the bare necessaries of life, they devote themselves to their proper occupations and, instead of coveting the property of their neighbours, prefer a life of labour to political activity and official power, except where office promises an opportunity of large gain. For the Many care more for pecuniary gain than for honour, as may be inferred from their ac-

CHAP. IV. The four forms of Democracy: p. 269.

(1), the agricultural,

---

[1] Reading τὸ δίκαιον καὶ τὸ ἴσον.

[2] Inserting τὴν βελτίστην before δημοκρατίαν.

[3] Omitting μή.

quiescence in the tyrannical governments of antiquity
and the Oligarchies of our own day, provided that
no one interferes with their labour or despoils them
of any of their property. The reason is that, *if they
are left to themselves*, they rapidly acquire riches or
at least are relieved from poverty. It may be added
that their control of the elections to the offices of
State and the responsibility of all the officers of State
to them fully satisfy any ambitious cravings they may
have. For there are some States in which the Many
are content to let the election to the offices of State
pass out of their own hands into the hands of a body
elected from all the citizens by alternation[1], provided
that they retain the deliberative functions in their
own hands. And yet even this we must consider to
be a form of Democracy, an example of which formerly existed at Mantineia. Thus it is at once a
beneficial and a customary condition of the Democracy already described that, while the officers of
State are elected by all the citizens and are responsible to all, and all exercise judicial powers, the
principal officers of State are appointed by suffrage
rather than by lot, and eligibility depends upon a
property qualification, which is raised in proportion
to the importance of the office, or that, if no property
qualification is required in any case, the offices of
State should be confined to competent persons. A
political constitution of this kind is sure to be ex-
cellent ; for the offices of State will always be in the
hands of the best men with the full assent of the
commons and without any feeling of envy on their

[1] Omitting ὥσπερ ἐν Μαντινείᾳ.

part against the better classes, and the better or
upper classes will certainly be content with such a
system, in virtue of which they will never be subjected to the rule of their inferiors, while in the
exercise of their own authority they will be prevented from violating the principles of justice by
their responsibility to the supreme authority of
others. For there is an advantage to the State in
the feeling of dependence on the part of the officers
and in the limitation of their arbitrary dealing, as
the power of arbitrary action is incompatible with
the control of the baser elements existing in each
individual. And thus the result will certainly be
the condition of things which is the most highly
beneficial in any polity, viz. the rule of the better
class provided that they behave themselves well without any infringement of the rights of the people.

It is evident then that this is the best form of
Democracy, and that it owes its excellence to the
character of its population. For the encouragement
of agriculture among the people there are certain laws
of [1] ancient date which are all effective, such as a law
absolutely prohibiting the possession of more than a
certain amount of land or prohibiting the possession of
more than a certain amount within a certain distance of
the city proper or the State. Another *similar measure*
was the legal regulation which formerly existed in many
States actually prohibiting the sale of the original
allotments. The law of Oxylus, as it is called, against
taking a mortgage upon a particular part of the
landed estate belonging to any citizen is calculated

---

[1] Reading παρὰ τοῖς παλαιοῖς and omitting τὸ ἀρχαῖον.

to have much the same effect. But at the present day, if we would effect the necessary reform we must have recourse to the law of [1]Aphytis which is suitable to the end of which we are speaking. For the citizens of Aphytis, although their number is large and their country small, are all engaged in agriculture, because they assess the value of estates not in the gross but in subdivisions so small that even the poor can more than attain the necessary standard of assessment.

(2) the pastoral.

Next to an agricultural people the best population is one consisting of graziers who depend for their living upon live stock. For the life of a grazing population has many points of resemblance to agriculture; nor are there any people who have a condition so well disciplined for military service or who are so active physically or so well able to endure exposure to the elements.

The other populations of which the remaining forms of Democracy are composed are practically all a great deal lower *in the scale of civilization* than

(3) the mechanical or commercial.

these. For the life of mechanics, tradesmen and labourers is a low one; nor has any of the occupations in which such people engage any necessary connexion with virtue. And further all this class of persons, always loitering as they are about the market and the town, is ready enough to attend meetings of the Assembly; whereas an agricultural population being scattered throughout the country does not assemble *so readily* or feel the same need of such meetings. Where the situation of the country hap-

---

[1] Ἀρυταίων in Bekker's text is a mere misprint.

pens to be such that [1]it is at a great distance from
the city, it is easy to establish a good form of Democracy or a Polity; for as the mass of the population is obliged to make its settlements in the fields,
the mob of the market, even if it exists, is bound not
to hold- meetings of the Assembly without the rural
population, *and therefore holds them only on rare
occasions.*

The proper method of establishing the best or primary form of Democracy has now been stated. Nor
is it difficult to see how to establish all the rest. We
must deviate step by step from the primary Democracy and separate *from the citizens an unenfranchised* body which will in each succeeding case
be worse than before.

The latest development of Democracy, admitting (4) the ex-
as it does all the citizens to an absolute equality of treme.
political privileges, is one which cannot be endured
by every State and cannot well have a permanent
existence *in any*, unless supported by a good system
of laws and moral habits[2]. It is with the view of
establishing this form of Democracy and of confirming the power of the commons that the popular
leaders usually [3]enroll the largest possible number
of persons *in the ranks of the citizens*, conferring
political rights not only upon all the legitimate
children of citizens but upon their bastards and upon

---

[1] Omitting τὴν χώραν.

[2] Omitting the sentence ἃ δὲ φθείρειν συμβαίνει καὶ ταύτην καὶ
τὰς ἄλλας πολιτείας, εἴρηται πρότερον τὰ πλεῖστα σχεδόν, which has
reference to the contents of Bk. VIII.

[3] Omitting τῷ.

children who are descended from citizens upon the
side of one parent only, whether the father's or the
mother's. For all such elements are particularly con-
genial to the extreme Democracy. It is, as I say,
the custom of demagogues to establish a Democracy
upon these principles ; but the right course is to
enroll new citizens only up to the point at which the
numbers *of the commons* just preponderate over the
numerical strength of the upper and middle classes,
and to advance no further. For if[1] their numbers
are in excess of this limit, they disturb the equi-
librium of the State and irritate the upper classes
into a spirit of dissatisfaction with the Democracy,
which proved to be the cause of the political disturbances at Cyrene. For although the mob element
may be overlooked, so long as it is small, if it
reaches large dimensions, it forces itself more upon
the attention. Again, the interests of the extreme
Democracy are subserved by such institutions as
were adopted by Cleisthenes at Athens in his desire
to strengthen the power of the Democracy and at
Cyrene by the founders of the democratical constitution. New and more numerous tribes and clans
must be created, the number of private religious rites
must be united in a smaller number of public cere-
monies, and no stone must be left unturned to secure
the intermixture of all the different classes in the
State and the dissolution of the former private associations. And finally the established characteristics
of Tyranny seem to be suited without exception to

---

[1] ὑπερβάλλοντας should of course be ὑπερβάλλοντες.

the extreme Democracy, such, I mean, as the licence
of slaves, women and children—although in the case
of slaves it may be a good thing up to a certain
point—and the connivance at a life of uncontrolled
liberty among all the citizens. For there are many,
different ways of strengthening this sort of polity, as
the Many prefer a life of irregularity to one of continence and control.

It is not the principal or sole business of the CHAP. V
legislator or of anyone who aspires to constitute such The means of pre-
a polity as we have described merely to establish it serving
in the first instance but rather to provide for its Democra-
security. For it is easy enough for people to endure cies.
for a single day or two or three days under any form
of polity; *but a polity, if it is to be permanent,
demands special provisions.* Hence it is proper[1]
to take measures for its preservation by guarding
against all destructive agencies and ordaining such
laws whether written or unwritten as shall best
embrace all the preservatives of polities, and to regard as eminently democratical or oligarchical not
such measures as will give the strongest democratical
or oligarchical character to the State, but such as
will enable it to preserve that character for the
longest time. But our modern demagogues adopt a
different line. They seek to gratify the commons of
their respective States by using the instrumentality
of the Courts of Law to confiscate a great part of

---

[1] Omitting the words περὶ ὧν τεθεώρηται πρότερον τίνες σω-
τηρίαι καὶ φθοραὶ τῶν πόλιτειῶν ἐκ τούτων, unless indeed it is
better to follow Spengel and Susemihl in reading θεωρήσομεν
ὕστερον.

the property of the rich. Hence the true friends of
the polity should seek to counteract these measures
by enacting a law that nothing that is paid into the
treasury by persons who are condemned in a lawsuit shall escheat to the public but that it shall all be
consecrated to the service of the Gods. For the result will be that, while malefactors will be quite as
cautious as before, as being liable to precisely similar
penalties, the mob will be less eager to return a
verdict of condemnation against accused persons, if
they have no prospect of getting anything for themselves. Another expedient[1] is to reduce as far as
possible the number of State cases by imposing
heavy penalties as deterrents upon the originators of
baseless prosecutions. For it is not the friends of
popular government but the upper classes that are
the favourite objects of impeachment; whereas it is
desirable that all the citizens should, if possible, be
well-disposed to[2] the polity or at least that they
should not look upon the supreme power in the
State, *viz. the commons*, as hostile. Again, as in the
latest development of Democracy the population is
large, and the citizens cannot well attend the Assembly without being paid, and where there are no
revenues of State the payment of members is prejudicial to the interests of the upper classes—for the
means are sure to be supplied by extraordinary taxes,
confiscation of property and judicial iniquity, causes
which have before now proved the ruin of many
Democracies—but to resume, where there are no

[1] Changing ἀεὶ to δεῖ.
[2] Omitting καὶ.

revenues of State, it is desirable to hold only few meetings of the Assembly, and to make the Courts numerically large but to allow them only to sit for a few days at a time. For this tends to relieve the wealthy from dreading the expense, if it is only the poor and not the rich who are the recipients of payment for attendance in the Courts of Law, and at the same time to secure a far better administration of justice, as the rich are willing to absent themselves for a short time, but not for many days, from the management of their private affairs. Where there are revenues of State on the other hand, it is desirable not to follow the example of modern demagogues in dividing the surplus. The poor no sooner receive the money than they require it again ; for the sort of assistance thus given them is like the proverbial leaky pitcher *of the Danaides.* But the genuine friend of the people should take measures to prevent the masses from being sunk in extreme poverty, as this is a state of things which produces a degradation of the Democracy. Accordingly a systematic effort must be made to secure a permanent prosperity. And as this is the interest of the rich as much as of the poor, the residue of the public revenues should be collected and distributed in large sums to the poor, especially if it is possible to collect enough to supply them with the means of acquiring a plot of land or, failing this, to start them in business or agriculture. And if it is impossible to subsidize all the poor citizens at once, there should be a distribution of money among them by a rotation of tribes or some other division. Meanwhile

the rich should contribute the necessary payment
for the indispensable meetings *of the Assembly and
the Courts of Law*, on condition[1] of being released
from all useless public burdens. It is by some such
political procedure as this that the Carthaginians
have secured the loyalty of the commons, as they
raise a certain portion of them to affluence from
time to time by sending them out as colonists to the
surrounding subject States. Again, it shows good
taste and good sense on the part of the upper classes,
if they take individual members of the poorer population and direct them to some industrial pursuit by
giving them the means of starting in it. Nor is it a
bad plan to imitate the method[2] of rule among the
Tarentines, who secure the [3]loyalty of the masses by
giving the poor a share in the practical enjoyment of
their property. Another of their artifices was to
divide all the offices of State into two classes, the
appointment to one of which was by suffrage and to the
other by lot, the object in the latter case being to
secure the participation of the commons in office and
in the former to improve the character of the administration. But it is possible to treat the same
office in this way by adopting a principle of division,
so that one part of the officers is appointed by lot
and the other by suffrage.

CHAP. VI.   The methods of instituting the different forms of
Democracy have been described, and we may say

---

[1] Reading ἀφιεμένους.

[2] τὴν Ταραντίνων ἀρχὴν is the reading which has the best MSS.
authority.

[3] εὔνους is a misprint for εὔνουν.

that the methods of instituting those of Oligarchy The form of Oligarchy. are evident at once from these. For we must infer the characteristics of the several forms of Oligarchy from their opposites by observing the analogy between each and the corresponding form of Democracy. Let us take e.g. the primary or best-tempered form of Oligarchy. It is the form which approximates to the so-called Polity ; and in it we have to distinguish two separate kinds of property assessment, a lower which is requisite as a condition of eligibility to the merely indispensable offices of State and a higher as a condition of eligibility to the offices of greater importance. It is a further characteristic of this polity that the exercise of political privileges is open to anybody who acquires the requisite amount of property, the number of the commons introduced[1] into the ranks of citizens on the strength of the property assessment being so large as to secure the predominance *of the enfranchised* over the unenfranchised classes in the State. We may add that the persons admitted to the citizenship should in all cases be taken from the superior elements of the commons.

Similarly the second form of Oligarchy is to be established by a slight intensification of the oligarchical principle.

The form of Oligarchy which is opposite to the extreme Democracy, i.e. the form of Oligarchy which is the closest approximation to a dynastic or tyrannical form of government, as it is the worst of all Oligarchies, is the one that requires the largest

[1] Reading εἰσαγομένους.

precautions. For as bodies which are in a thoroughly
healthy condition and vessels which carry a crew fit
to put to sea admit of numerous blunders without
being fatally injured by them, while sickly bodies
and crazy vessels manned by a bad crew cannot
sustain the smallest blunders, so in the case of
polities it is the worst that require the greatest precautions.

The means of pre-serving Oligarchies.
As in a Democracy then it is a general rule that
the best preservative is a large population—for it is
the plea of numbers which is the correlative to the
plea of merit—so on the other hand in an Oligarchy
it is plain that the safety of the State must be due
to a good adjustment of the polity.

CHAP. VII.
The four branches of the military service. Their adaptation to the several polities.
The population of the State may be subdivided
into four principal parts viz. husbandmen, mechanics,
tradesmen and labourers, and there are four branches
of the military service viz. cavalry, heavy infantry,
light-armed troops and marines. Accordingly where
the country happens to be suited to cavalry, there is
a natural propriety in instituting the Oligarchy there
in a pronounced form; for in this case the safety of
the inhabitants depends upon the force of cavalry, and
it is only persons of large property who can afford
to keep horses. Where again the country is suitable
to heavy infantry, the next form of Oligarchy is appropriate; for it is the rich rather than the poor
who are qualified to serve as heavy infantry. A
strong force of light-armed soldiers or marines on
the other hand is wholly democratical. Recent experience shows that, where there is a large number
of light-armed soldiers and marines, the Oligarchs

are often worsted in the event of civil war. This is a
danger which ought to be met by an expedient borrowed from strategy, where generals unite with their
cavalry and heavy infantry forces a proportionate
number of light-armed troops. It is the light-armed
service that gives the commons in different States
their victory over the rich in civil wars, as their light
armour enables them to fight without difficulty against
a force of cavalry or heavy infantry. If the Oligarchs
then in any State allow the light-armed force to be
taken exclusively from the commons, they are so
far forging a weapon of attack upon themselves.
The proper course, in view of the differences of age
and of the natural distinction between old and young,
is that the Oligarchs should let their sons in youth
receive instruction in the easy exercises of the light-
armed service, so that, when they have passed out
of the ranks of boys, they may be personally masters
of the system.

Admission to the governing class should be open <abbr>Admission to the governing class in an Oligarchy.</abbr> p. 327.
to the general population either upon the principle
already described, viz. to all who acquire the requisite property qualification, or as at Thebes to such
persons when they have desisted for a stated period
from mechanical occupations or as at Massalia by a
selection of deserving persons whether members[1] of
the polity or external to it.

Again the most important offices of State, which Oligarchical devices.
must be confined to members of the governing body,
should be saddled with public burdens, so that

[1] It is probable that ἐν τῷ πολιτεύματι and ἐν τῇ πολιτείᾳ below
should change places.

the commons may acquiesce in their exclusion and may not grudge the officers of State the authority for which they pay so heavy a sum. And the officers of State upon their accession to power may appropriately celebrate magnificent sacrifices and construct some public work, that participation in the entertainments which naturally follow and the view of the city with its rich embellishment of votive offerings and public edifices may induce the commons to welcome the permanence of the polity ; not to say that the offerings and edifices will serve in the future as memorials of the heavy expense incurred by the upper class. But our modern Oligarchs adopt an exactly contrary line of action. They are fully as eager for the spoils as for the honour of office, so that these Oligarchies may well be described as nothing better than Democracies on a small scale.

So much for the right method of establishing the different forms of Democracy and Oligarchy.

CHAP. VIII.

The number and nature of the executive offices. p 298.

p. 300.

The next step in our discussion is to subdivide the field of the executive offices properly, determining their number, nature and provinces, as has been already said. For as it is impossible that a State should exist without the necessary offices, so it is impossible that it should be properly administered without such offices as advance the cause of good discipline and order. And further as the number of the offices will necessarily be smaller in small States and larger in large ones, as indeed has been already remarked, it is necessary to ascertain the character of the offices which may appropriately be combined with each other or kept distinct.

Taking first the functions which are indispensable (1) political. in any State, we begin with the superintendence of the market, which should be under the control of a definite office having the oversight of commercial transactions and general good order. For a system of sale and purchase may be said to be indispensable to any State as a means to the mutual supply of necessary wants ; nor is there any other equally ready method of securing independence, which is *ex hypo-thesi* the object of association in a single polity.

Another function, which comes next to this and is closely allied to it, includes the superintendence of all public and private property in the city with a view to the maintenance of good order, the preservation and restoration of dilapidated buildings and streets, the supervision of boundaries between neighbours in order to prevent disputes, and any other similar duties of superintendence. The office in question is commonly called the commissionership of the city. It embraces however various departments, to each of which in the more populous States different officers are appointed, such as constructors of fortifications, superintendents of the water-supply and guardians of the [1]harbour.

There is a third office equally indispensable and similar to the last, as its duties are the same, except that its locality is the country and the suburbs of the city. These officials are sometimes called commissioners of public lands and sometimes commissioners of woods and forests.

---

[1] Reading λιμένος.

Apart from these three offices of superintendence there is a fourth consisting of persons whose duty it is to receive and hold in charge the public revenues and to distribute them to the different branches of the administration. The name of these officers is receivers or treasurers.

Another office is the one before which all private contracts and the decisions of the Courts of Law have to be registered. It is in the presence of the same officers too that indictments have to be laid and preliminary proceedings in a lawsuit taken. Although there are some States in which the functions of this office, as of the commissionership of the city, are divided among several officers, it is *practically* a single office which controls all such business, under the name of recorders, presidents, remembrancers or some other similar title.

Next to this is an office which is probably the most indispensable and most difficult of all, viz. the office which is concerned with executions upon the property of persons who have been cast in their suits or are posted according to the registers of public defaulters, and with the custody of their persons. The difficulty of the office lies in the fact that it involves a considerable amount of odium, and consequently in any State where it offers no opportunity of large pecuniary gain people either refuse to accept it or, if they do accept it, will not perform the duties in accordance with the laws ; its necessity in the fact that there is no good in having legal decisions upon disputed questions of right, if they never receive practical execution, and hence if civic

The levying of fines.

society is impossible without lawsuits, it is equally impossible without the levying of fines. *In view of the unpopularity of the office* it is desirable that these officials should not form a single body, but that different persons should be appointed by the different Courts of Law and that an effort should be made to effect a similar division in regard to the proscription of persons whose names are posted. And further it is desirable that in some cases the fine should be levied by the officers themselves, and especially that fines imposed by the officers[1] of last year should by preference be levied by the officers of the current year, while as regards fines imposed by the existing officers it should be one officer who imposes the fine and another who levies it, e.g. the city-commissioners should levy the fines imposed by the censors of the market and some third board of officers the fines imposed by the city-commissioners. For the smaller the degree of odium attaching to the levying officers, the more effectual will be the execution. Where it is the same persons who impose and levy the fines, they are subject to a double unpopularity; while where it is the same persons who levy the fines in all cases, they are placed[2] in a relation of hostility to all the citizens. There are many States in which the police-authority has itself a distinct organization from the levying authority, as at Athens in the case of the officials known as the Eleven, *who have the custody of prisoners in some cases but do not levy fines.* Thus *as there are successful precedents for*

---

[1] Reading τὰς τῶν ἔνων.
[2] Reading πολεμίους ποιεῖ πᾶσιν.

the division, it is better to keep the police distinct and in their case to have recourse to the same artifice as before. For although the police are quite as necessary as the levying officers, it is a fact that this is the office of all others which the respectable classes are most disposed to shirk ; while it is not safe to intrust the lower orders with such authority, as they are more in need of police-supervision themselves than in a position to exercise it over others. The proper thing then is that there should not be a single definite office or the same office perpetually engaged in the work, but that the younger citizens, where there exists a system of youthful volunteers or militia, and the officers of State in certain sections should undertake the charge.

These are the offices which must be placed in the first rank as being in the highest degree indispensable. We come next to those offices which, although not less indispensable, are invested with a higher dignity, as requiring a large degree of experience and trustworthiness. I refer to such as are concerned with the defence of the city or are appointed for military purposes. Warders of the city-gates and walls, reviewing officers and inspectors of the drill of the citizens are equally necessary in time of peace and of war. The number of offices appointed to these various duties is larger in some States and smaller than others ; in fact in small States there is sometimes only a single office for[1] all of them. The officers in question are called generals and members.

----

[1] Reading περὶ πάντων.

of the Council of War. And in addition to these, if there is a force of cavalry or light-armed troops or archers or marines in the State, there are sometimes distinct officers appointed to command these several[1] departments and known as admirals and cavalry or infantry commanders with their subordinate and departmental officers, such as naval captains, majors, colonels, and so for each subdivision of a regiment. But all these functions fall under a single general head, viz. military supervision.

Such is the condition then of the office we have described. And as there are some officers, if not all, who have a large amount of public money passing through their hands, it is indispensable that there should be a distinct board of officers, whose business it is to receive and audit the accounts, while there is no money passing independently through their hands. They are variously called auditors, accountants, inspectors of accounts and public prosecutors.

In addition to all these offices there is still the supreme office of all. For it is often one and the same office which enjoys the power of ratification as well as of initiation, or there is an office to which belongs the presidency of the popular Assembly in States where the authority of the commons is supreme; for there must be a body which convenes the supreme power in the polity, *viz. the commons.* It is sometimes called a Preliminary Council from its function of giving a preliminary consideration to bills *before they are presented to the Public As-*

The supreme office.

----

[1] Reading ἐπὶ τούτων ἕκαστον.

sembly, but more usually where the government is a popular one, a Council.

(2) religious.   This is practically a complete list of such offices as are political in their character. Another species of superintendence is the superintendence of divine worship, including such officers as priests and superintendents of the ordinances of religion, whose duty it is to keep existing buildings in a good state of repair, to restore dilapidated buildings and to look after the general apparatus of divine worship. These duties are in some places, i. e. in small States, all placed in the same hands, while in others they are confided to a number of officers distinct from the priesthood, such as masters of the sacrifices, warders of sanctuaries and treasurers of the sacred funds. Next to these are the officers who are appointed to direct all such public sacrifices as are not assigned by law to the priesthood but are solemnly celebrated' upon the hearth of the State. They are in different States termed archons, kings and presidents.

Speaking summarily then we may say that the objects of necessary superintendence are religious services, the science of war, the revenue and expenditure of the State, the market, the city, the harbours and the country, the system[1] of the Courts of Law, the registration of contracts, the levying of fines, the custody of prisoners, the audit, inspection and scrutiny[2] of the officers' accounts. There is finally the deliberative agency in matters of State.

---

[1] Reading τὰ περὶ τὰ δικαστήρια.
[2] Reading προσευθύνας.

There are certain other officers who exist only[1] in such States as enjoy a larger degree of leisure and prosperity and have also a regard for general decorum, such as censors of women, guardians of the laws, censors of boys, presidents of gymnastic exercises and lastly the superintendents of gymnastic and Dionysiac contests and any other similar performances that may take place. But of the offices in question some, e.g. the censorship of women and boys, are evidently not suited to a Democracy, as the poor having no slaves are obliged to use their wives and children as attendants. Lastly, of the three forms which may be adopted in the election of the supreme office of State, viz. a Guardianship of the Laws, a Preliminary Council and a Council, the first is an aristocratical, the second an oligarchical and the third a popular institution.

The different offices of State have now practically all been described in general outline.

---

[1] Reading ἴδιαι.

BOOK VIII.

Chap. I.
Political
revolutions. THE discussion of the various subjects of which we undertook to treat with one exception is now practically complete. We have next to consider the nature, number and character of the circumstances which produce political revolutions, the agencies destructive of the several polities, the general sequence of polities in a revolutionary age and lastly the preservatives of polities both generally and [1]individually.

The cause
of a variety
of polities. It is right at the outset to assume the principle that the cause of the appearance of many different polities in History is that, while all people agree in the conception of justice as proportional equality, they pp. 123 sqq.
134 sqq. fail to realize this equality, as has been already said. Thus Democracy originated in the theory that persons, if equal to others in any respect, are equal absolutely, for it is because all are free alike that they suppose themselves to be all equal absolutely; and Oligarchy in the assumption that persons, if unequal to others in a single respect, are wholly unequal, for

---

[1] The clause ἔτι δὲ διὰ τίνων ἂν μάλιστα σώζοιτο τῶν πολιτειῶν ἑκάστη is, as Susemihl suggests, a διττογραφία, and is omitted in the translation.

then to adopt the principle partly of arithmetical and partly of proportional equality. Still there is more *Comparative stability of Democracy and Oligarchy.* stability and less danger of sedition in Democracy than in Oligarchy. For in an Oligarchy there occur two forms of seditious disturbance, one among the Oligarchs themselves and the other between the Oligarchs and the commons ; but in a Democracy sedition can only take the form of an attack upon the Oligarchs *who aspire to exclusive power*, while no sedition worth speaking of ever occurs within the ranks of the commons themselves. And finally the polity which rests upon the middle class has more affinity to Democracy [1]than to Oligarchy, and there is no polity among the class we are now considering, *i.e. with the exception of the best polity*, which has a character of so much stability as this.

But as we are investigating the circumstances Chap. II. which give rise to seditions and political revolutions, we must first ascertain generally their predisposing occasions and causes. These[2] are practically three in number, which must first be roughly distinguished in the abstract. We have to ascertain the conditions under which people are seditious, the objects which they have in view, and thirdly the occasions predisposing them to political disturbances and seditions.

The principal cause which produces in people *The conditions favourable to sedition.* more or less of a disposition to revolution must be generally defined as the one of which we have already spoken. For it is the aspiration after equality which provokes the commons to sedition when they suppose

---

[1] Omitting ή.
[2] Reading εἰσὶ δέ.

that they have a smaller share *of political advantages* although they are the equals of the privileged Few, and it is the aspiration after inequality or in other words after superiority which provokes the Oligarchs to sedition, when they imagine that despite their inequality their share of *political advantages* is not greater than that of others but is equal or even smaller. This ambition of equality or inequality may be either just or unjust; *but the fact is such as I have described,* for in the one case it is from a position of inferiority that people are encouraged to sedition by the hope of equality, and in the other from a position of equality by the hope of predominance.

Such are the conditions under which people become the authors of sedition. The objects of sedition on the other hand are gain, honour and their opposites; for it is sometimes in the effort to avoid dishonour and pecuniary loss or to shield their friends from them that people raise seditions in their States.

The objects of sedition.

The causes predisposing to sedition.

The causes and predisposing occasions of political disturbances, which produce in the agents the disposition we have described and produce it in reference to these objects, are from one point of view seven and from another more numerous. Two of these are identical with the objects we have already mentioned, although they have a different bearing. For gain and honour are in this case the causes of our exasperation against one another not in the hope of acquiring them for ourselves, as in the last case, but from the sight of others enjoying either justly or unjustly a larger share of them than we do. The other predisposing causes are insolence, fear, predominant influence, contempt, the

destroyed, *as is the case* when the foot e.g. is four
cubits and the rest of the body only two spans long,
or sometimes would actually be metamorphosed into
the form of another animal, if the disproportionate
growth were not only quantitative but qualitative, so
a State is composed of various parts, and it often
happens that there is an imperceptible increase in one
of these, let us say in the poorer population in Democracies or Polities. This may sometimes even be the
result of accidental circumstances. At Tarentum e.g.
the defeat and destruction of a large number of the
upper classes by the Iapygians a little subsequently
to the Persian wars led to the substitution of a
Democracy for a Polity. At Argos again after the
destruction of the members of the seventh[1] order
by the Lacedaemonian Cleomenes it was necessary to admit some of the Periœci *or surrounding
subject population* to the citizenship, and at Athens
the reverses sustained by the army led to a diminution in the number of the upper classes, as every
man whose name appeared on the register was compelled to serve in the ranks during the Lacedaemonian war. And the same result, although not to
the same extent, occurs in Democracies, where an
increase in the numbers of the poorer classes or
in the amount of property *possessed by the Few* effects
a revolution to an oligarchical or dynastic form of
government.

---

[1] It is impossible to attach any precise or certain meaning to
the phrase τῶν ἐν τῇ ἑβδόμῃ; but the context is in favour of the
notion that it describes a class of the citizens rather than a time
or place.

Polities may be revolutionized without actual sedition in consequence of party-spirit, as at Heraea
where the change from suffrage to lot in the appointment of the officers of State was due to the prevalent
habit of electing none but the candidates of a party,
or in consequence of neglectfulness in allowing the
admission of persons disloyal to the polity to the
supreme offices of State, as was the case at Oreos
where the overthrow of the Oligarchy arose from the
accession of Heracleodorus to an official position, who
converted the existing Oligarchy into a Polity and
afterwards a Democracy.

Another cause of revolution is insignificant change.
It happens not infrequently that a great alteration
has[1] been imperceptibly wrought in the institutions of
a State from a failure to observe the insignificant
steps. In Ambracia e.g. where the property qualification for office was originally small, people eventually
came to hold office without possessing any property
qualification at all from the idea that there was no
difference between a small qualification and none at
all or that they came to very much the same thing.

Diversity of race among the citizens is another
cause of sedition, so long at least as the different
elements have not been welded together. For it is
as little possible to create a State in any arbitrary
period of time as to create it of any arbitrary population. Accordingly the great majority of States to
which a number of alien colonists have been admitted
at the time of their foundation or at a later date have

---

[1] Reading γενομένη.

been the scenes of [1]violent sedition. Thus the Achaeans who united with the Troezenians for the coloniza-
tion of Sybaris afterwards attained a numerical superiority and expelled them from the State ; the result
of which was the [2]curse that fell upon the Sybarites.
Again, at Thurii the Sybarites quarrelled with their
fellow-colonists and were expelled for preferring a
claim to exceptional privileges upon the plea that
they were the proper lords of the country. And there
are other similar cases, as at Byzantium, where the
later colonists being detected in a conspiracy against
the original citizens were driven out at the point of
the sword, at Antissa where the Chian exiles who had
been admitted to the citizenship were expelled in the
same way, and at Zancle where the citizens were
themselves expelled by the Samians whom they had
welcomed within their walls. Again, the Apolloniates
on the Euxine sea were involved in civil war by
the admission of a fresh body of settlers, the Syracusans after the [3]era of the tyrants were divided
owing to the aliens and mercenaries upon whom
they had conferred the citizenship and came to an
actual pitched battle, and the Amphipolitans were
expelled almost to a man by the colonists whom they
had themselves received from Chalcis.

[1] Reading διεστασίασαν.

[2] "The curse that fell upon the Sybarites" was probably the
destruction of their State B.C. 510, as related by Diodorus xii.
9, 2 sqq.

[3] By " the era of the tyrants " is meant the Gelonian dynasty.
It was in B.C. 466 that Thrasybulus, its last member, was driven
from Syracuse.

It sometimes happens too that the cause of sedition in States is their localities, when the country is not naturally adapted to the existence of a single State. We may instance the feuds at Clazomenae between the inhabitants of [1]Chytron and the islanders and at Colophon between the Colophonians and the [2]Notians. Nor is there a complete harmony *of democratical sentiments* at Athens; but the inhabitants of the Piraeus are more advanced Democrats than the population of the city. For as in war the passage of streams however small breaks up a regiment, so it seems that every distinction in a State is a cause of division. The greatest division perhaps is that between virtue and vice, the next that between wealth and poverty, and there are other divisions more or less striking, one of which is the local division we have described.

CHAP. IV.
Distinction between the objects and the occasions of sedition.

It is not the objects of sedition that are unimportant but the occasions; the objects are always important. And the effects of quite unimportant seditions are serious, when the parties to them are the powerful people in the State. It was so at Syracuse in the olden days when a political revolution was the consequence of a quarrel between two youths of official rank about a love-affair. In the absence of

---

[1] Chytron or, as Strabo calls it, Chytrion was on the Ionian coast, probably occupying the site of the old Clazomenae, from which the inhabitants had withdrawn in the earlier part of the 5th century B.C., to the island lying opposite to it. Alexander the Great united the island-city to the mainland by a mole.

[2] Notion, as appears from Thuc. iii. 34, was the harbour-town of Colophon.

one of them one of his companions seduced the object
of his affections, and the aggrieved person in his
indignation against the offender retaliated by inducing
his wife to commit adultery. The result was that
they gradually collected adherents among the members of the governing class until they had arrayed the
whole body in two opposing factions. It is necessary
therefore to be on our guard against dangers of this
kind at their commencement and to put a *speedy* end
to the feuds of leading and influential people in the
State. For it is at the beginning that the mistake
is committed in these cases, and as the beginning
according to the proverb is half the whole, *i.e. is as
important as all the rest*, it follows that even a small
mistake at the beginning *of any affair* bears the
same proportion, *i.e. is equivalent*, to the mistakes
made at all the other points. It is a general rule
that feuds among the upper classes involve the State
as a whole in their effects. This was the case at
Hestiæa subsequently to the Persian wars in consequence of a dispute between two brothers about[1]
their patrimonial estate; for the poorer of the
two, finding that his brother refused to produce
the property and the treasure discovered by their
father, made himself a party among the Democrats,
and the other being a man of large property, among
the wealthy class. So too at Delphi it was a dispute
arising out of a matrimonial question that was the
beginning of all the subsequent seditions. The bride-
groom, interpreting as an omen of evil some accidental

---

[1] Reading περὶ τῆς πατρῴας νομῆς.

occurrence at the time when he came to fetch his
bride home, went away without her, and the bride's
relations [1]feeling themselves to be insulted threw
some consecrated property into the flames while he
was sacrificing and then put him to death for sacri-
lege. At Mitylene again it was a feud arising about
heiresses that proved to be the beginning of a world
of troubles and *more especially* of the war with the
Athenians in which their city was captured by Paches.
The circumstances were as follows. A rich citizen
named Timophanes died leaving two daughters.
[2]Dexandros who had been a rejected suitor for them
on behalf of his sons became the prime mover in
the feud and, as he was Athenian consul at Mitylene, incited the Athenians to declare war. Again, in
Phocis it was a quarrel of which an heiress was the
subject between Mnasias the father of Mneson and
Euthycrates the father of Onomarchus that proved to
be the beginning of the Phocian sacred war. And
lastly the polity of Epidamnus was revolutionized in
consequence of a marriage engagement. A person
who had secretly betrothed his daughter to a young
citizen, being fined by the father of his future son-in-
law in his official capacity, felt the indignity so acutely
that he formed an alliance with the unenfranchised
classes in the State *to effect a revolution.*

One cause of revolution in polities, although it
may equally lead to an Oligarchy, a Democracy
or a Polity, is the accession of high repute or

[1] Reading οἱ δ᾽ ὡς ὑβρισθέντες.
[2] Dexandros and Mnasias are the forms which have the best
MSS. authority.

influence to some particular office or class in the State. Thus it was apparently the reputation won by the Court of Areopagus in the Persian wars which intensified the character of the polity, *i.e.* *rendered it more oligarchical;* and on the other hand the sea-faring population by its services in winning the victory at Salamis and [1]thereby founding the Athenian supremacy, which rested on the command of the sea, succeeded in increasing the strength of the Democracy. So too at Argos the nobles were emboldened by the renown they won in the battle fought at Mantineia against the Lacedaemonians to attempt the overthrow of the Democracy; at Syracuse the commons, to whom had been due the victory in the war with the Athenians, revolutionized the existing Polity into a Democracy; at Chalcis the commons after allying themselves with the nobles to destroy the tyrant Phoxus proceeded at once to keep the control of the polity in their own hands; and similarly in Ambracia again the commons after aiding the conspirators to expel the tyrant Periander got the polity into their own power. It is indeed a general rule of which we must not lose sight that all who have been instrumental in augmenting the power of a State, whether private individuals or executive officers or tribes or any class or body whatever, become a cause of political disturbance, as it happens either that there are persons who disturb the peace out of envy at the honour paid to these public benefactors or else that they are themselves so much

---

[1] Reading διὰ ταύτην.

elated by their preeminence as to refuse to acquiesce any longer in mere equality.

Another occasion of political disturbance is when the classes that appear antagonistic in the State, viz. the rich and the commons, are evenly balanced, and there is no [1]middle class or it is extremely small ; for if one of the two classes has a great and manifest superiority of power, the other is unwilling to undergo the risk of a contest. And this is the reason why the class distinguished by conspicuous virtue is hardly ever guilty of seditious action ; they constitute an insignificant minority.

Such is broadly the state of the case as regards the predisposing occasions and causes of sedition and The modes revolution in the various polities. But political disturb-
of political
revolution. ance may be effected either by force or by fraud, and force may take the form either of initial or of subsequent compulsion. For the fraud as well as the force may be of two kinds. It sometimes happens that the revolutionary party begins by fraudulently inducing the people to consent to a political revolution and afterwards employs force to maintain it against their will. Thus the Four Hundred during their régime at Athens first deceived the people by the pretence that the Persian king would supply money for the war against the Lacedaemonians and after this false statement made a protracted effort to maintain the polity by force. There are other occasions when persuasion is successfully employed at a later stage as well as in the first days of a revolution to secure the acqui-

---

[1] Reading μηδὲν ἢ μικρὸν.

escence of the people in the authority of the Government.

Speaking broadly then of polities in general, we may say that these are the causes which have resulted in revolutions. We have now to take the various CHAP. V. kinds of polity severally and by the light of the principles at which we have arrived consider the actual results in detail.

The main cause of revolutions in Democracies is Revolutions the intemperate conduct of the demagogues who force cies. the propertied class to combine partly by instituting and nature. malicious prosecutions against individuals—for the worst enemies are united by a common fear—and partly by inciting the masses against them as a body. We may see this actually [1]occurring in many cases. At Cos e.g. the democracy was revolutionized through the appearance of unscrupulous demagogues in the State and the consequent combination of the nobles. [2]At Rhodes the demagogues were in the habit of supplying the people with fees *for their attendance in the public Assembly and the Courts of Law* and of preventing the payment of dues to the trierarchs, so that they were compelled by fear of the lawsuits with which they were threatened *by their creditors* to form a conspiracy and abolish the Democracy. It was the fault of the demagogues again that the Democracy of Heracleia was abolished immediately after the foundation of the colony ; for the nobles fled one after another from the oppression to which they were subjected, until at a later date the exiles

[1] Omitting οὕτως.
[2] Reading καὶ ἐν 'Ρόδῳ μισθοφορὰν οἱ δημαγωγοὶ ἐπόριζον.

23—2

collected in a body, returned home and abolished the Democracy. It was much in the same way that the Democracy at Megara was overthrown. The demagogues in order to have an opportunity of confiscation ejected large numbers of the nobles from the State, until they had swelled the ranks of the exiles to such an extent that they returned home, 'conquered the Democrats in a pitched battle and established the Oligarchy. The same was the case at Cyme with the Democracy overthrown by Thrasymachus. And if we look at the generality of other States, we may discover the same characteristics in their revolutions. The demagogues drive the nobles to combine sometimes by direct oppression in the hope of currying favour with the people, whether they make an actual re-distribution of their properties *among the lower orders or cripple* their incomes by heavy public burdens, and at other times by vexatious prosecutions intended to afford an opportunity of confiscating the possessions of the wealthy.

It usually happened in ancient times, whenever the functions of demagogue and general were united in the same person, that Democracies were revolutionized into Tyrannies. The great majority of ancient tyrants had been demagogues. The reason why this was the case in those days and is not so now is that the demagogues of that age belonged to the class of active generals, as at that early date there were no practised rhetoricians *to become popular leaders,* whereas in our own day, when Rhetoric has become so important, it is able speakers who play the part of demagogues, and their ignorance of military matters prevents them from attempting to seize supreme power, although there may have been some trifling exceptions to this rule. One reason for the creation of Tyrannies in former times rather than in our own day was the importance of the official positions intrusted to individuals. Thus at Miletus a Tyranny was the outcome of the Presidency owing to the wide and important jurisdiction of the President[1]. Another reason is that, as States were not large in those days, and the people lived in the country busily engaged in their occupations, the popular leaders, whenever they were men of military genius, attempted to make themselves tyrants. They were enabled to do so in all cases by possessing the confidence of the commons, the ground of this confidence being their detestation of the wealthy classes. This was the case at Athens with Pisistratus in consequence of his feud with the *wealthy landed* proprietors of the plain, with Theagenes at Megara after his slaughter of the live stock of the wealthy whom he found encroaching upon the pasture-land by the river, and with Dionysius who was elevated to the tyranny as a reward for his accusation of Daphnaeus and the propertied class, because his hostility to them won him confidence as a friend of the people.

·   Yet another species of revolution is from the traditional to the most modern form of Democracy. Where the offices of State are elective, but there is no requisite property qualification, and the election is in the hands of the commons, candidates who are eager for office go so far in their desire of popularity

[1] The πρύτανις or President was, as Susemihl thinks, the highest officer of State in republican Miletus.

as to invest the commons with an authority superior
even to the laws. The means of preventing or at least
mitigating this evil would be to place the appointment
of the executive officers in the hands of the tribes
instead of the whole body of commons.

The causes which I have specified are practically
productive of all the various revolutions in Democracies.

CHAP. VI. ` Revolutions in Oligarchies on the other hand
Revolutions
in Oligar- generally assume two most conspicuous forms.
chies.
Their forms   The first is the case where the Oligarchs oppress
and causes. the masses. For any champion of the people is good
enough at such a time, especially when it happens
that the leader is taken from the ranks of the Oligarchs themselves, like Lygdamis at Naxos who subsequently made himself tyrant of the Naxians.

But secondly when the sedition arises among the
actual[1] Oligarchs, it may take a variety of forms.

Sometimes the destruction of the polity is effected
by persons who are members of the propertied class,
although not of the official body, when the honours of
State are in the hands of a narrow clique. This has
been the case at Massalia, at Istros, at Heracleia and in
other States where the members of the propertied class
who were excluded from office kept up an agitation
until first the elder and at a later date the younger
brothers obtained admission. It must be explained that
there are some States in which a father and a son and
others in which an elder and a younger brother are not
allowed to hold office simultaneously. And while at
Massalia the [2]Oligarchy assumed more the character of

[1] Reading ἐξ αὐτῶν.
[2] Reading ἡ ὀλιγαρχία.

a Polity, at Istros it ended eventually in a Democracy and at Heracleia was transferred from the hands of a smaller body to a body of Six Hundred. Again, the revolution of the Oligarchy at Cnidos was due to an internal quarrel among the nobles arising from the fact that the admission to office was confined to a few persons and, as has been said, if a father was a member of the official class, the son was excluded, and if there were several brothers in a family, it was only the eldest who was admitted. For the commons seizing the opportunity of these feuds and finding a champion in the ranks of the nobles rose in insurrection and overcame the Oligarchs ; for a house divided against itself can never stand. It was the same at Erythrae with the Oligarchy of the Basilidae in olden times. The strict limitation of the official class, despite the wise administration of the persons who possessed political privileges, produced such a feeling of indignation in the commons that they revolutionized the polity.

Another occasion of disturbance in Oligarchies arising within the oligarchical body itself is when personal rivalry induces the Oligarchs to assume the rôle of demagogues. But this demagogy may take two forms. It may be within the oligarchical body itself. The appearance of a demagogue is possible even in a narrow clique of Oligarchs. Thus it was within the ranks of the Thirty at Athens that the party of Charicles rose to power by courting like demagogues the other members of the Thirty, and it was within the ranks of the Four Hundred that the party of Phrynichus rose to power in the same manner. It may be the mob on the other hand to whom the members of the Oligarchy pay court, as at Larisa where the Guardians of the citizens were always toadying the mob upon whom they were dependent for election. This is liable to occur in any Oligarchy where it is not the class from which the officers of State are taken that constitutes the body of electors but, while eligibility to office is conditional upon a high property qualification or upon membership in a political club, the electing body consists of the heavy-armed soldiers or of the whole body of commons, as was long the case at Abydos. It is the same where the Courts of Law are not constituted of members of the governing class. The result of the court paid to the people in order to secure favourable verdicts is a revolution of the polity, as actually happened at Heracleia upon the Pontus. Another occasion of revolution is when an effort is made by a certain party to narrow the Oligarchy still further, as the advocates of equality *among all the members of the oligarchical body* are then obliged to invite the assistance of the commons.

Again, revolutions occur in an Oligarchy when *some of the Oligarchs* have wasted all their private means in riotous living, as in this case they are eager for innovation and either affect a Tyranny themselves or set up somebody else as tyrant. It was thus that Hipparinus helped to place Dionysius on the throne of Syracuse, that at Amphipolis a man named Cleotimus introduced the Chalcidian settlers and upon their arrival arrayed them in opposition to the rich, and that at Ægina the person who conducted the negociation with Chares attempted for a similar reason to effect a revolution of the polity. The spendthrifts in question sometimes make a direct[1] attempt at political innovation and at other times plunder the Treasury; and in the latter case the result is that an attack is made upon the Government either by the offenders, *if it offers a resistance to their proceedings*, or, *if it is favourable to them*, by the opponents of their malversation, as was the case at Apollonia upon the Pontus.

[2]Another occasion of seditions *arising within the oligarchical body itself* is when some of the actual Oligarchs suffer a repulse at the hands of others or are the victims of party violence in matrimonial or legal cases. We may instance as the results of a matrimonial question the seditious disturbances which have been already described as well as the overthrow of the Oligarchy of the Knights at Eretria by Diagoras in consequence of the wrong done him in an affair of marriage. A judicial sentence was the motive cause of the sedition at Heracleia and at Thebes, where Euetion[3] in the one case and Archias in the other were subjected on a charge of adultery to a punishment which no doubt was merited but was prompted by a spirit of factious partisanship; for their enemies carried the vindictiveness of rivalry to such an extent as to have them confined in open market in the pillory.

It has frequently happened too that the over-des-

p. 352.

---

[1] Reading εὐθὺς ἐπιχειροῦσι,

[2] It seems best to follow Susemihl in transposing to this place the passage γίνονται δὲ στάσεις......ἡ ἐν Χίῳ ὀλιγαρχία p. 206, ll. 17—30, as describing other forms of sedition which arise within the oligarchical body.

[3] Εὐετίωνος is the form of the name which has the best MSS. authority.

potic character of Oligarchies has led to their overthrow by exciting a sentiment of indignation in the
breasts of some members of the governing class.
Such was the case of the oligarchies in Cnidos and
Chios.

But where harmony prevails among the Oligarchs
an Oligarchy is not easily destroyed[1]. This we may
infer from the case of the Pharsalian polity in which
the Oligarchs, although they form only a small minority of the population, are able to retain authority
over the Many by being on good terms among themselves.

Oligarchies are sometimes destroyed on the other
hand by the creation of a second Oligarchy within the
first; and this is liable to occur when the entire governing class is numerically small, and yet the highest offices
of State are not open to all the members of this small
body. Such was once the case at Elis where the polity
was in the hands of a Few, and it was only a small
fraction of the Few who were admitted to the Senate,
as the Senators who were always ninety in number
held office for life and the method of election was
dynastic, *i.e. characteristic of a narrow Oligarchy,*
and similar to the election of the Senate at Lacedaemon.

A revolution in an Oligarchy[2] may take place in
time either of war or of peace. The occasion in the
former case is sometimes that the Oligarchs from
distrust of the commons are obliged to employ mercenary troops, and thus the individual in whose hands

---

[1] Omitting ἐξ αὐτῆς.

[2] Reading ὀλιγαρχιῶν.

they place the command not infrequently makes himself tyrant like Timophanes at Corinth or, if there are several commanders, they found a dynastic government in their own interest, and at other times that the fear of this induces the Oligarchs to admit the masses to full political privileges, as they cannot dispense with the assistance of the commons. The circumstances in which an Oligarchy is revolutionized in time of peace are when the mutual distrustfulness of the Oligarchs is so great that they put the police of the city into the hands of mercenary troops and an arbiter between the factions who sometimes succeeds in making himself master of both, as happened in ¹the case of Simus at Larisa during the reign of the Aleuadae and at Abydos in the era of the political clubs, among which the club of Iphiades was one.

Lastly, accidental circumstances may be the cause of revolutions whether in the so-called Polity or in Oligarchies, i. e. in all governments where a certain property assessment is requisite for the Council, the Courts of Law and the offices² of State. If we take e.g. the property qualification originally fixed with reference to existing conditions, admitting a Few only in an Oligarchy and the middle class in a Polity to the enjoyment of political privileges, it often happens that a season of prosperity due to *long-continued* peace or some other fortunate circumstance multiplies so greatly the value of the same estates as to admit the entire body of citizens to full privileges, sometimes gradually by a slow and imperceptible process of re-

¹ Reading ἐπὶ τῆς τῶν Ἀλευαδῶν ἀρχῆς περὶ Σίμον.
² Omitting ἄλλας.

volution and at other times with an excessive ra-
pidity.

We have now enumerated the causes of revolutions
and seditions in Oligarchies. It is to be observed as
a general rule applicable both to Democracies and
Oligarchies that they are sometimes altered not to the
antagonistic polities but to other polities of the same
kind, e.g. from the restricted forms of Democracy and
Oligarchy to the absolute forms and *vice versa.*

CHAP. VII.   Coming to Aristocracies, we find that one cause of
Revolutions sedition is the limitation in the number of persons
in Aristo-
cracies. admitted to the honours of State, a cause which has
Their causes
and occa- been already described as an element of disturbance in
sions.
p. 358. Oligarchies. (For an Aristocracy itself is in a certain
sense an Oligarchy, as in both the ruling class is numerically limited. But the ground of the limitation
is different; in fact it is only in appearance that Aristocracy, as being so limited, is an Oligarchy[1].) This
cause of political disturbance is necessarily most
operative when there is a considerable[2] body *of unprivileged persons* within the State who have a proud
feeling that they are the equals[3] *of the privileged
class* in virtue, like the so-called Partheniae at Lacedaemon on the strength of their descent from the
Peers[4] or *fully enfranchised citizens;* for the Partheniae were detected in a conspiracy and sent away out
of the country to be the colonists of Tarentum. Again,

---

[1] The sentences enclosed in brackets are virtually parenthetical.
[2] Reading τι πλῆθος.   [3] Reading ὁμοίων.
[4] The ὅμοιοι or Peers at Lacedaemon, as opposed to the ὑπο-
μείονες, were the fully enfranchised and privileged members of the
State.

sedition is apt to occur when a stigma is put upon
persons of consequence who are fully the equals of any
citizen in virtue by other citizens who hold a position
of greater dignity, as e.g. upon Lysander by the Lacedaemonian kings. *'Other occasions of sedition in an
Aristocracy are* when there is an individual of strong
character who is excluded from the honours of State like
Cinadon the author of the conspiracy and insurrection
against the Spartiates in the reign of Agesilaus, or again
when there is excessive poverty on one side and excessive wealth on the other within the State—a condition
of things which is especially incident to warlike times
and actually occurred at Lacedaemon about the time
of the Messenian war, [1]as appears from the poem of
Tyrtaeus called Eunomia (Good Order); for it was
under pressure of the war that a certain number of
the citizens demanded a re-distribution of the soil—
or lastly if there is an individual already powerful and
capable of extending his power, *who heads a sedition*
in the hope of making himself monarch, as according
to the popular view was the case of Pausanias the
commander-in-chief in the Persian war at Lacedaemon
and of Annon at Carthage.

But the main cause of the dissolution of Polities
and Aristocracies alike is a deviation from their
proper principles of justice in the constitution of the
polity itself. Its origin is the unsuccessful fusion of
the democratical and oligarchical elements in the
Polity and of these elements with virtue added
in the Aristocracy, but especially of the first two,
as it is a fusion of these elements only that

---

[1] Omitting καὶ before τοῦτο.

is attempted in the majority of so-called Aristo-

Compara-
tive sta-
bility of
Aristocra-
cies and
Politics.

cracies as well as in Polities. For the difference between Aristocracies and Polities in the limited sense of the word and the reason why the latter are more permanent than the former is that all constitutions of the kind *we are considering* which incline to Oligarchy are called Aristocracies, while those which incline to popular government are called Polities. And thus the comparative stability of all such Polities is due to the fact that in them the numerical majority have the upper hand, and they are sooner satisfied with mere equality, while the propertied class, if invested with superiority by the political constitution, is eager to display an insolent and aggressive spirit. It is a general rule however that, whatever may be the bias of a polity, it is in that direction that it is usually revolutionized, as the two parties in the State, *the rich and the poor*, respectively extend their power, viz. Polity in the direction of Democracy and Aristocracy in the direction of Oligarchy. It may happen on the other hand that these polities are revolutionized to their opposites, viz. Aristocracy to Democracy, when the poorer classes feeling aggrieved effect a violent circumvolution of the government, and Polity to Oligarchy. For the only conditions of permanence are proportional equality and security of rights. There was an instance of a polity being changed to its opposite at Thurii where the excessive amount of the property assessment requisite for office led to its reduction and to an increase in the number of the official boards, and the illegal acquisition of the entire soil by the nobles—an encroachment facilitated

by the excessively oligarchical character of the Polity
—resulted in the commons who had been disciplined
in the war getting the upper hand of the Guards *or
military force maintained by the Oligarchs and never
resting* until a surrender had been made by all who
were in actual possession of an exorbitant amount of
land. Another cause of revolution is that the tendency of all aristocratical polities to be oligarchical
affords the nobles an opportunity of self-aggrandisement. At Lacedaemon e.g. the wealth of the country
is gradually falling into the hands of a Few, and the
nobles enjoy a greater freedom of action and *especially*
of matrimonial alliance.   And while we are upon this
point, it was the marriage connexion[1] with Dionysius,
we may remark, that led to the destruction of the
Locrian State ; which would never have happened in a
Democracy or in an Aristocracy where there was a successful fusion of the different elements.

But an imperceptible revolution in Aristocracies is
effected principally by a gradual process of dissolution.
It is a remark which has been already made in this   p. 348.
work, as applicable to all forms of polity generally
that insignificant change is one cause of revolutions.
For no sooner has some one constitutional point been
surrendered than it is easier to introduce another
slightly more important innovation, *and so on* until
an innovation has been effected in the whole existing

[1] One of the wives of the elder Dionysius was Doris a native
of the Epizephyrian Locri. It was this connexion that led the
younger Dionysius upon his expulsion from Syracuse B.C. 356 to
flee to Locri, where he was generously received and requited the
hospitality of the citizens by making himself their tyrant.

system. This was the case with the polity at Thurii among others. There was a law there that nobody should be general a second time except after an interval of five years. Upon this some of the younger generation, who had displayed military talents and were in the enjoyment of a high popularity among the masses[1], in contempt of the executive authorities and in the expectation of an easy success began by making an attempt to abrogate this law so as to allow the same people to be generals continuously, as they saw that the commons would be only too glad to vote for them. The officers appointed to watch innovations in the laws, the Councillors as they were called, although eager at first to resist the proposition, were prevailed upon to acquiesce in it under the impression that the young citizens, if they succeeded in altering this law, would leave the rest of the polity undisturbed; but at a later date their desire to prevent further innovation proved absolutely ineffectual, and the entire system of the polity was revolutionized to a dynastic government in the hands of the party who had originated the revolution.

Polities generally are liable to dissolution not only from within but from without, when there is *a State having* an antagonistic polity either near to them or distant but possessed of considerable power. This is a truth that was continually verified in the case of the Athenians and Lacedaemonians, the former of whom abolished the Oligarchies and the latter the Democracies wherever they found them.

---

[1] Omitting τῶν φρουρῶν.

The origins of revolutions and seditions in polities
have now practically been described. We have next
to discuss the means of preserving polities both generally and individually.

CHAP. VIII.
The pre-
servatives of
polities.

It is evident at the outset that, as we know the
means of destruction in the different polities, we know
also the means of their preservation; for opposite
effects are produced by opposite causes, and destruction is the opposite of preservation.

In any polity, in which a successful fusion of various
elements has been achieved, we ought above everything
to be on our guard against illegality and especially to
take precautions against insignificant steps in this
direction. ¹For illegality is imperceptibly admitted
into States *and brings them to ruin*, as small expenses
frequently incurred are the ruin of properties. The
reason why the deception² is not observed is that
it does not take place all at once ; for the judgment
is deluded by petty acts of illegality according to the
sophistical argument that if every part is small, so is
the whole. But although there is one sense in which
this is true, there is another in which it is false. The
truth is that the whole or the sum total is not small
but is only composed of small parts.

We must be on our guard then in the first place
against this beginning of revolution, and secondly
we must put no trust in the measures concocted
as artifices to impose upon the masses, as they are
proved by experience to be failures. What we

¹ Reading λανθάνει γὰρ παραδυομένη ἡ παρανομία ὥσπερ τὰς
οὐσίας τὸ μικρὸν δαπάνημα ἀναιρεῖ πολλάκις γινόμενον.
² Reading ἡ ἀπάτη.

W. A.   24

understand by political artifices has been already described.

Further, it is to be observed that there are some polities, not only Aristocracies but even Oligarchies, which owe their permanence not to the stability of the polities in themselves but to the good terms on which the persons in official positions live with the citizens who do not enjoy political privileges as well as with the members of the governing class, in that they abstain from all oppression of the unprivileged body, admit to full political privileges the members of it who show a capacity for command and never wound the honour of the ambitious spirits on the one hand or injure the pecuniary interests of the Many on the other, while in all their relations to one another and to the members of the privileged body generally they display a true democratical spirit. For the principle of equality, which it is the ambition of the popular party to realize in the case of the masses, is not only just but actually advantageous in the case of the Peers *or privileged class in an Oligarchy or Aristocracy.* And from this it follows that, if there is a considerable number of members of the governing class, there are not a few popular institutions which are advantageous, one such being the limitation of the tenure of office to a period of six months as a means of admitting all the Peers in turn to an official position. For the Peers in virtue of their equality form a sort of Democracy among themselves, and it is thus that demagogues often make their appearance among them, as has been already remarked. Another advantage *of a system of short tenure* is that there is not the same

p. 350.

danger of Oligarchies and Aristocracies being merged in Dynasties. For abuse of power on the part of the officers of State is not so easy where the tenure of office is limited as where it is long, as it is the long tenure which in Oligarchies and Democracies is a cause of the establishment of Tyrannies. For the attempt to seize tyrannical power is made either by the most influential individuals in the two polities, viz. by the demagogues in the one case and the Dynasts *or most powerful Oligarchs* in the other, or else by persons holding the highest official positions, whenever the system is one of long tenure.

Again, polities are preserved not only by their remoteness from destructive agencies but in some cases by their very proximity to them, as fear induces the citizens to keep a stricter control upon the polity. It is proper therefore for the friends of the political constitution to suggest alarms, that the citizens may be on their guard instead of neglecting the defence of the polity like a watch in the night, and to bring what is far off home to them.

And further, an effort should be made by legal regulations among other means to keep a watch upon the rivalries and feuds of the upper classes before[1] the infection has actually spread to those who at present stand outside the rivalry, as it is not in the power of any ordinary person but requires the ability of a statesman to discern the evil at its commencement.

As a precaution against the revolution from an Oligarchy or Polity which is occasioned by the property

---

[1] Omitting the comma after ὄντας.

assessment when there is a large influx of money while
the assessment requisite for office remains unchanged,
it is well to revise by comparison with the former
assessment the total amount of assessed property in
the State, either annually[1], wherever there is an an-
nual assessment of property, or in larger States at intervals of three or five years and, if the total amount
of assessed property is many times larger or smaller
than the last by which the assessments of individuals   ·
for political purposes were regulated, to fix according
to legal rule an increase or diminution of these assessments, an increase corresponding to the multiplica-
tion of the total value, if it has risen, and a corresponding diminution and reduction, if it has fallen.   For in
Polities and Oligarchies, if there is no reduction of
the requisite assessment from time to time, an Oligarchy in the one case and a Dynasty in the other is
the result, while if there is no increase, a Polity is
converted into a Democracy and an Oligarchy into a
Polity or Democracy.

It is a rule equally applicable to Democracy, Oligarchy and all other constitutional governments not
to invest any individual with an excessive and disproportionate authority but to aim at assigning unimportant honours of long duration rather than high
honours with rapid change—for high honour has a
corrupting influence, and [2] *as the saying is*

"Not everyone is equal to good fortune,"

[1] The words κατὰ τοῦτον τὸν χρόνον should stand after κατ'
ἐνιαυτόν.

[2] Stahr is probably right in regarding these words as a quotation.

or at least, if this is impossible, not to assign all these honours at once and afterwards revoke them all at once, but to proceed gradually and to try, if circumstances are favourable, so to use the regulating[1] influence of the laws that no citizen may appear who is vastly superior to the rest in the number of his *clientèle* or the amount of his wealth or, failing this, to banish his supporters from the land.

Again, as one cause of revolutions is to be found in the private lives of the citizens, it is proper to create certain officers in the State whose province it is to have supervision over all who by their manner of life exercise a prejudicial influence upon the polity, viz. upon the Democracy, if the polity is democratical, upon the Oligarchy, if it is oligarchical, and similarly in each of the remaining polities.

And further, the same reason, *viz. the danger of unconstitutional conduct*, will justify precautions against any class or order in the State which in the vicissitudes of human fortune is at the time in the enjoyment of remarkable prosperity. A certain safeguard against this danger is to be found in always entrusting the conduct of business as well as the official positions to' the antagonistic elements in the State —I refer to the antagonism between the respectable classes and the masses or between the poor and the rich—or in endeavouring either to effect a fusion of the poorer and richer population or else to increase the strength of the middle class, as it is this class which composes all such feuds as arise from a sense of inequality.

1 Reading οὕτω ῥυθμίζειν ὥστε.

But the chief requisite in any polity is that the system of the laws and the general administration should be so ordered as to afford the officers of State no opportunity of personal gain. This is a point to be especially observed in oligarchical polities. For it is not so much exclusion from office that excites a feeling of indignation in the Many, who are actually thankful if they are allowed leisure to attend to their own business, as the idea that the officers of State appropriate the public money. When this is the case, they feel a double annoyance in being excluded both from the honours and from the gains of State. The only possible means of combining Democracy and Aristocracy is by a system in which official gain is impossible, as this is the only way of satisfying equally the wants of the upper classes and of the commons. For while universal eligibility to office is a characteristic of Democracy, it is a characteristic of Aristocracy that all official positions are in the hands of the upper classes. But this latter condition will be realized whenever office affords no opportunity of gain, as the poor having no prospect of gain will not be desirous of office but will prefer to attend to their own business, while the rich will be capable of holding office, as having money enough of their own to do without the public money. The result will be that, while the poor will acquire wealth by devoting themselves to their occupations, the upper classes will not be subjected to the rule of persons who possess no special qualifications; *and both will be satisfied.* Now as a means of preventing malversation of the public money, it may be suggested that the transference of

the commons, and the oaths they take should be exactly the opposite of those now in vogue. Instead of swearing as they do now in some Oligarchies "I will be a foe of the commons and will devise whatsoever ill I may against them," they should take or pretend to take a precisely opposite view, emphasizing in their oaths the pledge "I will do the commons no wrong."

But the greatest safeguard for the permanence of any polity, greater than any we have hitherto mentioned, is one which is universally disregarded at present, viz. the education of the citizens in the spirit of the polity. For the wisest of laws, although ratified by the consentient voice of the whole civic body, are of no avail unless the citizens are trained by habit and education in the lines of the polity, i.e. democratically, if the laws are democratical, and oligarchically, if they are oligarchical. For the same[1] intemperance which is found in an individual may be equally found in a State. But an education conducted in the spirit of the polity does not imply the performance of such actions as are agreeable to the friends of Oligarchy or Democracy, but of such as will facilitate an oligarchical or democratical administration. The actual fact however is that in Oligarchies the sons of the ruling class live in luxury, while the sons of the poor are subjected to a severe and laborious discipline which tends to produce in them at once the desire and the capacity for revolution, and in such Democracies as are considered to exemplify the most pronouncedly democratical character the state of

Education in the spirit of the polity.

---

[1] Reading ἥπερ.

Misconception of liberty. things is just the contrary of their true interest. The reason in the last case is the erroneous conception of liberty. For there are two things which are popularly regarded as the determining characteristics of Democracy, viz. the supremacy of the numerical majority and personal liberty. For it is assumed that justice is equality, that equality consists in the supremacy of the will of the masses, and that it is a characteristic of liberty[1] that every citizen acts as he chooses. The result is that in this kind of Democracy each individual lives as he chooses or in the language of Euripides[2] "as he likes it." This however is a serious mistake; *for the citizens should live and live gladly in the spirit of the polity,* as such a life ought not to be regarded as a bondage but rather as a means of preservation.

Such then are broadly the various causes of revolution and destruction as well as the means of preservation and permanence in polities. It remains to discuss the natural destructives and preservatives of Monarchy.

CHAP. X. Monarchy. Its dangers and preservatives.

The actual history of kingly and tyrannical forms of government is much the same as our description of constitutional polities. For while Kingship corresponds to Aristocracy, Tyranny is a compound of the extreme form of Oligarchy and Democracy and is thus of all governments the most prejudicial to the subjects, as being composed of two evils and containing in itself the perversions and errors of both these polities.

Contrast of Kingship and Tyranny.

The very origins of these two forms of monarchical government are precisely opposite. Whereas Kingship

[1] Omitting καὶ ἴσον.
[2] *Fragment* 883, in Dindorf's *Poetae Scenici Graeci.*

is instituted for the protection of the better classes
against[1] the commons, and a king is appointed from
among the members of the better classes on the
ground of his personal superiority in virtue or actions
which result from virtue or of the superiority of a
virtuous race, the tyrant is taken from the mass of The origin
the commons to act against the nobles and to protect nies.
the commons from injury at their hands. This is a
truth which is evident from the facts of History. It is
an almost universal rule that persons who have succeeded in making themselves tyrants have been ex-
demagogues, who had won the confidence of the
people by abuse of the nobles. Some Tyrannies were
established in this way, *i.e. in the person of demagogues*, from the time when States had attained considerable dimensions, others at an earlier date in
the person of kings who exceeded their hereditary
privileges and aspired to a more despotic authority,
others again in the person of citizens elected to the
supreme offices of State, as it was the ancient custom
of the commons in different States to allow a long
term of office to the civil and religious magistrates,
and others finally as the outcome of Oligarchies by
the election of an individual with supreme power to
the highest offices of State. In all these cases it was
no difficult matter for the individuals in question to
effect their object, if they had but the will, as the
power was already theirs in their kingly authority or
high official status. It was thus that Pheidon at
Argos and others made themselves tyrants on the

---

[1] Reading ἐπὶ τὸν δῆμον.

basis of an existing Kingship, that the Ionian tyrants and Phalaris rose from high honours of State, that Panaetius at Leontini, Cypselus at Corinth, Pisistratus at Athens, Dionysius at Syracuse and others in the same manner rose from the position of demagogues. But to resume: Kingship, as we said, so far corresponds in principle to Aristocracy as it is based upon merit, whether upon the virtue of an individual or of a family, or upon public services or upon the combination of these with power. For it was in virtue of services they had rendered or were capable of rendering to their States or races that people in all cases attained regal dignity, whether by having defended them from subjugation on the field of battle like Codrus, or by having liberated them from slavery like Cyrus, or as founders of the State or conquerors of new territory like the kings of the Lacedaemonians, Macedonians and Molossians.

The origin of King-ships.

In theory the king is a guardian appointed to protect the propertied class on the one hand from spoliation and the commons on the other from insolence. Tyranny on the contrary, as has been frequently remarked, is absolutely regardless of the public weal, except so far as it subserves the personal interest of the tyrant. And while the object of the tyrant is pleasure, that of the king is moral elevation. It is thus that the tyrant is distinguished by the ambition of [1] exorbitant gain, but the king by that of extravagant distinction, and that, while the body-guard of the latter consists of citizens, that of the former is exclusively composed of mercenaries.

pp 120, 280.

---

[1] Reading τὰ μὲν εἰς χρήματα.

It is evident that Tyranny combines in itself the The vices of
evils both of Democracy and of Oligarchy. It borrows Tyranny.
from Oligarchy *firstly* the pursuit of wealth as its
summum bonum—for it is only wealth that enables
the tyrant to maintain his body-guard and gratify his
luxurious tastes—and *secondly* its absolute distrust of
the masses which leads to a general seizure of arms and
to other measures equally characteristic of Oligarchy
and Tyranny, such as the oppression of the common
people, their banishment from the city and distribution through different parts of the country. It borrows from Democracy its hostility to the upper classes,
so that the tyrant makes away with them by secret and
open measures and banishes them from the State as
rivals and obstacles to his authority. For it really is
the case that they are the authors of conspiracies
against tyrants from their desire in some cases of
personal rule and in others of deliverance from slavery.
It was this feeling that prompted the counsel of Periander to Thrasybulus when he cut off all the overtopping stalks as a sign that he ought from time to time
to put the overtopping citizens out of the way.

[1]It appears then, as has been already remarked, The causes
that the predisposing causes of revolutions must be ing to in-
considered to be practically the same in Monarchies in Monarch-
as in constitutional polities. It is injustice, fear and p. 380.
contempt that commonly cause the insurrections of
subjects against monarchical governments; and the
injustice consists principally in insolence, although
sometimes in the spoliation of private property. Also

---

[1] Reading καθάπερ οὖν ἐλέχθη, σχεδὸν τὰς αὐτάς, κ.τ.λ.

the objects of the insurgents are the same in Tyrannies and Kingships as in constitutional polities; for monarchs are in the possession of great wealth and honour, and these are the objects of universal desire.

Forms of insurrection.

Insurrections may take the form of an attack either upon the person or upon the authority of the rulers. Where an insurrection is occasioned by insolence, it assumes the first form. There are various kinds of insolence, any one of which is provocative of the anger which incites to insurrection; but where anger is the motive, it almost always happens that the object is revenge rather than personal predominance. Thus the insurrection against the Pisistratidae was a consequence of the insult offered to the sister of Harmodius and the humiliation inflicted upon Harmodius himself; for Harmodius was incited to rebel by regard for his sister and Aristogeiton by regard for Harmodius. Similarly the cause of the conspiracy against the Ambracian tyrant Periander was an insulting question he put to his favourite, when he was sitting with him over his cups. The conspiracy of Pausanias against Philip was due to his having suffered him to be insulted by Attalus and his friends, that of Derdas against Amyntas the Less to his having boasted of the liberties he had taken with him, that of the eunuch against Evagoras of Cyprus whom he murdered to his resentment of the insult offered him by Evagoras's son in seducing his wife. Again, a frequent cause of insurrections is the personal affront[1] offered to their subjects by some monarchs. It was so in the insurrection of

---

[1] Reading αἰσχῦναι.

Crataeus against Archelaus. It was because of the
disgust he had always felt on this account that he
was satisfied with so comparatively trivial an excuse
for assassination as that Archelaus had violated his
agreement to give him one of his daughters in marriage, and had given the elder under pressure of the
war with Sirras and Arrabaeus to the King of Elimeia
and the younger to his own son Amyntas in the hope
of thereby reducing to a minimum the chance of a
quarrel between him and his son by Cleopatra. *This
was the immediate motive of the assassination*, but
the beginning of his alienation was the old feeling of
disgust. It was the same reason which induced
Hellanocrates of Larisa to associate himself with the
conspiracy. As Archelaus who had been his lover did
not fulfil his promise of restoring him to his country,
he conceived the idea that it was simply insolence
which had prompted · the king to the intimacy.
Python[1] and Heracleides of Ænos assassinated Cotys
in revenge for their father's death, and Adamas was
incited to revolt from him by a sense of the insult to
which he had been exposed in childhood at Cotys's
orders. Again, people have often been goaded to such
fury by the degradation of corporal punishment
that their sense of the insult has led them either to
murder or attempt to murder their insulters, even
although these were persons holding high official
positions or members of regal dynasties. At Mitylene
e.g. the Penthalidae, as they were going their rounds

---

[1] Pyrrhon is the form of the name which has the best MSS.
authority here ; but we know from other writers that it was properly Python.

and dealing blows with their clubs, were attacked and killed by Megacles and his friends, and at a later date Penthilus himself was assassinated by Smerdis whom he had visited with corporal punishment and had forcibly dragged from his wife's side. Lastly, in the conspiracy against Archelaus it was Decamnichus who took the lead, being the first to incite the conspirators. The cause of his anger was that Archelaus had handed him over for scourging to the poet Euripides who was annoyed by some remark of his about the foulness of his breath. And there have been many others who for similar reasons were the victims either of assassination or conspiracy.

Fear again is similarly a cause of conspiracy. We have already seen that this is one motive in Monarchies as well as in constitutional polities. It was thus that Artapanes assassinated Xerxes for fear of the accusation that would be brought against him because he had put Darius to death by hanging without the authority of Xerxes himself in the expectation that the king would overlook the act, as his hard drinking at the time would prevent his remembering the circumstances.

Another cause of conspiracy is contempt. Thus it was the sight of Sardanapalus carding wool among his wives that incited someone to the assassination, if indeed the story is true, and if it is not true of him, it may well be so of somebody else. It was contempt that led Dion to rise against Dionysius the Younger, as he saw the citizens ready for revolt and Dionysius himself perpetually drunk. It sometimes happens too that contempt leads the personal friends of the

take two forms; one in consequence of a sedition among the members of the royal family, and a second when the kings endeavour to adopt a method of administration which approximates to Tyranny by claiming more extensive and unconstitutional powers. Kingships are no longer created in modern times but, *The reason why Kingships are not created in modern times.* if monarchical governments are created at all, they are generally Tyrannies. For while Kingship implies voluntary obedience on the one hand and comparatively high authority on the other, there is *in modern times* a large body of persons who stand on the same level and no individual of such preeminent distinction as corresponds with the importance and dignity of the regal office. There is thus no voluntary submission to the rule of an individual; but if such rule is founded upon fraud or force, it is admitted to be *ipso facto* a Tyranny.

If we take hereditary Kingships, there is yet one *Hereditary Kingship.* further cause of their destruction to be found in the contemptible character displayed by many of the kings and the insolent conduct of which they are guilty, when it is not tyrannical but regal dignity that they enjoy. For in this way the abolition of Kingships was facilitated, as no sooner is the good will of the subjects lost than the ruler will cease to be a king, although he may be a tyrant, for the good will of the subjects is not a necessary condition of Tyranny.

These then and other similar circumstances being *Chap. XI. The preservatives of Monarchy, (1) of Kingship,* the causes of destruction in Monarchies, it is clear[1] that the means of their preservation are generally the opposites and in the case of Kingship more particu-

---

[1] Reading δῆλον ὅτι.

larly a tendency to moderation. For the narrower the limitation of the kings' authority, the longer is their power sure to continue without diminution, as the kings themselves display a less despotic spirit and in character stand more on an equality with the citizens and are less liable to the envy of their subjects. This accounts for the long duration of the Kingship among the Molossians as well as among the Lacedaemonians, where it was due to the original bi-partition of the regal authority and again to the restrictions put upon it by Theopompus in various ways, and especially in the institution of the Ephoral office as a check upon the kings. For as by diminishing the power of the Kingship he increased its permanence, it was true in a certain sense that he made it greater rather than less. It is said in fact that when he was asked by his wife if he did not feel ashamed that the Kingship as he bequeathed it to his sons was not so great as he had inherited it from his father, "Certainly not," he replied, "for as I bequeath it it is more permanent."

(2) of Tyranny. Oppressive measures. There are two modes exactly opposite to each other in which Tyrannies are preserved. The first is the traditional mode adopted by the large majority of tyrants in the exercise of their authority. It is Periander of Corinth who gets the credit of having introduced most of the rules, but there are many others of a similar kind which may be borrowed from the Persian government. I refer to the measures p. 389. mentioned in an earlier part of this treatise for the preservation of Tyranny, so far as possible, viz. the practice of cutting off the prominent characters and

proximating the regal authority to a Tyranny, so it is a safeguard of Tyranny to approximate it to a Kingship, securing however one point only, viz. the power of the tyrant, so that he may maintain his authority not only with but also without the goodwill of his subjects. For the surrender of this point is the surrender of tyrannical rule altogether. But while this must necessarily remain as a fundamental principle, the tyrant except in this one point should always either in reality or pretence successfully play the part of a true king[1]. He should affect primarily to be careful of the public money by not lavishing it in such presents as excite the indignation of the masses, when the money extorted from their labour and thrifty toil is squandered upon mistresses, foreign favourites and artists, and by rendering formal accounts of all receipts and expenses, as has been already the practice of some tyrants. For an administration so conducted will assume the character of Domestic Economy rather than of Tyranny. Nor is there any reason why a tyrant, *if he so rules*, should dread a deficiency of funds so long as he retains supreme authority in the State. So far is this from being the case that it is actually better for tyrants who are obliged to go abroad to have acted thus, *i.e. to have been moderate in their pecuniary exactions*, than to leave behind vast sums of money which they have amassed, as there is less danger of an attempt upon their power being made by the guardians *of the royal treasure* who, as remaining at home, are an object of greater dread to tyrants during their absence from home than the citizens who accompany them in

[1] Reading τὸν βασιλικὸν.

Further precautions of Tyranny. their expeditions. Again, it is proper for the tyrant to make a show of collecting the taxes and imposing public burdens upon the citizens solely for economical purposes and in case of need in military emergencies, and generally to assume the attitude of a guardian and treasurer of funds which he treats as the property of the State rather than as his own. And further his address should be not stern but dignified, so as to inspire all who meet him with a feeling of reverence rather than of fear. But this is a result difficult of attainment, if he is personally contemptible. Accordingly even if he disregards all other virtues, he should still devote his attention to political virtue and infuse into the minds of the citizens a high opinion of his excellence in this respect. Again, neither the tyrant himself nor any member of his court should ever be seen to offer an insult to any of his young subjects whether male or female. There should be not less prudence in the behaviour of their wives to the wives[1] of the other citizens, for insolent actions on the part of the wives have been one frequent cause of the destruction of Tyrannies. In regard to sensual indulgences the tyrant should adopt a contrary line to that which is taken in modern times by some tyrants who not only begin their indulgences at early dawn and continue them without intermission for many days, but are actually anxious to let their conduct be seen by the citizens generally in order to excite an admiration of their happiness and felicity. So far from acting in this way the tyrant should, if he is wise, be

---

[1] Reading πρὸς τὰς τῶν ἄλλων.

moderate in his sensual pleasures or should at least avoid publicity; for it is not one who is sober or vigilant but one who is intoxicated or asleep that exposes himself to contempt and insurrection. And almost all the actions already described he should reverse. He should enrich the city with edifices and decorations in the spirit rather of a guardian of the public interests than of a tyrant. Again, he should always display a conspicuous zeal in the service of the Gods; for people are less afraid of unconstitutional treatment at the hands of their ruler, if they regard him as religiously minded and attentive in his duties to the Gods, and are more likely to abstain from conspiracy against him in the belief that he has the Gods as his allies. Yet he must not go to such lengths in his religious observances as to incur the reproach of a weak superstition. Citizens who display excellence in any respect he should treat with signal honour, so as to inspire them with the idea that they would never have received higher honours from the citizens, if they had been independent. And further while he personally dispenses these honours, he should inflict his punishments by other agencies, such as officers of State and Courts of Law. It is a precaution suitable to every form of Monarchy not to elevate any individual to a position of greatness but, if such elevation is necessary, to elevate several people, as they will then keep an eye upon each, or, if it really is necessary to elevate an individual, anyhow not to choose a person of intrepid character; for such characters are preeminently disposed to aggressive action in all the affairs of life.

Similarly, if it is the tyrant's pleasure to remove any-body from his position of power, he should do so gradually instead of stripping him of all his preroga-tives at a single stroke. Also he should restrain him-self from every form of insolence and from two forms more particularly, viz. corporal chastisement and in-decent conduct. This precaution he must 'especially observe in dealing with the ambitious spirits. For as it is neglect of their pecuniary interests which is resented by the avaricious, so it is such neglect as issues in dishonour which is resented by the ambi-tious and respectable of mankind. And thus the tyrant should either abstain from all dealing with these ambitious spirits or should make it clear that his punishments are inflicted in a paternal spirit rather than from contemptuous thoughtlessness, and that his addresses are prompted by the motions of love rather than by the mere wantonness of power; and generally he should redeem the apparent humilia-tions by more than equivalent honours. The authors of attempts upon the lives of tyrants are most formid-able and demand the strongest measures of defence when they are willing to sacrifice their own lives if only they succeed in the assassination. It is ne-cessary therefore to adopt the gravest precautions against persons who conceive that an insult is offered either to themselves personally or to the objects of their affection. For anybody who is incited by passion to a murderous attempt is not in a mood to spare himself, *and is therefore formidable* accord-ing to the saying of Heracleitus that "it is a hard battle with passion, as the passionate buy vengeance with their lives." Finally, as States are composed of two elements, viz. the rich and the poor, it is desirable that both, if possible, should see in the authority of the tyrant the basis of their own security, and that neither party should be subject to oppression at the hands of the other or, failing this, that the stronger party of the two whichever it is should be made the creatures of his authority; for if this support is assured to the existing order of things, the tyrant has no need to resort to a general emancipation of slaves or disarmament of the citizens, as the accession of this one party to the side of the tyrant's power is a guarantee of ability to crush all insurrectionary efforts. But it is superfluous to discuss all these measures in detail. The object is clear, viz. that the tyrant in the eyes of his subjects should wear the appearance not of a tyrant but of a householder or king, not of a self-seeker but of a guardian of the public interests, that he should aim at all that is moderate rather than at all that is extravagant in his life and that, while he wins the hearts of the upper classes by affability, he should conciliate the masses by flattery. The result is sure to be not only that his rule will assume a higher and more enviable form, as the subjects instead of being degraded will be morally elevated and he will not himself be always an object of hatred or fear, but that it will be also more permanent, and, we may add, that his own moral disposition will either be *absolutely* noble and virtuous or *at least* half-virtuous and not *absolutely* bad but *at the worst only* half-bad.

Still there are no polities which have so short a CHAP. XII.

duration as Oligarchy and Tyranny. The Tyranny of
Orthagoras and his descendants at Sicyon, which had
the longest existence, lasted only a hundred years.
The explanation of its permanence is that they treated
their subjects with moderation and submitted themselves in many instances to the laws, that the military
genius of Cleisthenes prevented him from becoming
an object of contempt and that they won the hearts
of the commons as much as any demagogues could
have done by the constant attention which they devoted to their interests. It is said at least that Cleisthenes, *when he was a competitor for a prize,* bestowed
a crown upon the judge who had refused him the
victory; and there are some authorities who assert
that the sitting statue in the market is the effigy of
the judge who pronounced this decision. It is said
too that Pisistratus himself submitted on one occasion
to appear in answer to a summons before the Areopagus.
Next to the Sicyonian Tyranny the most permanent was
that of the Cypselidae at Corinth which lasted seventy-
three years and six months. For Cypselus was tyrant
for thirty years, Periander for forty years and six months[1]
and Psammitichus[2] the son of Gordias for three years.
The causes of permanence were the same in this case
as in the last, viz. that Cypselus played the part of a
demagogue and never employed a bodyguard during
the whole period of his rule, while Periander with the

---

[1] The substitution of ἐξ μῆνας for τέτταρα seems to be the most
satisfactory means of making the items tally with the total given
above.

[2] The MSS. authority is in favour of Ψαμμίτιχος as the form of
the name.

character of a tyrant had also the genius of a general. The third longest Tyranny was that of the Pisistratidae at Athens, although it did not continue without intermission, as Pisistratus was twice banished during his Tyranny and consequently in a period of three and thirty years was not tyrant for more than seventeen. These with the eighteen years' Tyranny of his sons make a total of thirty-five. The longest Tyranny with these exceptions was that of Hieron and Gelon at Syracuse[1], although it too did not last a great number of years, only eighteen in all. For Gelon died after seven years of tyrannical power, Hieron enjoyed it for ten years and Thrasybulus was expelled in the eleventh month of his rule. The majority of Tyrannies have not lasted more than a very short time.

The causes of destruction and preservation in constitutional polities and in Monarchies have now practically been all discussed.

In the *Republic*[2] the subject of revolutions is discussed by Socrates, but not satisfactorily. For *in the first place* there is no particular treatment of the revolution incident to his best or primary polity. He assigns as a cause the fact that nothing in the world is permanent, all things change in a certain cycle, and the principle of change is contained in certain figures[3] *Criticism of the Socratic theory of revolutions.*

[1] Reading περὶ Συρακούσας.

[2] The discussion occupies nearly the whole of the 8th and 9th Books of the *Republic*.

[3] *Republic*, VIII. p. 546 C. The 'Platonic number' was a standing puzzle of scholarship, at least as early as Cicero's time (*ad Att*. VII. 13. 5). Some account of the proposed explanations is given in Prof. Jowett's *Dialogues of Plato*, Vol. III., Introduction to the *Republic*, pp. 113—117.

whose root, which is in the ratio of 4 : 3, by combination with the number 5 produces two harmonies *or proportional numbers*, i.e. when the number of the diagram is cubed. The theory is that Nature from time to time produces bad men who defy all educational influences; and so far perhaps Socrates is not far wrong, as there may well be persons whom it is impossible by any educational process to convert into virtuous men. But the question arises why this form of revolution should be peculiar to the best polity of his nomenclature rather than to any other polity and indeed to anything that comes into being. Secondly, as regards the period of time which according to Socrates works a revolution in all things, it may be asked whether things which did not come into being simultaneously experience a simultaneous revolution, e.g. whether[1] a thing is revolutionized with the rest, if it came into being only on the day preceding the change. And further why should the revolution from the best polity be *always, as Socrates says it is*, to the Lacedaemonian? For all polities are more often revolutionized into opposite than into closely similar polities.

The sequence of polities.

The same remark will apply to the other revolutions *described by Socrates*. The Lacedaemonian polity, he says, is revolutionized to Oligarchy, Oligarchy to Democracy and Democracy to Tyranny. But it may be objected that revolutions occur equally in the reverse order, e.g. from Democracy to Oligarchy and in fact more frequently to Oligarchy than to Monarchy.

[1] Reading ἆρ' ἅμα μεταβάλλει;

Another point is that Socrates does not state whether Tyranny will be liable to revolution or, if it is not, what is the cause of its exemption and, *if it is,* what sort of polity will succeed it. The cause of the omission is that he would have had a difficulty in settling the question. No precise determination of it is possible, whereas his theory requires that Tyranny should be revolutionized to the primary or best polity, if there is to be continuity and a complete cycle *of revolutions.* The truth however is that one Tyranny may give place to another, as the Tyranny of Myron at Sicyon to that of Cleisthenes, or to Oligarchy, like the Tyranny of Antileon at Chalcis, or to Democracy, like the Tyranny of the Gelonian family at Syracuse, or to Aristocracy, like the Tyranny of Charilaus at Lacedaemon or the Carthaginian.

There are also revolutions from Oligarchy to Tyranny, as in the great majority of the ancient Oligarchies of Sicily, where the Tyranny of Panaetius at Leontini, that of Cleander at Gela and that of Anaxilaus at Rhegium were all the outcomes of Oligarchies, and the same has been the case in many other States.

It is a strange idea[1] too *of Socrates* that the cause of revolution to an Oligarchy is simply the love of money and the habit of commerce existing in the official body rather than a feeling on the part of the class which enjoys a great superiority of property that there is an injustice in allowing people who possess nothing to exercise equal political rights

---

[1] *Republic,* VIII. pp. 550 sqq.

with the possessors of wealth. We may add that there are many Oligarchies in which lucrative business is not allowed *to the governing class* but is prohibited by special laws and that in Carthage[1] the citizens engage in business pursuits and have never yet passed through a revolution.

Again, it is a strange remark[2] *of Socrates* that an oligarchical State contains in itself two States, one of the rich and another of the poor. Why is this more true of an Oligarchy[3] than of the Lacedaemonian or any other State, where there is not an equality of property or a similarity of virtue among all the citizens?

It may be added that without the impoverishment of any citizen it still happens that polities are revolutionized from Oligarchy to Democracy, if there is an increase in the number of the poor, or from Democracy to Oligarchy, if the rich are stronger than the poor and are on the watch *for opportunities*, which the poor disregard.

Again, although there are various causes of revolutions in Oligarchies, Socrates mentions only one[4], viz. the impoverishment of the citizens by profligacy and usurious interest, as though they were all or nearly all originally rich. This is not however a true statement of the case. The truth is that, if it is some of the leading citizens who have wasted their properties, they introduce innovations, but, if it is others, no serious consequence ensues. Nor, if there is any seri-

---

[1] Omitting δημοκρατουμένη.
[2] *Republic*, VIII. p. 551 D.
[3] Reading αὕτη.
[4] *Republic*, VIII., 555 D.

ous consequence, does the revolution take the form of
a Democracy rather than of any other polity.

Again, if there are persons who are excluded from
the honours of State or subjected to oppression or
insult, they become the authors of seditions and political revolutions. They may do so, even if they have
not squandered their property, simply for the sake of
attaining the privilege of acting as they choose—a
result which in the view of Socrates[1] is due to a spirit
of excessive liberty.

Lastly, *it may be objected that,* although there are
various forms of Oligarchy and Democracy, Socrates
in describing the revolutions of each speaks as though
there were but one.

[1] The reference is apparently to *Republic,* VIII. pp. 562 sqq.

INDEX.

CAMBRIDGE: PRINTED BY C. J. CLAY, M.A. AND SONS, AT THE UNIVERSITY PRESS.

Lightning Source UK Ltd.
Milton Keynes UK
UKOW06f1908051017
310500UK00008B/148/P